DAUGHTER *of the* YELLOW RIVER

DAUGHTER of the

DIANA LU

YELLOW RIVER

An Inspirational Journey

Image Global Impact

Image Global Impact
One Market St.
Spear Tower, Suite 3600
San Francisco, CA 94105
Phone: 415-293-8218
Fax: 415-293-8001
E-mail: books@igimpact.com

Ordering information:
Distributed by Midpoint Trade Books
27 West 20th Street, Suite 1102
New York, NY 10011
Phone: 212-727-0190
Fax: 212-727-0195
E-mail: midpointny1@aol.com

ISBN: 1-933726-00-8
LCCN: 2005938838

To my dear mother and father for their
unconditional love and support,
and for giving me wisdom and strength.

And to my motherland, China, for giving
birth to me, raising me, and forming me.

And to my home, the United States,
for stimulating me and refining me.

And to the people in the world who cared and
shared my vision, for without their encouragement
and acceptance of who I am, this wonderful
journey would not have been possible.

Contents

Acknowledgments

When I reflect on the process of creating *Daughter of the Yellow River*, I am refreshed by the images of every person who supported me and who had a hand in this accomplishment. From the moment of the first hunch to make this book to the day of publication, it has been a rewarding year. So many people have helped by brainstorming with me, intensifying my thoughts, clarifying my memory, making suggestions on the many drafts of the manuscript, and making the book much better than it would have been without their contributions. I am overwhelmed. Whatever other merits the book may have, it is a masterpiece of a true team effort. I would like to offer thanks . . .

To my beloved family, especially my mother, my father, and my little nephew. Despite how much my parents would like to keep our lives private, they have given me unconditional love and support, knowing that the purpose of the project is to inspire other people, in particular the younger generation. Their love is the major source of my strength to accomplish this work. Their tolerance and patience, their remarkable wisdom, and their knowledge of history, along with my nephew's innocent suggestions, made my work easier and more enjoyable.

To my assistant and friend Patricia Weinstein, a very talented woman and an amazing mother of five. I am deeply grateful for her faithfulness, her recognition of my heart and my capabilities, and her devotion to my vision of making a positive impact on people's lives. She worked with me day and night and accompanied me everywhere to seek inspiration and resources. When I was reluctant to relive and write out the painful parts of my history, she was there by my side, holding my hand firmly and giving me the confidence and strength to keep going. This project never would have been started, let alone completed, without her push and encouragement.

To my writer Margaret Lucke. I was blessed with good fortune to have met such an extraordinary person. Her contribution to this book was absolutely vital. Her remarkable intuition and intelligence broadened my horizons, and her ability to discover my most soulful feelings and experiences was the key to making the book real and human. She refined my thoughts and my words, and, in a way that was always encouraging, she helped me to face and reflect on the parts of my life that made me most vulnerable. She had a huge impact on me as I strove to deepen the book's purpose and value. I have been inspired by her profound and philosophical understanding of human nature, her exquisite taste in literature, and her high professionalism and ethics. Working with her was a stimulating and joyful adventure.

To the wonderful people at Wilsted and Taylor Publishing Services, who crafted the manuscript into a real book: Christine Taylor, for her expert knowledge, sound advice, and skillful management of the project; Rachel Bernstein, for her excellent copy editing, her wise suggestions, and her patience and sense of humor; Janet Wood, for the elegant text design and for a cover that so beautifully captures the book's essence; and Nancy Evans, Melody Lacina, Andrew Patty, Tag Savage, Yvonne Tsang, and Jennifer Uhlich for the many contributions that made this a better book.

To my mentors, James Pammenter and John Edward, and my great team with Image Global Impact—Darryl Quan, Mike Yell, Dr. Stefan Hunsche, Ahmed Mustafa, and Chester Hurtado. Thanks to their dedicated support and wisdom, our enterprise and this book have become more solid and convincing.

To Ellen King, Steven Hemminger, and their firm White & Case LLP, who fought for my integrity with their high professionalism, their wisdom, and their rich legal experience. They have taught me the meaning of being a true winner.

To James Burns and Christopher Vejnoska (Clifford Chance LLP, Orrick LLP), two of the world's most extraordinary litigators, as well as people of noble spirit and humanity. Their heartfelt empathy and sincere belief in me pulled me out of depression and brought back my strength.

To my best friend, Sally Li, and her family. For more than a decade, they have honored me with their loyalty and friendship. Wherever I have been, whatever my situation, the door to their home and their hearts has been open to me. One reason I wanted to write this book was to give something back to them for their unconditional love and support.

To Ms. Mo Hui Xing, who believed in me and supported

my dream and my pursuit of a better life at a very critical stage.

To Guo Jun Ming, my great high school friend, who was the first person to have faith in me and who remained so cheerful and supportive throughout the most difficult time in my life.

To Ginger Onishi and David Godfrey, my very first American friends and teachers, who opened their hearts to share, support, and embrace my culture, my beliefs, and my dream. They taught me that love, compassion, kindness, and acceptance have eternal and universal power. Ginger and David have been my role models of the great people and nation of America.

To my friends all over the world who believed in me, cared for me, and shared my vision.

To my beloved motherland China, which gave me birth, strength, knowledge, and wisdom.

To the Western world, which refined me and improved me, and especially to my home, the United States, and the great American people.

To the people in the world. They inspire me to create joy and happiness, and they give me more courage to do what I can to make the world a better place. In this way, they give my life meaning and purpose.

Introduction

The Yellow River, or Huang He, rises high up in the Kunlun Mountains. Tinted by silt, the river follows a meandering, eastward course, traveling more than three thousand miles across deserts, plateaus, and plains. At last it reaches a gulf of the Yellow Sea, not far from Beijing. Considered the mother river of China, it runs through the very heart of the country.

I am a daughter of the Yellow River. Its waters flow within me like the blood in my veins. I was born, raised, and educated in China, and I was shaped by the culture and traditions of that great land.

I have also become a citizen of the world. I have traveled on several continents and in many countries, and I now make my home in one of the world's most cosmopolitan cities, San Francisco. I have lived my life fully and passionately, driven to follow my heart, find my true calling, and embrace my own personal power. I knew that this would be my route to success. And I was right.

My journey has taken me along a path that has led me from hardship and poverty to a life of comfort, glamour, and wealth. Starting with no money, no power, and no formal business education, I became a successful international entrepreneur in a highly sophisticated technology industry, working with major corporations worldwide—an amazing accomplishment for a young Chinese woman in a male-dominated business environment.

The road has sometimes been bumpy and rough, but the adversities I encountered became valuable assets. They gave me opportunities to learn, challenges that made me grow stronger, and experiences that made me value my life even more.

This book is the story of my growth and success. I am telling my story in the hope that it will inspire you to pursue and attain your own dreams. I have included much of the wisdom I've gained about business and about life, as well as specific techniques that are part of an efficient, practical, and usable system I've developed to enable me to achieve my goals. At the end of each chapter I've summarized what I learned during the phase of my life that the chapter covers into a list of stepping-stones to success. I hope that they will be helpful guides on your own journey.

* * *

Most of my years as a small child were spent in a remote, impoverished coal-mining village in the Gobi Desert, where my educated, middle-class family was sent to be "re-educated" during the Cultural Revolution. Relying on our strong spirits and our love for one another, we managed to survive the hardships of those dark, depressing, and frightening years.

When I was eleven my family moved to the city of Lanzhou, on the Yellow River's banks. There I went to high school and medical school. Realizing that a career as a physician didn't suit me at all, I found a teaching position in a university. Though this job was a better fit, it still left me restless and unfulfilled, and I began to dream of a better life.

Acting against societal pressure and the objections of my family, I broke with tradition and left my family and my secure, privileged job, determined to seek out opportunities that would be true to my talents and passions. I moved to Shenzhen, China's most capitalistic city, with few contacts, no job, and almost no money in my pocket. What I did have was a strong resolve and an understanding of how to set and achieve my goals. I worked hard at a series of jobs, learning from each everything I could. Within three years, I was a senior manager of a British company in China.

Then I took on another level of challenge and adventure—I moved to the United States and started my own international consulting business, involving sales and marketing in the optical fiber industry. I found it exciting to deal with a male-dominated industry, but also sometimes lonely. I learned I was the youngest and only female entrepreneur in that fast-paced competitive industry in China. Employing a unique blend of Western business strategy with Chinese business culture, I dealt with clients and vendors from all over the world.

Defying the advice of experts who said it couldn't be done, I took a huge risk on an unknown product. With strategic thinking, solid knowledge of the market, a winning marketing package, and a resolute spirit, I established a winning brand and took it from a zero market share to a market worth hundreds of millions of dollars in China within two years.

Unfortunately, my success, combined with my youth and femininity, created jealousy and resentment in some quarters. When I believed that a contract that my company had entered into had been breached, I didn't back down. I fought back, filing a lawsuit against the giant corporation in a U.S. court. Four years of legal battling made me stronger and more knowledgeable about international business law. With solid evidence, a powerful legal team, and my tenacious spirit and unbreakable confidence, I am winning this fight.

While I was conquering the optical fiber market in China, I explored additional opportunities in other business ventures in the Western world. My personal vision and sense of purpose and hard work have brought me substantial rewards.

At the age of thirty-four, I took the opportunity to enter into retirement, enjoying a life of luxury and leisure in my San Francisco home and the cities I visit during my worldwide travels. One of my joys has been pursuing my lifelong love of singing and dancing. I have been developing my talents and skills with formal professional training from top teachers, and I've loved the opportunities I've had to perform onstage. Soon I will release my first vocal CD, a collection of arias from Western operas and Broadway show tunes.

I've also been engaged in the fascinating realm of spiritual and motivational studies, finding many sources that have guided and inspired my personal growth in profound and fundamental ways. Through this work I have renewed my commitment to my life goals.

* * *

Living and working in different cultures has been a wonderful experience. I am so fortunate to have been formed by the waters of the Yellow River, polished by the currents of San Francisco Bay, and refined by the tides of the world. My experiences have given me unique insights about people, business, and personal accomplishment. Now I want to share what I've learned with you, so that you can make your life the kind of miracle that mine has been.

Therefore, supported by a team of prominent entrepreneurs, professionals, and senior executives, I am launching a new business—Image Global Impact. *Daughter of the Yellow River* is the first in a series of books, seminars, consulting services, and networking centers that are designed to carry out our twofold mission: to help Chinese and Western companies do business together more effectively, and to help individuals like you achieve greater success and happiness, personally and professionally.

If you would like to know more about Image Global Impact, I invite you to visit us at our website, www.igimpact.com.

The story I'm telling in this book may seem incredible, but it is true. Throughout the book I have taken the liberty of putting conversations in quotation marks for ease of reading and have tried to capture the essence of what was said even though the precise words may not be accurate. I have described the events from my own perspective, but I have made the accounts as accurate as I could, based on my memories and understandings as well as on documentary records and the recollections of other people who were involved. I have changed the names of some of the people mentioned in order to respect their privacy.

The miracles that have happened to me can happen to you if you truly want your dream to come true. I hope that you enjoy reading this book, and that it will serve as a friendly guide on your own journey to success. I wish you joy, friendship, and many satisfying accomplishments along the way. Good luck!

DAUGHTER *of the* YELLOW RIVER

*Diana as a newborn baby and enjoying a ball game
at the grammar school in Shandan Meikuang.*

煤矿小村

One Coal-Mining Village, 1970–1978

My earliest memories are of chaos, confusion, and fear.

When I was three years old, a little girl in pigtails, my world turned upside down. The government of China yanked my family out of our familiar, comfortable, urban way of life and thrust us into a remote rural place filled with poverty and despair.

Anguished and frightened, my parents embarked on the long journey from Beijing with my baby sister and me. We didn't have anything to bring with us except a few clothes. We traveled by train for three days to the city of Lanzhou, then for another day to the town of Shandan. There we transferred to a truck for a long ride to Shandan Meikuang, the coal-mining village that was our destination.

Mama clutched me tight as we rattled along the bumpy, unpaved road.

"Hush, Jing-Jing," she whispered when I fretted. "Do not be afraid. It will be all right." But I could hear the pain and worry in her voice.

Shandan Meikuang was isolated and undeveloped, too tiny

to be found on a map. Though the village was only ten miles from Shandan, the last leg of our journey took more than two hours. The road wound through a rocky desert surrounded by mountains. The landscape was stark; we saw few trees, just stands of camel weed. At last we came upon a view of a long, narrow valley filled with heavy gray and black smoke.

"Down there," our driver told us. "That's the village."

In this cold, barren, and strange place, we would make our new home.

We were not alone in our predicament. All over China, families like ours were being uprooted from their homes and forced to relocate long distances away. The government claimed that its motive was to "re-educate" people from the professional and intellectual classes, teaching them how to better serve the principles of communism. What we learned instead were lessons about courage, strength, and the determination to survive.

* * *

Let me back up a little and explain what was happening. From the mid-1960s to the mid-1970s, China went through a dark and confused period—Mao Zedong's Cultural Revolution.

Mao Zedong was the founder of the People's Republic of China. He was born in Hunan province in 1893, on the brink of a century that brought China tremendous conflict and change.

In 1911, after more than a decade of political and social upheaval, the emperor of China was overthrown. This ended the 267-year-old Qing dynasty and with it the tradition of imperial rule that extended back four thousand years. In its place a republican government was established. The following years saw various factions struggling for influence and control.

Mao, who came from peasant stock, was angered by the oppression experienced by China's peasants and distrustful of the more elite classes. He embraced communism as a young man and was one of the earliest members of the Chinese Communist party. He helped organize the Red Army and became a formidable military leader as the Communists attempted to seize power from the Kuomintang, the Nationalist Party that ruled China under Chiang Kai-shek. Although originally the two parties worked together, they split with great acrimony in 1927, beginning a civil war that raged for more than twenty years.

In 1937 Japan invaded China, intent on taking over the Chinese mainland. The Sino-Japanese War brought China into World War II. The Japanese finally surrendered to China in September 1945, a month after capitulating to the Allied nations, but the civil war raged on. China plunged into a deep economic crisis. Because the Nationalist Party was seen as protecting the financiers, industrialists, and other tycoons, it lost the support of the majority of Chinese people. Mao's Communist Party had inspired and empowered the poor, the oppressed, and the exploited, who were backing Mao as they fought to improve their lives. By the late 1940s the Communists occupied nearly all of China. In 1949 the People's Republic of China was born, with Mao Zedong as chairman of the central government council.

In addition to leading the government, Mao was China's most prominent political theorist. The ideas he espoused profoundly influenced the development of the communist ideology. In the mid-1960s a collection of passages from his writings was published in the famous Little Red Book, officially called *Quotations from Chairman Mao*. It set forth the stringent principles that he considered fundamental to true communism. The book was distributed all over China, even in remote corners of the country where other reading material was almost nonexistent. The Little Red Book quickly came to be regarded as an instruction book for life. Everyone was expected to think and behave according to its ideals and directives.

In my understanding and memory, the Little Red Book was intended to encourage the Chinese people to revere Mao and unify their beliefs with his. This was important to Mao and his supporters, who were concerned that their firm grip on the country might slip. Large numbers of people were suffering under his regime. In the late 1950s and early 1960s, twenty million people had died of starvation as a result of his disastrous economic policies. Some party members had begun to oppose his leadership.

In 1966 Mao came up with another strategy to consolidate his power and impose his vision of communism. He initiated the Cultural Revolution. According to Mao's government, the Cultural Revolution was intended to transform China's culture into one of equality, to wipe out the distinctions between the proletariat and the elite. To accomplish this, the regime forced educated people like my father, a teacher of philosophy at a college in Beijing, to give up their homes and careers. They were sent into the distant countryside to work and live with the peasant class, who would "re-educate" them to know hard labor and deprivation. Somehow this would serve society's greater good.

To carry out this new policy, Mao enlisted the help of several top officials, including his wife, Jiang Qing. This group, which became known as the Gang of Four, was determined to eliminate any threat of opposition and to punish people for activities, or even beliefs, that were contrary to official policies. The government mobilized thousands of Chinese youth to join the Red Guard, and it used these forces to persecute and purge anyone who might not be totally loyal to Mao and his ideology. The Red Guard units achieved their objectives through intimidation and violence. Their targets included dissenters within the Communist party, as well as professionals, intellectuals, technicians, and anyone else who might have counterrevolutionary or capitalist leanings. Proof of wrongdoing was not needed; merely belonging to a suspect group, or owning foreign novels or other bourgeois books, was enough to render a person guilty in the minds of zealous Red Guard members and their adherents in the government.

For China's upper and middle classes, this was a time of suffocating fear, intense paranoia, and little hope. Intellectual people lived so timidly that they were like dogs with their tails between their legs. Someone was always watching. Friends, neighbors, and colleagues backstabbed each other to protect themselves. You could trust no one. You had to be cautious not to offend anyone and extremely careful about what you said to someone else, because that person might be setting you up to get you in trouble. If you were accused of saying or doing something that did not align with the government's philosophy, your life could be ruined in a moment.

My family was actually very lucky to suffer no real physical harm during this time. Others were not so fortunate. Large numbers of people lost their lives, and millions suffered brutalization and severe emotional distress, as well as the total loss of their homes, jobs, careers, and way of life. Many people never recovered.

It was under these circumstances that we arrived in the tiny coal-mining village, far away from everything and everyone we knew. We were frightened and despairing. We had no idea what the future might hold. But we were grateful to be together, grateful to be alive.

* * *

My father, affectionately known to me as Baba, and Mama were dismayed to find themselves living in such an inhospitable place as Shandan Meikuang.

The physical environment was harsh. The village was in Gansu province in northwest China, set among rocky mountains at the fringe of the Gobi Desert. The surrounding area was nearly devoid of natural resources except for coal. Digging the coal from the ground provided the villagers with their livelihood. The climate was cold and the landscape bleak. Rain almost never fell on the parched land, and the drinking water was bitter.

The social environment was severe as well. No warmth,

no compassion, no welcome greeted us when we arrived. One or two other families had been relocated here, and they were treated as coldly as we were. The local residents lived in poverty and great hardship, and it's little wonder that they disliked the newcomers from the city. They peered at us through hostile, suspicious, and defensive eyes. The isolation was made worse by a language barrier; we did not understand the dialect spoken here, nor did they understand ours. This was a lonely place for a stranger.

The village was arranged along a central street of packed earth. The buildings included a cluster of houses and a store that sold basic goods. Another shop sold vegetables, which had to be trucked in from sixty miles away. The grammar school and high school sat side by side. My father had been assigned to be their new principal.

Like most Chinese towns, this one had an auditorium where political meetings and entertainment programs were held. No doubt it was modest in size, but to me it seemed like a vast space that must be capable of holding everyone in the village. Once a month or so, movies were shown there to people who were lucky enough to bribe or cajole a local official into letting them buy tickets. In the center of town, a large loudspeaker was mounted outdoors. It was used to broadcast official announcements and also to wake up the town. Each morning at six-thirty music blasted from the speaker, jolting everyone from sleep and summoning people outside for their daily calisthenics.

The new home that the government provided for us was scarcely more than a crudely built hut. Situated on a dirty, bleak hill, the house had straw and brick walls packed with mud for "insulation." The windows were small and sparse. Needless to say, this was a cold, drafty, damp, and dark place to live. We had two bedrooms, a kitchen, and a fifty-square-foot living room. A cellar had been dug out under the house for storing vegetables, which pretty much meant cabbage and potatoes.

Our peasant homestead also had a shabby, dirty coop for the chickens that laid eggs for our family. Chickens were extremely valuable to every family. They provided fresh eggs, a main source of nutrition for the villagers. When our chickens didn't lay enough eggs to feed us adequately, Mama would save up old clothing so she could exchange them for eggs with neighbors.

Without chickens, people were devastated, and to lose them was a disaster. We constantly heard horror stories about this family or that who suffered after their chickens were stolen and killed by thieves or wild animals or even their neighbors. My parents were very careful to make sure that our chickens stayed alive. The chicken coop outside our house was vulnerable and unsafe, so Mama moved them to stay with us. Our tiny living room became a de facto chicken coop.

The chickens were in heaven; it was warmer inside than out in the real chicken coop. The climate was cold, and keeping warm was an issue for people as well as animals. Our beds were hollow structures made of mud. Chimneylike tubes connected them to the coal-burning stove in the kitchen that was our only source of heat. The warmth flowed into the hollow spaces, heating the beds so that the sleepers wouldn't freeze at night. The stove was both a blessing and a curse. It filled the kitchen with choking, blinding smoke. When Mama was cooking, she would often step out of the kitchen, coughing from deep in her lungs, gasping for fresh air, her eyes filled with tears. I patted her back to comfort her, wishing I could do more. That smoke is one of my most vivid early memories.

Another strong memory is of hunger. In my first days in this scary place, I was tormented by hunger pangs; I could hear my stomach making noise as if begging for a meal. There just was not enough food for us. My parents were accustomed to vegetables, rice, and dishes mixed with a little meat or fish. But here food was scarce, and what there was, was unfamiliar. Besides eggs, cabbages, and potatoes, the other staple of the local diet was a yellow bread made of coarse cornmeal. Mama didn't know how to bake it, and when she tried, the loaves that emerged from the smoky oven were acrid and inedible. She felt desperate and afraid when her family went hungry due to her lack of skills and supplies.

Mama hated herself for not doing a better job taking care of us. Angry and frustrated, she complained endlessly about the harshness of life in this village and the cruelty of the fate that forced us to live in a land with such poor food and such unfriendly people. She could not understand why we had to endure such hardship and misery, and since she had no good way to ease her fear and anger, the negative emotions spilled over onto us. My father bore the brunt of her blame for being incapable of changing our unfortunate situation. Baba, on the other hand, had a stoic resolve to make the best of a bad situation. At least we were still all together and alive and able to work.

The two of them fought constantly—a natural result of the fear, hopelessness, and paranoia they were experiencing. Raising their voices helped ease their pain. While they were fighting, we children—my sister, Yan-Yan, and I, and our little brother who was born the year after we arrived—would hide in the corner and huddle together as we listened to them yell. We were too frightened to make a sound. Sometimes my sister was so terrified that she wet her pants. But Mama and Baba were exhausted from figuring out how our family would survive, and they had no energy or time to comfort us. Their incessant battling created an environment inside the house that was nearly as difficult to cope with as the one outside.

* * *

To understand my mother's frustrations and fears, it helps to look back at her own family's history. My mother was born in 1943 in the province of Hubei, a subtropical place of great natural beauty. Her family had means and social position, and its members were cultured and educated. Her grandfather and father were well-known teachers who drew students from all over the county. Mama's father was not only a talented scholar; he was honest and straightforward, and quite outspoken in his opinions about the government. In the political climate of the mid-twentieth century, the family's social status and her father's candidness worked against them, and they paid a heavy price. The authorities labeled the family as right wing and looked on them with suspicion.

Eventually the government arbitrarily removed Mama's father from his job and blacklisted him from taking any other position. The family lost their financial resources and their standing in society. Mama's father suffered from depression, which compromised his health, and he suffered an early death at the age of fifty-two. With four children to care for, her mother struggled to earn a living by washing clothes. Mama and her older brother were nearly grown, but her two sisters were much younger. Their mother was unable to provide for her littlest child and was forced to give up this daughter to be raised by a relative.

Because her family was no longer in its good graces because of her father's political status, the government disqualified my mother from seeking a college education even though she was very bright. That meant she could not obtain a professional job. Yet she was burdened with the responsibility of helping to support her mother and siblings. Here was this lovely, gifted, sensitive young woman looking at closed doors everywhere.

To make a living, Mama capitalized on her beautiful voice and her grace as a dancer. At the age of seventeen, she was selected to join the entertainment troupe sponsored by the county government. Most counties in China had a professional ensemble of singers, dancers, and actors who performed in local auditoriums and theaters. Mama sang folk songs, danced, and performed opera roles. She became a popular local celebrity, acclaimed for her beauty and talent.

In 1960, she was introduced to the young man who would become my father. Their parents arranged the meeting, as was the custom of the time. She found him very appealing—he was handsome and intellectual, a student at Wuhan University, one of the most prestigious institutions of higher learn-

ing in China. Always a profound thinker, he had chosen philosophy as his field of study.

The two of them fell in love, and in 1963 they were married. Like nearly all weddings in China, theirs was a low-key
occasion in keeping with the style of the so-called new revo-
lutionary wedding mandated by the government. Mama and
Baba simply went to the government office in Hubei and reg-
istered as man and wife. Afterward they invited relatives,
friends, and coworkers to gather at home for an announcement
of the marriage. There was no ceremony, no vows, no banquet. The bride and groom just bowed three times, once to
each other, once to their parents, and once to Chairman Mao.
Then they handed out candy, a symbol of their union, to the
assembled guests.

By marrying my father, my mother saved her family from ob-
scurity and poverty. But that's not to say they enjoyed wealth
or luxury. In the early years of their marriage, they did not
even live together. My father returned to Wuhan to complete
his graduate studies. In 1965, he received his degree and was
appointed to teach at a college in Beijing that trained managers for the coal-mining industry. He moved to China's capital city, where he lived in a single room in the university housing complex, ate in the canteen, and took part in academic
activities.

Four years later, the government assigned my father to a
training school in Heilongjiang province, way up in China's
northeast corner, a land famous for its frigid temperatures and
festivals of ice and snow. Along with other academics who
were sent there from Beijing, he became a student rather than

a teacher. The purpose of the school was to have farmers "re-educate" the intellectuals, instilling in them the virtues of farmers and the rural life. In addition to reading Mao's Little Red Book every day, my father and his colleagues learned how to brew Chinese wine and do farm chores like feeding the pigs.

All this time my mother remained behind in Hubei. When the government dissolved her entertainment troupe, she was assigned temporarily to teach music in a high school, and then given a permanent teaching post in a grammar school. She too resided in government housing. Although they were able to arrange visits from time to time, for long periods my parents' communication was limited to letters. Such luxuries as telephones were available only to people who were very rich or very powerful.

When I was born on October 28, 1967, Baba was able to come back to Hubei for a month to spend time with us. He did so again when my baby sister, called Yan-Yan, came along two years later.

In 1970 my father received a notice he had been dreading. It informed him that he was being assigned to work in a coal-mining village in a remote part of Gansu province. This time the government had arranged for my mother to move there with him. Our family reunited in Beijing, where we made preparations for this huge change in our lives.

To a wide-eyed child, Beijing looked like an ocean of red. Everywhere I looked, red flags and red banners with quotations from Mao fluttered in the wind. Even many of the walls had been painted red. Because of the political climate, Beijing, like all of China, was a chaotic place, full of fear and distrust and confusion. But our family was overjoyed to finally be all together, and we had happy times there. My father bought Mama a gift—her first wristwatch—and we all went sightseeing. There is a photo of me that was taken near the entrance of the Forbidden City. It shows a small girl eating watermelon. The juice covers her entire face. The two pigtails on top of her head are pointing to the sky. I remember that moment. All of the tourists around us were laughing at the cheerful spectacle I presented, and I was so happy.

* * *

The year after we arrived in the coal-mining village, my brother, Hui-Hui, was born, bringing my family great happiness. Yan-Yan enjoyed having her status elevated from baby to big sister.

My parents, my sister, and I were not the only ones who welcomed the new arrival. My brother's birth gave great hope to my father's conservative family, who still adhered to the Chinese tradition of favoring boys over girls; after all, boys were entitled to inherit property, and they brought honor to the family by carrying on its name.

One day when Hui-Hui was about three months old, my grandmother—Baba's mother—arrived for a visit. She had been delighted beyond words when she heard that my parents' third try at last had given her a grandson, and she had decided to make the long journey alone so she could see him. With no one's help, this woman in her mid-seventies, hobbling with her cane, took a nine-hour bus ride from her home to Wuhan, changed to a train that took her to Lanzhou, and then caught another train from Lanzhou to Shandan County. When she asked at the station how to get to Shandan Meikuang, she was dismayed to learn that there was no public transportation; one had to take a truck to get there. Luckily, some of Baba's colleagues happened to be at the station. They brought my grandmother to our home in the village. My parents were distressed at how much difficulty she'd gone through to reach us, but my grandmother didn't care. She just wanted to see my brother.

It was fortunate for my mother that her third child was a boy; otherwise, my grandmother would have pressured her to keep having babies until she produced a son. Throughout her visit, which lasted several months, my grandmother pampered and indulged Hui-Hui, giving him 100 percent of her attention. She reserved the best food for him and hid it from my sister and me.

To Yan-Yan and me, she was cold and mean. Being small children, we could not understand why simply being girls should make our grandmother dislike us so much. Yan-Yan and I fought her constantly over her prejudice and unfairness, and we complained to our mother about the way we were mistreated. No doubt our behavior only made things worse, confirming to my grandmother that we didn't deserve her affection or attention. But we never backed down. We even took the food from my brother when she was not there.

Our grandmother was distant and uncaring to Mama too, a typical attitude for a Chinese mother-in-law. It seemed that, to our grandmother, only my father and brother were real human beings, deserving of respect and love. I carried the sting of her rejection with me for a long time.

* * *

Like everyone else in Shandan Meikuang, my parents had to go to work—my father as the school principal and my mother as an assistant in the village administrative office. But what were they to do with their three small children? While my grandmother was with us, she could babysit, but she had returned home, and, at that time, in that place, there was no such thing as kindergarten or preschool. How could they keep the children safe?

My parents decided that their best option for keeping us out of harm's way was to lock us up with the chickens.

To a Westerner, my mother and father may appear cruel and uncaring. Quite the contrary. They didn't like it, but they felt that they had no other alternative for protecting us while they were gone all day. As sometimes happens with parents, in attempting to do what was best for their children, they actually put us in a worse situation.

The living-room-turned-chicken-coop might have been a safe place for the chickens, but it did not feel safe at all to three little children. I was five years old, Yan-Yan was three, and our brother, Hui-Hui, was just one. To us, this place was dark and scary. It was locked from the outside so we had no way to escape into the kitchen or bedrooms. The only light came from a tiny window at the top of the big front door.

It was noisy, too. Let me tell you, in case you're not familiar with chickens, they are noisy. The cacophony of their squawking never ends. The cocks were especially loud and frightening. We chased those noisy, nasty birds around to try to quiet them down, but that only made them mad, and when they got mad they screeched even louder.

Hui-Hui was still wearing a baby's split-seamed pants, and one day the cock managed to grab his most tender parts. The scream that emitted from his lungs sent the chickens into a frenzy of flapping and shrieking. At first Yan-Yan and I didn't realize what had happened. We knew only that our brother was crying and the chickens were upset. We tried to comfort Hui-Hui and stop his tears, but he wouldn't be consoled because his fright and pain were too great. At the same time, we had to fight off attacks from the evil chickens. All three of us ended up in tears. I held my little sister's and brother's hands tightly and desperately wished for my parents to come home.

Worst of all was the disgusting odor. The stench from the chickens and their poop was so bad that I can smell it in my nostrils to this day. Anything with that chicken stink puts me right back into that frightening and uncomfortable time.

Trapped every day inside the "chicken coop," we felt lonely and abandoned. We were frantic to escape this scream-filled, smelly, dark, and scary little room. We had no clock with which to judge the time, and the hours seemed unending until Mama and Baba came home from work. We were desperate for their hugs. The one good thing is that there were many, many hugs when they finally arrived, especially from Baba.

My mother was determined that we should keep ourselves clean, but that was impossible. Needless to say, when our parents got home at the end of the day, we were not a pretty sight. Our faces were always dirty and stained, our shoes were covered with chicken droppings, and our shirts weren't much better. It took a long time each day to clean ourselves up. Mama, in her frustration, would raise her voice in anger. It was a hopeless situation for her.

I didn't want her to be angry with me, so I asked if I could help her out with the cleaning. I was willing to do anything to see my mother smile again.

She gave me a special job. I was to keep the chicken coop clean by taking ash from the stove to cover up the chicken droppings. I would throw the ash on the ground, sweep up the mingled ash and poop, then throw new ash down and repeat the whole process until the place was excrement-free. Anyone who has lived with chickens, or any bird, knows how pointless this chore was, since birds eat and poop constantly. I would sweep and sweep until finally the old brick floor appeared clean, only to see it become dirty again within minutes. Those chickens never stopped.

It was a very un-fun task—dirty, smelly, disgusting, and unpleasant in so many ways. I hated it. I didn't want to do it, but I wanted to help Mama and make her happy. So I conscientiously performed the tiresome chore, suffering through it without expressing my resentment. In fact, I made up a little song to cheer up my family and myself: "I am the big sister. I love working. Cleaning the floor and table is my job, tra-la-la. . . ."

Nowadays I always work diligently to overcome obstacles, and I try to endure hardships with a positive attitude. Maybe this experience is what cultivated those abilities in me. But I have to confess that I still hate cleaning anything at all. I would rather cook a twelve-course dinner every night than clean my home. This is why I hire people to help me do so. I'm not lazy, just severely traumatized from my chicken-coop days.

The past always creeps up in little ways to affect your life in the present. The resentment, the sadness, and the fear that I felt as a child abandoned in the chicken coop still surface in my adult life. Feelings like these are hard to erase from your subconscious. They stay buried, wait to pop out and torment you at the slightest provocation. Part of succeeding as an adult is learning to cope with these hidden emotional demons.

* * *

My father has always been my ally—affectionate, comforting, patient, and supportive about anything that I do. During my frequent arguments with my mother, he always stepped in to find a point of compromise.

As I grew older, my mother's complaining became more bothersome. I was upset with the way she would argue aggressively and angrily with my father, and I urged him to put a halt to her outbursts. But he was determined to be patient with her constant complaints and criticisms. He felt responsible for her plight. He believed that the political philosophies he'd expressed while teaching in Beijing had made him and his family a target for government oppression. Mama had suffered so much and lost so many opportunities due to the actions of others. The least he could offer was silence and tolerance. If her complaints made her feel better, then enduring them was worthwhile. He knew who he was and what he was worth, and that was enough for him. My father truly loved my mother, and he felt she deserved to be happy, even if sometimes her happiness came at his expense.

He was then and still is my hero, my source of security and love. My father's acts of love—nonjudgmental, never weary, never complaining, always tolerant—served then and now as examples to help me appreciate what real, meaningful, and timeless love is all about. He set a high standard, one that I seek for myself and for others around me. True love is not always comfortable, but it is always kind and forgiving and understanding. From my father I have learned that a great relationship is about giving without always getting; it is about protecting and honoring the one you love. This is not easy to find or achieve, but I am not going to stop seeking it.

> *True love is not always comfortable, but it is always kind and forgiving and understanding.*

I'm not saying my mother didn't have a loving nature. She just displayed it in different ways. A harsh life sometimes brings out a harsh voice, but the tender voice can be heard under the words if you pay attention. Sometimes the tenderness is expressed in deeds rather than words. Despite her pain and endless exhaustion, Mama in fact was affectionate, and she was always generous. Even when we did not have much food, she would not turn away a hungry stranger. I remember the time a hungry teenage girl came to our house begging for food. Mama cooked a huge bowl of rice and pigs' blood and bread, placed it in the center of our table, and asked the girl to join us. What greater love is there than compassion for a total stranger?

My mother was strong-willed, outspoken, and hardworking. She always fought for the truth. Once she became angry because the village shopkeepers were setting aside the top-quality goods for the political leaders and well-connected officials; ordinary villagers had to settle for inferior goods. Mama thought that this was unfair. She made a big poster denouncing the shopkeepers and put it on display on the bulletin board of a major county center. This was highly unusual—normally, only the government put up posters, and rarely did people find ways to protest when they were treated unfairly. The villagers were amazed that Mama would do such a bold, outrageous thing. No one else in the county had that much courage, but they admired her for taking action and gave her their enthusiastic support. Afterward, the shopkeepers treated Mama with more respect, and the quality of the goods our family bought was a little higher. Her campaign became the talk of the village for a while. Whenever I heard someone praise my mother's brave spirit, I felt proud.

I remember the day in January 1976 when I found Mama crying in her office. She had just heard over the radio that Zhou Enlai, a man she respected, admired, and loved, had died. Mama took the pink silk butterfly ribbon off my pigtail to express her grief and her condolences to him. When I asked Mama why she was so sad, she explained that Zhou Enlai had become a legend in China. He was a prime minister of China, a founder of the Chinese Communist party, and a former foreign minister. Despite the abuses that occurred during the Cultural Revolution, he had worked to improve relations with other countries, and he had protected many people from the insanity and oppression of the Gang of Four's regime. Here was a man who fought for justice and human decency, who had sacrificed his whole life and his heart for his country. Now he was dead, and my mother mourned him bitterly and completely. Her heart broke on that terrible day.

Zhou Enlai's death clouded the whole village in sorrow, and it only added to China's political confusion. Everyone shared my mother's anguish and fear as they wondered what further destruction the country would now endure. I admire my mother for her personal resolution to survive whatever would befall us.

* * *

I was delighted when the time came for me to enter grammar school. It meant that I would finally be sprung from the chicken-coop prison. Going to school didn't relieve me completely of unpleasant chores, though. In addition to my duties at home, I now had tasks at school. The students took turns going to school before class to clean the classroom and light the stove. I hated it when my turn came. It meant rousing out of bed early—as soon as the village loudspeaker blared at six-thirty AM—and rushing through the frigid dawn to the school. The classroom would be freezing until I could get the fire lit with my icy-numb fingers. Sometimes, to add to the unpleasantness, the lengths of metal tubing that made up the chimney would come apart. The room would fill with smoke, and I would have to wrestle the chimney pieces back together again.

But for the most part I liked going to school. I enjoyed learning new things, and I proved to be an apt student—a well-behaved child who earned good grades. The teacher handed out little red flags for good academic performance. Receiving one was an honor, and the children competed for them. I was pleased to earn three or four red flags each month.

We studied the basics of reading, writing, and arithmetic. Our reading text was Mao Zedong's Little Red Book. The hardest thing was learning to write the Chinese characters. To do it properly, we had to sit up straight and hold our wrists perfectly still as we made the strokes. We used a pen with a brush at the end of it, and special ink. The teacher gave us a model of the character to follow. We copied each one fifty times to make sure we knew it correctly. How boring. I much preferred work that was more creative. But I practiced carefully anyway so I would earn good reports from my teacher and make my parents proud.

* * *

When I was seven years old and my sister was five, I became fiercely jealous of her beautiful dimple. Yan-Yan was a cheerful, good-natured little girl with an adorable dimple on her chin. Everyone loved her, and I was sure that the dimple was the reason. I spent a lot of time looking hard into the mirror and poking at my face, trying to create a dimple for myself. I never succeeded. But as time went on, I learned that what made my sister so loveable was her easy nature. Because I had a stubborn and determined spirit, I just didn't come across as being bubbly and adorable, and I was quite shy and quiet. But the very quirks in my personality that made me seem a little prickly turned out to be the source of strength I needed to make my mark in life.

One time, when I was eight years old, my willful and fierce personality proved to be a definite asset. My brother, Hui-Hui, was just four. The poor little guy had bad allergies and some chronic sinus problems, and as a result he had a rather unpleasant appearance: a trail of thick yellow mucous was always discharging from his nose. This made him a target for the neighbor kids, who were clearly repulsed by the way he looked. The bullies laughed at him, made fun of him, and pushed him around. I could not tolerate my brother being abused like this. How could I get even with these people, especially the big bully neighbor boy who instigated the abuse? I knew that I could not defeat him with my fists, since he was big and I was so tiny.

The personality quirks that made me seem a little prickly turned out to be the source of strength I needed.

One day I had an inspiration. Finally those pesky chickens would have some value. I gathered their droppings and spread them all over the courtyard of the bully's home, covering the muck with ash to disguise it. When the bully and his mother came outside, they stepped all over it and got filthy.

"Eek!" the mother screamed. "Who did this?"

I was watching from a distance, and when I saw how distressed they were, I laughed myself silly. I laughed so hard that tears rolled down my cheeks.

However, no good deed goes unpunished. When the bully realized that I was the culprit who'd done this to him, he ran straight to my father to complain.

Baba called me into the house. Calmly he asked, "Jing-Jing, can you explain your actions?"

Why should I explain, I wondered. The bully deserved what I had done to him.

"I want you to apologize immediately," Baba said.

The boy and his mother stood by, waiting for my words. I, of course, righteously refused. Instead of apologizing, I kept silent. No amount of encouragement from my father could budge me from my moral position. I believed I was right and therefore did not have to explain my actions to anyone.

Eventually, when the boy and his mother left, all the tension inside me came to a head and I burst into loud sobs. Going to Mama, I told her all about Hui-Hui's suffering. I defended my decision to try to protect him and get even for the pain the bully had inflicted upon him.

Mama was not impressed. "You have two choices, Jing-Jing," she told me. "Either you will apologize to this boy and his mother, or you will receive a spanking on your buttocks and hand. The choice is yours."

What a dilemma. I did not like pain, but I was justified in what I'd done. There was no doubt in my mind at all. Finally, with the strength of will that would guide me throughout my adult life, I made my choice. I would take the spanking.

I fetched the ruler that we kids had all come to hate. I handed it to Mama in silence. Reluctantly I lowered my pants and bent down to receive my spanking. The blows hurt, and

I cried out loudly and for a long time. I learned that there would always be a reckoning if I chose to disobey my mother. But I still think it was worth it.

* * *

Life in the coal-mining village probably doesn't seem like much fun for small children, and it certainly wasn't. When I think back to those years, I mostly remember the cold winters, the spiteful local people, and the brats who bullied my sister and brother. I remember the times when we didn't have enough vegetables and fruits to eat. I remember the loud arguments between my parents and the feelings of depression and paranoia about our future, which everyone felt in various ways, some expressed, some hidden. We were all so fearful of the political environment during that dark time in China's history.

My family did not have many possessions. Nobody did. We learned how to value our few belongings, like our radio and sewing machine. Each family had a limited number of tickets for the purchase of necessities like meat, bread, clothes, and oil. Too often, the supplies that the tickets entitled you to were inadequate. To get what you needed, you had to be extremely nice to the people who controlled the distribution. People were always competing with each other for power and money and political favor.

One day Mama found that our tickets for purchasing clothes had mysteriously disappeared. She searched everywhere in the house, and she almost went crazy when she could not find them. What was she going to do? We kids were outgrowing our clothes, and the tickets couldn't be easily replaced. Mama was in despair when my sister arrived home. Upon hearing what was wrong, Yan-Yan took the tickets from her pocket and handed them over. She had taken them thinking they were tickets for the movie show in the village auditorium; with such a stash she might never need to buy movie tickets again. You can imagine the spanking my poor sister endured. She never touched any of the tickets again.

When I think back to my life in the village and reflect upon the fickle nature of fate, a sad memory surfaces. The village had one small reservoir that provided all our water, and the kids would go swimming in it during the summertime. One day a little boy drowned there, and we were never allowed to get close to the reservoir again. This taught me a serious lesson about the uncertainty of life and the fragility of happiness.

But happiness does exist, and children, who can be very resilient, will find ways to achieve it. My nature, even back then, always led me to seek it out. And while our village had residents who were malicious and rude, we also had kind, friendly neighbors. So to balance the dark memories, I can summon up some that are bright and fun.

Here is one particularly pleasant memory. Every morning at around eight o'clock, I went to visit my neighbor, whom I referred to as my sister. Her name was Zhang Li, and her family, like mine, had been relocated to Shandan Meikuang because of the Cultural Revolution. I would go to her home, and she would comb my hair and braid it into a thick, black, glossy pigtail. I prided myself on that beautiful pigtail. Even when you do not have much to be proud of, you take pride in whatever you can; at least I did.

Zhang Li had a gentle voice. She was warm and nurturing, and she was always calm and patient with me. She told me fairy tales and shared her snacks. Her little brother entertained us with practical jokes. I wanted to spend more and more time with them.

Zhang Li was a beautiful twelve-year-old when I met her. She had such a lovely, dainty face, with affectionate brown eyes. I remember thinking, "Why is she so beautiful? I wish that she were my real sister. Why isn't she my real sister?"

Beauty comes from doing and from being.

Later, as an adult, I came to understand the true nature of beauty. This is not to say that Zhang Li wasn't really pretty; she was. But her real beauty came from the way she behaved. Her generosity with her time and her heart made her glow in my mind. Today, as a successful female entrepreneur, I maintain a philosophy that beauty comes from doing and from being. I try to create beauty all around me by the way I treat other people and my environment. As a result, I feel that an aura of beauty surrounds me wherever I go.

Zhang Li was a great teacher without knowing it. We all have the potential to be great teachers if we pay attention to the needs of others around us. My personal commitment to teaching and reaching out to others is a subject I will discuss later on. But now you have an idea of how it came about.

* * *

Some wonderful memories also came from the performances of the local entertainment troupes. Before remote areas like ours had movies and television, people had to be creative regarding entertainment. As in Mama's home county, the government sponsored troupes that visited our village, performing in the village auditorium or on the school playground. I loved watching them, and what I loved even more was being part of the show.

I was my mother's daughter in that singing and dancing came naturally to me. I felt happy when I was imitating the movements that I saw the dancers perform. Singing was my companion and my sanity when I had to do those tedious and disgusting chores. When I sang and danced, I felt normal, even beautiful.

Imagine my thrill when I was selected by the high school's music instructor to participate in a performance. Several students from the high school were chosen, but I was one of the few pupils from the grammar school. Soon I was going onstage regularly, often with my mother and Zhang Li. We would sing and dance together with the local entertainment troupes.

This was an absolute privilege for me. It was such a joy to see my mother look and feel her best. She loved to sing, and she looked so beautiful in her makeup and costume. The people loved her; when she took her bow, the whole audience would pop up and applaud loudly. No one wanted my mother to leave the stage. I was so proud of her. When she performed, I could see in her face a little bit of the mother I used to know. This made me feel happy.

It was exhilarating to dress up in costumes, vibrant with color and texture. Even more fun was the elaborate makeup. Oh, how glamorous it made me feel. I adored wearing it.

Waiting in line to put on my makeup, I felt excited, and after the show I threw a fit when it was time to take it off. I still love my makeup to this day, although I've learned to use it for nontheatrical purposes. Whenever I put it on, for a moment I still feel that old tremor of excitement and anticipation.

I still feel joyful and giddy when I think about singing and dancing with the local entertainment troupes. It was an especially happy time that I shared in an intimate way with my mother. When I sang and danced with her, it felt as if I were lifted up to another level. No longer was I a little peasant girl stuck in a dreary mountain village. No, I was a great creature flying in the air. Free and graceful and utterly beautiful, and at one with a higher universe.

One day I was in a big dance demonstration, rehearsed in front of everyone at the high school. I decided that I didn't exactly have to follow the movement of the other dancers. I chose instead to move in my own unique way to the rhythms that I felt within my very being—an internalization of cadence and melody that compelled me to move this way and that. All the time I sensed that I was in perfect synchrony with the music's true rhythm.

Unfortunately, I was not in synchrony with the other dancers. I stood out like a sore thumb. The other dancers were annoyed, and the audience laughed at me. I was mortified and shocked. How could they laugh at such perfection? How could they not see and feel what I was seeing and feeling? What made me so different that they could not share the profound experience I was having? I was so embarrassed that I wanted to hide under a rock.

Later, at home, Baba comforted me. "Jing-Jing, you are very brave, very creative. Don't let yourself be upset by those people." He told me he liked my dance movements.

Those were just the right words for me to hear. My dad's support and belief in me helped me develop the courage and self-belief that I carry with me today. He let me understand that it is okay to be creative and different, and this belief has empowered me to try unique things even at the risk of ridicule and laughter from others. His kind, supportive, honest words kept me from abandoning the very thing that today gives me so much joy. To this day I am developing my voice and dance skills, and, in fact, I believe that I am coming into my own right now. I owe it all to this gentle, patient man, my father.

It is okay to be creative and different.

* * *

Other bright moments in my life come back now and then like flashes of light in a dark sky.

Games we played provide glowing memories. I remember laughing with my brother and sister as we played with mud toys, and romping until I was out of breath as I played hide-and-seek with the village boys and girls. A game I particularly liked was *yaang gala*. It was a sort of juggling game that developed dexterity skills, and we played it for hours in the kitchen. The playing pieces were ping-pong balls and a particular type of oddly shaped bones that came from lambs' feet. We

painted the bones bright colors like purple. They were col-
lector's items. I recall trading hair ornaments for good *yaang
gala* bones.

A high point in my memories is the spring festival, when
we celebrated the Chinese New Year. This was an exciting
time for all the children in the village. It was traditional for
parents to present us with new clothes for the festival. New
clothes were a rare treat, and we eagerly awaited our New
Year finery. No one could afford to buy new clothes, so our
mothers made them. Since moving to Shandan Meikuang,
Mama had learned to make simple clothes so we wouldn't be
totally without them, but she was not a talented seamstress
or knitter. Sometimes her collars were uneven or her pants
legs were different lengths. We cheerfully wore the clothes
because they were new. Her younger sister, my favorite aunt,
was a highly skilled dressmaker. Sometimes she was able to
send us beautiful clothes that she'd made for my siblings and
me. We cherished her gifts.

Right after midnight on the New Year, the sky would ex-
plode with noise as firecrackers burst everywhere. All of the
neighbors came out of their homes to greet each other with
cries of "*Bai nian!*"—"Happy New Year!" Children jumped up
and down, showing off their new clothes. Bold kids would
throw firecrackers into the crowd to scare the other children.
Once or twice I was frightened to tears when they went off
with a boom close to me. But I loved the warmth of the crowd
and the passion we all felt on that occasion, the excitement
and warm atmosphere. I felt excited to be alive, and I wished
that the moment would last forever. Even in this dismal
town, the light of hope appeared. I carry that light with me

today wherever I go and in whatever circumstance I find myself.

Many of my happy memories relate to food.

Apricots. We had few fruits available in the village, and my parents rarely had money to buy any for us. So fruit was a real indulgence. I still recall the thrill of swiping apricots from the market in the summer. We kids would mingle with the crowd, each of us with a steel stick in hand. We would squeeze between the people in front of the apricot stand and use our sticks to stab an apricot and pull it away. Then we would run away, afraid and excited that we might get caught. Out of breath and laughing, we would enjoy the sweet, juicy reward of eating our purloined treasure. That was great fun. And I still love apricots.

Watermelons. The Gobi Desert's soil and long period of summer sunshine are excellent for producing sweet, crunchy watermelon. As a special treat we could go to a farm twenty miles away where they were grown and eat as much as we wanted; if we took any home, we had to pay for them. The farmer was kind and generous. As many as ten kids would go out there together at one time, and he allowed us to grab a big watermelon and eat until our small stomachs stuck out like little drums. We patted each other's tummies and compared to see whose was biggest.

In the summer, on occasion, the village government pro-vided watermelons as gifts to the local families. Whenever we got extra watermelons at home, my parents had to keep a close eye on them. My clever sister was always figuring out ways that she could eat more and eat earlier than the rest of the family. One time Yan-Yan sneaked under the bed where

Mama had hidden the watermelons and picked holes in every single melon with her little hands. The next day she declared that we should eat the watermelon because the chickens had dug holes in them.

"Yes, indeed," Mama said, "and that little chicken is called Yan-Yan."

Yan-Yan winked at my parents and smoothly confessed. We were able to eat the watermelons much earlier than my parents planned because of my sister's tricky masterwork. From that time on, my parents kept the watermelons with the fresh vegetables in the small storage room with a big lock on it. The three of us spent a lot of time trying to figure out how to find the key, open the door, and replace the key once we'd swiped our watermelon. Unfortunately, we never succeeded. As an adult I've tried many kinds of melons in many countries, and none are as sweet as the watermelons in that little village. And when they were forbidden, they were even tastier.

Candies. These sweet confections were strictly for special occasions. Only at festivals and weddings did we get the chance to eat candies. One of the most popular kinds—sweet, creamy, and quite chewy—came wrapped in colorful paper printed with illustrations from an old fairy tale called *Xi You Ji*, or *Journey to the West*. It is the story of a gold monkey king with magical powers who helps the famous monk Xuanzang retrieve the true secret of Buddhism from India. Whenever I got a piece of the candy I saved the wrapping; I liked to collect things, and this was one of my favorite collections. One day a dozen kids came over to my house, and they all wanted to trade me something for those beautiful papers. I felt so proud and important at that moment.

Chive dumplings. I can still taste those delicious, fragrant treats. Whenever we had one of our infrequent rains, it would produce an abundance of raw chives. We would harvest them, along with the hair mushrooms that also sprang up, and make chive dumplings. Such a delicacy required a celebration. Neighbors gathered together in a festive manner to make the dumplings and eat together. Harmony and peace, fellowship and fun—these events yielded precious memories during that otherwise bleak time.

Then there were the tomatoes, bright red and yellow. So sweet and seductive and tempting, especially since they were not always available. Tomatoes also taught me a valuable lesson about honesty.

One day my sister and I walked into the vegetable shed, which was usually locked but not that day. We discovered a trove of ripe tomatoes. Yan-Yan grabbed one, and I grabbed two. She took a great big juicy bite. I hid mine in my trousers to savor later.

Suddenly my mother appeared and demanded to know what we were doing.

"Nothing," I said, looking her straight in the eye.

"You are stealing tomatoes," Mama said sternly.

Yan-Yan, her mouth full of red, sweet fruit, couldn't deny it. But she tried to justify herself. "It was my sister's idea. I just followed her."

Mama did not believe either of us. "Step forward, Jing-Jing," she commanded.

I didn't move. I pretended that my stomach was hurting.

She said it again. "Step forward."

So I did, and the two tomatoes rolled out of my pants onto

the floor right in front of my mother. I was so embarrassed. When I looked at her unsmiling face, I knew that more trouble was to come from this little misadventure.

Mama instructed me to go into the house, and she followed me there. Trouble was brewing; I could just feel it.

"I will not tolerate a liar," Mama said. "When you make a mistake, then you need to have the courage to admit it. Do not lie."

Then she gave me a choice. One option was to bring her the dreaded ruler and a chair, and be prepared to receive three strokes from the ruler. If I chose not to get the ruler and chair, then I would get five strokes.

> *When you make a mistake, you need to have the courage to admit it.*

I thought hard. Neither choice was good. Finally I decided to take my punishment. I went and brought the ruler and chair. Three strikes were quickly dispensed, and they hurt so much. But she taught me my lesson—do not lie.

My brother and I still hate that ruler. Once we were grown, we tried hard to find it, but we never could.

To this day, I link lying to the pain I felt from that experience. I do my best never to lie to my friends, colleagues, or even enemies.

* * *

One day in October 1976, I was resting on my bed, listening to the radio. The newscaster proclaimed that the Gang of Four was no longer in power.

This was huge news. The Gang of Four had directed the worst oppressions of the Cultural Revolution. Chairman Mao had died the previous month, and this group of radical politicians had been trying to seize control of the nation.

I looked up to my father nearby and asked, "Baba, is it true? The broadcast says they've been arrested."

"Let's go and see." My father took my hand, and together we walked to the center of the village. The big public loudspeaker was blaring the news, repeating it again and again.

A large crowd gathered. People started out talking in whispers, but gradually their voices grew louder and louder until everyone burst into cheers. Someone cried out, "Let's light some firecrackers to celebrate."

In a few seconds, we heard firecrackers exploding everywhere. The noise was deafening. The bursts of light made by the firecrackers acknowledged our emergence out of an era of darkness.

My mother joined us. She, too, held my hand, as she wept out of pure happiness and relief. For the first time in many years, she felt hopeful for her country. A sense of joy and celebration filled the air. To me, it seemed to spread to every corner of the earth and heaven.

Nearly one year later, in August 1977, the Eleventh National Communist Party Congress officially declared an end to the Cultural Revolution. Deng Xiaoping, a moderate who had opposed the Cultural Revolution at the beginning, became a deputy premier. He was put in charge of charting a new direction for China, and soon he became one of the country's most powerful leaders.

Deng launched significant political, economic, social, and

cultural reforms. He implemented a new recovery policy addressed to the professionals, intellectuals, and other educated people who had been devalued and displaced over the past decade. They would be allowed to use their talents to help rebuild the country.

Once again, the lives of my parents, my siblings, and myself were turned topsy-turvy, but this time for the better. In 1978 my family received good news—we were going to move. The government appointed my father to be a lecturer in the philosophy department at Lanzhou University in the capital city of Gansu province. After eight years of feeding chickens and pigs, coaxing food to grow in barren soil, digging coal, and riding herd on unwilling students in a crude village school, he would be allowed to begin a new life. At last he would be a true educator in a place that valued academic achievement and intellectual interests. His new position would take us out of the dark hell of the coal-mining village and into the light of the modern world again. We were overwhelmed with joy at this opportunity.

Life is like a mirror. If you smile at it, it smiles back at you. If you frown or weep in front of it, it will frown or weep back at you.

We left the coal-mining village in the autumn of 1978. Before we departed, a farewell dinner was held for us. Zhang Li's mother cooked more than ten dishes—so many delicacies. That was the first time I ate a salted, marinated, boiled egg. Its yolk was creamy and tasty, and it helped me tremendously to avoid getting carsick on our journey. Our spirits were high as my parents, my siblings, and I climbed aboard the big truck that would take us to the city of Lanzhou.

I am happy to say that we left the chickens behind.

* * *

So let this chapter close with the thought that the life we live is full of experiences. Some are good; some are bad. But all of them are part of the creative process of becoming a human being in this world.

A wise Chinese philosopher once said: "Life is like a mirror. If you smile at it, it smiles back at you. If you frown or weep in front of it, it will frown or weep back at you." Our experiences guide us and influence us throughout our lives. How we respond to them—whether with a smile or with tears—makes an incredible difference. My desire is to introduce you to my experiences in the hope that I can show you how you can move beyond your past or present circumstances and achieve a future that honors your passion and power.

Diana's Stepping-Stones on the Journey to Success

Stay positive and hopeful. Even in the darkest times, we can find sources of light. The ability to seek out brightness and maintain hope is what carries us through.

Be grateful. We should always take time to appreciate life and the small things that can contribute to our joy.

Give unconditional love, compassion, and support to those you care about. And expect the same in return. Our loved ones and friends are our most valuable treasure.

Maintain your dignity, honesty, and principles. No matter what the situation, no one can rob us of these things but ourselves. If you conduct yourself with integrity, you can trust that the universe will reward you with a better life.

With junior high school classmate and volleyball team member Sun Peng in Lanzhou.

牛肉面城

———

Two   Beef Noodle City, 1978–1981

———

We arrived in Lanzhou early on an autumn morning. The sunlight was thin and cold, filtered through a haze of smoke from the petrochemical plants and other factories. As we made our way through an endless maze of streets lined with tall, boxy buildings, I stared open-mouthed at all the people—hundreds of them, thousands, on foot, on bicycles, in buses and trucks. How crowded this place is, I thought. How noisy. How vast. I was eleven years old and in awe.

Because my father would be teaching at Lanzhou University, we were assigned an apartment in a faculty housing complex. There were two dozen apartment buildings clustered tightly together. I noticed children playing in the walkways that connected them.

"How many people live here?" I asked Mama.

"I don't know, Jing-Jing," she replied. "Quite a lot. Probably more people live in just this one little corner of Lanzhou than in all of Shandan Meikuang."

When we reached Building 13, where we would reside,

my family stopped to gaze at it, to take in its contours, its colors, all the details about it, and make them ours.

"It's so big," I murmured, rising on my tiptoes in excitement. I could hardly believe we were going to live in such an amazing place.

Our apartment house was five stories high—a giant structure compared to the buildings in the coal-mining village we had left behind. Each floor had four units fronted by a common balcony, and the balconies were lined with drying laundry that flapped in the breeze as if banners had been hung out to welcome us.

"Our apartment is on the third floor," Baba told us. "It is number 307."

I ran up the stairs, Yan-Yan and Hui-Hui at my heels. We all held our breath as our father opened the door.

"Here we are," he said as we entered our apartment for the first time. "Welcome to our new home."

Home—that thrilling word made me shiver. In Shandan Meikuang, we were in exile, outcasts. Even within the mud-packed walls of our little house, we had never felt as though we belonged. But now we lived in Apartment 307. I will always remember that number, because it meant that at last I had a real home.

The apartment was tiny—around 160 square feet. There were two small bedrooms, plus a room that served as kitchen and living room both. We kids explored the whole place in just a few minutes.

Right away I noticed that we didn't have a coal-burning stove; instead there was a steam-heated radiator. Curious, I touched the pipes and marveled as their warmth seeped into my fingers. What a wonderful invention, so modern, so new. No longer would I have to start the stove, shovel in coal, clean out the ashes, and be choked by the strong smoke and soot.

Life in the city was going to be fine.

* * *

Though Gansu is one of China's poorest, most remote, and most undeveloped provinces, its capital city, Lanzhou, has been an important place for more than two thousand years. Once it was known as the Golden City because the precious metal was mined nearby, and it was an important stop along the legendary Silk Road, the ancient trade route linking China and the Mediterranean. The Yellow River flows through the city, and mountains rise on either side of it.

By the time we arrived, whatever golden sheen the city might have had was gone. Even on sunny days, the sky wasn't blue but the pale color of ash, the result of polluted air. The many factories, including one of China's largest oil refineries, spewed smoke, which became trapped in the narrow river basin. Dust blowing down from the Gobi Desert only made the terrible smog worse.

Even so, much delighted me about the changes in my life and the big city I was now living in. There were so many people around us, and they were so different from our neighbors in Shandan Meikuang. Lanzhou's two million residents came from many places, especially around Lanzhou University, which had gathered professors from Beijing, Shanghai, and other well-developed and modern cities. I loved all the variety of the faces and the clothing and the ways that people spoke. I was also impressed by their politeness. Instead of rudeness and hostility, people greeted each other with courtesy. They didn't yell all the time, but modulated their voices. This kind of civility was a new experience for me.

Another new experience was a culinary one. The city was famous for a special dish—Lanzhou beef noodle. This flavorful concoction quickly became one of my all-time favorite foods. To make it, the dough is rolled for hours; the dough ball is then stretched into a single lengthy noodle of whatever thickness the diner desires, from hair-thin to inch-wide. The noodle is cooked and served in a beef broth seasoned with vinegar and spicy peppers—the perfect food to warm you on a cold, foggy winter's day. Every neighborhood has several noodle restaurants, all of which claim to have the best broth, made from a secret family recipe. Long lines form outside the best places, which become so crowded that the customers spill out the doors, crouching down outside the restaurant to consume their lunch with loud slurping sounds.

My family found a fancy restaurant that became our favorite. At that time it was called Lanzhou Fandian, and it served really tasty, high-quality food. When Mama and Baba took us kids to eat pot stickers or fried dumplings called *baozi*, it seemed just like a festival.

Our lives became centered around Lanzhou University, since Baba was on the faculty there and we lived on its grounds. With more than fifteen departments or faculties and a little less than ten thousand students ranging from undergraduates to postdoctoral candidates, it is one of China's most

prominent universities, recognized for its academic excellence. At long last my father would be working in the kind of
stimulating intellectual environment he loved. I was so glad
for him.

* * *

Though we were happy to be living in Apartment 307, it
truly was a humble place. The bedroom I shared with Yan-
Yan and Hui-Hui was so small that only one bed fit within it.
Instead of lying on it with our heads and feet in the proper
places, the three of us slept on it crossways. As we grew
taller, Mama added a wooden extension to the side of the
bed so we could stretch out without our feet dangling over
the edge. In the daytime she leaned this contraption against
the wall so we would have a little space in the room in which
to walk.

Like most of the apartments in the complex, ours didn't
have a private washroom. Instead, everyone went to a big
public bathhouse. In the coal-mining village, we had to stoop
in a narrow basin and sponge ourselves off. Here, we were issued tickets that entitled us to two hot showers every week.
It was such a pleasure to get thoroughly clean.

At first it felt uncomfortable to expose our nakedness to
strangers. But we lost our fear as we realized that everyone
else was stripped bare too. Soon Yan-Yan and I were giggling
as we made note of all the different shapes of womanhood—
tall bodies and short bodies, thin ones and fat ones, pendulous
breasts and tiny buds.

We squeezed ourselves into narrow shower stalls, which

were usually shared by three or four women. The stalls were made of concrete, which could get very slippery. One day my feet skidded on the slick floor and I fell against a hot water pipe, burning my left leg badly; I have a little scar to this day.

Even if we'd had a private shower at home, we would have preferred the bathhouse because our apartment had no hot water. In our old home, when we needed hot water we boiled some on the stove. That was no longer necessary. The residential complex was served by a central water-boiling house, called *kaishui fang*. To obtain the day's hot water supply, everyone brought large thermos bottles to fill from the huge, simmering vessel. The *kaishui fang* was located in the center of campus, about two miles away from the residential areas. People stood in long lines in a steamy room, getting hot and sticky as they waited for their turn. Every one of the ten or so lines had at least about fifteen people.

My mother assigned me this errand, which I did twice a day. The thermos bottles, made of glass and steel, were awkward and bulky. They held five quarts and were about three feet high—almost as tall as I was—and they were hard for me to handle. When filled with water they were very heavy, and I had to carry them all the way there and back with both hands. It was hard work and a boring chore that I hated.

One day, shortly after we arrived in Lanzhou, I grew fidgety as I waited in line. Moving about to ease my restlessness, I failed to notice how close someone was standing behind me. All of a sudden I heard a huge crash. I didn't know what had happened. All I could see was that two hot water thermoses were smashed into small, shining pieces.

Uh-oh. This was bad. But what made it worse was that they were not my thermoses.

I became aware of two sets of dark eyes staring at me. The eyes belonged to the two girls who stood in line behind me. They were near my own age, and they looked like sisters. I quickly realized that the broken thermos bottles were theirs.

I was scared. The girls no doubt were angry with me, but not half as much as my mother would be when she found out about this transgression. I know that my family could ill afford the expense of replacing the thermoses.

My voice trembled as I said, "I am so sorry, *yatou*." This was an informal word that everyone used in the coal-mining village; it meant "miss" or "girl."

The two girls frowned. I felt worse and worse. I could tell by their expressions that somehow I had affronted them, on top of the offense of breaking their bottles.

Finally one of them spoke. She was a tall girl with freckles on her face, and she said, kindly and calmly, "It is no problem about the bottles. But we are not *yatou*."

"N-not *yatou*?" I stammered. "What do you mean?"

"You come from the country, don't you?" she asked.

I nodded slowly. What difference did that make?

"In the country, people speak differently than we do here. You are in the city now, so you should know that *yatou* is very rude slang. To city people, *yatou* means 'maid.'"

So I had my first lesson in my own "re-education" into the ways of the urban world—never call a girl *yatou*; she is just "miss" or "girl."

I apologized again, this time for the vulgar insult I'd given them without intending to. I felt so relieved. I couldn't believe how kind these girls were.

A few days later when I was walking on the balcony I saw a familiar freckled face. Oh, my God—the girl whose thermoses I broke lived in the same apartment building I did. I felt extremely nervous as she approached me. What if she told my mother about my little accident?

Pushing that scary thought from my mind, I greeted her, "Hello, miss." I knew better than to call her *yatou* this time.

"Hello again," she said. "Do you live in this building?"

"Yes, on the third floor. Oh, miss, I beg you, please don't tell my mother about . . . about what happened in the hot water house."

She smiled. "Don't worry, I can keep a secret. I live on the fifth floor. My name is Li Huang." And that is how I met one of my closest friends. Li Huang has given me encouragement and emotional support my whole life. She challenges me and protects me at the same time, and I deeply appreciate her friendship.

* * *

Instead of a small school heated by a smoky stove, I now attended the large, modern Lanzhou University Grammar School, a subsidiary of the university where my father taught. It had so many students that there were four classes for each of the five grades.

Except for my father, my whole family went to school together: my siblings and I as students and my mother as a teacher. She taught second and third graders and was highly regarded for her warm, passionate teaching and caring personality. She encouraged the kids and gave guidance to the parents as to how to best educate their children. Some of the students she taught then still write to her. I was very proud of my mother, although I couldn't understand how she could be so nice to her students and yet so often be strict and severe with her own children.

I was in the fourth grade. Because I was small for my age, I was seated right up front; throughout my school career, I never sat farther back than the second or third row. I was too shy and quiet to speak up in class, but I purposefully set out to meet everyone and make as many friends as I could.

One advantage I had in this campaign was my new eyeglasses. My mother had noticed that when I read, I put my face too close to the book. She insisted that I sit up and hold myself in the proper position while doing my homework, and I would try, but soon I had my nose to the page again. I was also complaining of headaches. Mama realized that I wasn't being willful; the problem was that I couldn't see well. So she took me to get glasses. I was very proud of them; they made me look smart and distinguished. No one else in my class wore glasses, and I got lots of attention because everyone was curious about them. They were a great help in getting acquainted, and I felt privileged to have them.

Fourth grade was a high point in my life because it was then that I discovered what has become a lifelong passion— the English language. We had an introductory class taught by a teacher called Miss Ma. Though I only saw her that one time, she gave me a gift in the form of a moment that would change my life forever. It came when Miss Ma pronounced an English word—"careful."

"Careful." Such a beautiful sound. The way Miss Ma said it made me feel as if I were listening to music. I said the word too, imitating her as precisely as I could. It was the first English word I spoke. It was such a special word, this word "careful."

For days I walked around mumbling the word under my breath, trying to get the sound exactly right. I practiced it over and over: "Careful, careful, careful."

One day my mother overheard me. "Jing-Jing, what are you saying?"

"It's an English word, Mama." I explained what it meant.

She was amazed, and she became very supportive of my learning English because I was so very interested. After all the struggles with my mother, it felt good to have her support for something I was doing. That meant a lot to me.

* * *

In grammar school I made two great friends. One was Liang Yian, the daughter of the head of Lanzhou University. We were in the same class, and I was drawn to her because she was quiet like me, and also pretty, gentle, and affectionate. We often played games together after school.

I also became close to Liang Roujun, whose family lived on the first floor of our apartment building. Her mother was the principal of another grammar school, and she was a hospitable, warmhearted, and powerful woman. She welcomed her daughter's friends into their home and provided such a cheerful environment that the neighborhood kids loved spending time there. But we would have visited even if her mother had been as mean as a witch. Liang Roujun's home had a special draw—a television set.

No one else we knew had one of these marvels. Obviously her family had more money than the rest of us. My own family's financial situation was tight; it was beyond my imagination that we might ever afford a TV. I went to Liang Roujun's home to watch TV as often as I could.

My favorite program was called *Follow Me*. The government had enlisted the British Broadcasting Corporation to produce the show as a way to help Chinese viewers learn English; it was part of the effort to mend an educational system that had been ripped apart by the Cultural Revolution. The first time I saw *Follow Me*, I was one of five kids jostling for position in front of the TV, but the others decided the show was too much like school. After a month, I was the only one still watching. Even Liang Roujun, who lived there, didn't join me most of the time.

I watched the half-hour show every Tuesday and Thursday for nearly ten years. Whenever it was on I sat absolutely still, staring at the screen through the glasses perched on my nose. My whole body tingled with excitement. I didn't want to miss a single minute.

My mother had never seen me so well behaved, and she was impressed by my ability to focus on learning something that I was interested in even though most people found it hard and boring. But she was concerned at first that I was spending too much time at Liang Roujun's home, getting underfoot and being in the way.

"Don't worry about Jing-Jing," Liang Roujun's mother replied when Mama expressed this concern. "She minds her manners, and she's so enthusiastic about learning English. We're happy to have her here."

After that, when I wanted to watch the program my mother gave her support. It was the only interest I had at the time that gained me her full enthusiasm.

The instructor on *Follow Me* was named Kathy Flower, and she was the most beautiful foreign woman I had ever seen— slender and graceful, with an oval face that was framed by short, dark hair. I especially admired her fashionable clothes. She wore a new outfit for each show. Every time I heard her voice and saw her face it soothed me.

Compared to my drab and routine life, the world that Kathy Flower opened up to me seemed like a wonderland. Each episode told a story, an adventure in the lives of the handsome hero, Francis Matthews, and his blonde girlfriend, Jean. I recall one in which Francis courted Jean in a coffee shop and another in which a fat, ugly fellow tried to ask Jean for a date; Francis, of course, ran him off. There was a mystery story, too, that featured a detective. All of the episodes were designed to teach certain English phrases—"How do you do?" "Where is the train station?" "We are having sunny weather." "Would you like a gin and tonic?" It wasn't until more than a decade later, when I worked for a British firm, that I found out what a gin and tonic was. That's also when I finally tasted roast beef and Yorkshire pudding, exotic foods I'd watched

Francis and Jean enjoy. I loved the glimpses of foreign culture that the show gave me.

The episodes were re-run repeatedly, but I never grew tired of them. Eventually I was able to understand what was happening in the stories. When I explained to the kids in school what a particular episode was about, they demanded, "How did you get to know that?"

I didn't want them to think I was showing off too much, so I said, "I'm just guessing. I really don't understand the language very well."

But I was beginning to understand quite a lot. I found myself gradually speaking the language better and better, and I felt thrilled.

One day, looking through the window, I saw two tall, fair-haired, big-nosed foreigners in the backyard of the building. I asked my father, "Baba, who are these foreigners?"

He answered, "Oh, they are visiting scholars here to teach the Chinese students in the university how to speak English."

That piqued my curiosity. I immediately felt an urge to speak to them, but I was afraid they would reject me.

"Can I talk to them in English just for a simple hello?" I asked my father. "Do you think they would like to talk to me too?"

My dad was surprised by the questions. He paused for a second and then said, "Are you sure you want to do that? Can you say hello to them properly in English? I am not sure that's polite for us to do."

"Yes!" I said, full of excitement. "I know how to say hello. I can introduce myself to them, that's all. I will be really polite and I won't cause you trouble, I promise you. I'm so curious to know if they understand my English, and I want to know how it feels if I talk to a real foreigner. Please let me do this, just once?" I was begging him and pulling on his left sleeve.

At this point Mama joined the conversation. My parents looked at me and looked at the foreigners who were standing outside in the backyard talking to each other. Then they said the magic words: "All right, but be polite and make it quick!"

I was overjoyed to receive the permission. I ran out of our apartment to meet these foreigners. When I reached them, they seemed like giants because I was so tiny. I felt nervous, but I stood straight and still. In a little trembling voice, I said my first English word to them, not knowing what would happen next: "Hello!"

They bent over with big smiles. I could tell they were surprised to hear a little Chinese kid, a complete stranger, greeting them in English. Amazingly I heard another magic word, spoken back to me from these two tall foreigners: "Hello."

Encouraged, I continued: "How do you do!"

"How do you do!"

What should I say next to continue the conversation? I tried to recall the phrases I had memorized.

"Fine, thank you! My name is Jing-Jing. It is nice to meet you."

"I'm Tom," said one.

"I am Henry. It's nice to meet you too!"

I was so happy with their smiles and kindness. I couldn't wait to impress them with my last words. "Have a nice day. Good-bye!"

"Good-bye!" They shook my hand, which I didn't expect at all. I was blushing at such a friendly treat. Right away I ran home, so excited that I jumped up and down while I told my parents what had happened. They had watched the whole exchange and were very proud of me.

After that I took every chance I could get to speak in English to a Westerner. Each time was an adventure. I sought out the experts from Western countries who had been invited by Lanzhou University to give lectures or teach classes as visiting scholars. Everybody was amazed at how brave I was to approach these big-nosed white people, and I was surprised that I really could make them understand me in my awkward British-accented English. I collected quite a few Western stories that let me brag in front of the other kids. It was worth any risk of a rebuff from a stranger.

English wasn't the only language I learned. In my last year of high school, TV programs started that gave me the basics of French and Japanese. My enduring love of languages has helped to define me and has opened the door to perceptions and opportunities that I never would have gained in any other way.

* * *

A Chinese student's progress through school is governed by examinations. You must pass an exam to move from one level to the next—from grammar school to junior high, from junior high to senior high, and the most important and scariest exams of all, from senior high to university. When I finished the fifth grade, it was time to take the first set of exams, which would admit me to junior high school. I knew I was a good student, so I didn't worry too much about them. As it turned out, I passed them easily.

In junior high, as in grammar school, the many students in each grade level were divided into several classes. I was assigned to class six. At twelve years old, I was still very small for my age; even though I had a big appetite, it didn't help me grow taller. I continued to sit in the first or second row.

I enjoyed the new academic challenges that junior high offered. We remained in one classroom all day as teachers paraded in and out to teach us different subjects—Chinese literature, social studies, science, and math. My best grades were in math and English. I was delighted that English was part of the junior high curriculum. The language seemed to come naturally to me, and I was proud that I didn't have to work hard, like the other kids did, to learn vocabulary words and grammar rules.

But the best part of junior high was sports. I played a lot of basketball and badminton, and I earned a spot on the track-and-field team with my short-distance racing abilities. My favorite sports, though, were volleyball and ping-pong.

The whole school had volleyball fever. The gymnastics department organized a series of games and provided the referees. Each class had a team, and they were all fiercely competitive. Every team wanted to be the school champion.

To my surprise, I was elected captain of the team for class six. We were an odd group compared to the teams from the other classes. Here was this tiny girl surrounded by five much taller, bigger, and stronger girls. But most of the other groups had better training and more experience in competition than we did. So the six of us showed them a different way to win through our dedication, our teamwork, and, most of all, our spirit.

I kept my volleyball with me in class. Every day, as I thought the bell was about to ring to signal the start of recess, my feet started working the ball out from underneath my chair. Once I heard the first ring, I grabbed the ball and raced to the volleyball field to practice for fifteen minutes. Then I rushed back to the classroom without even stopping to catch my breath.

"Jing-Jing, you shouldn't do this anymore," my mathematics teacher told me. "You must leave time to get yourself back from your practice. Otherwise, you're so winded you can't focus on your studies."

I just made a little face in reply.

At the end of the day, I raced out again. I had to be quick if I was going to beat the other classes to the practice field; there weren't enough nets to go around, and every team wanted to use one. I loved playing the game, and I really wanted to practice with my team. I tried to organize regular practices so we could improve our skills. I worked hard, and my service from the line and my style of attack became famous for being fast and tricky despite my diminutive size.

When a game was coming up, I spent a lot of time at home working on my movements. I used a big wall outside as a backdrop for my serves. I also went to watch the other teams practice. I wanted to see who they were, how they were organized, what we could do to compete with them. My teammates came too, to observe and tell me what they noticed. I used the information we gleaned to develop a strategy for beating our competitors. The next day the whole class wanted to know what my strategy was, and how we planned to win.

Everyone in class six showed up at the games to applaud and cheer. With the six of us working together, and our class-mates supporting us, we were unbeatable. Our dedication and teamwork paid off in victory after victory.

Class six won the school championship for three straight years. What made us exceptional was the fact that we weren't afraid to show our spirit in competition. To prove it, I lost my voice twice cheering at the final games.

Our dedication and teamwork paid off in victory after victory.

At the time I didn't comprehend how capable, how passionate, and how encouraging I must have been to inspire the other five girls to work with me as a team to win the championship. This experience was the beginning of my sense that I could be a strong and ca-pable leader. It gave me confidence, self-esteem, and a sense of power. Only I didn't know where it was going to take me un-til much later in my life.

I still maintain that championship spirit. I love to win any competition that life has to offer, to conquer the difficult chal-lenges, and to achieve my goals.

My love for ping-pong led me to a different sort of victory. Even though ping-pong was a popular national game, my school didn't have many ping-pong tables. So Li Huang and I went to the Lanzhou University campus, which had an outdoor recreation area with some cement tables we could use. Many kids wanted to play, and the competition for the tables was fierce. We had to arrive early if we were going to claim one.

One day when all the tables were busy, a big, rude boy came along with his friends and kicked us out. "You've had your turn. Give us this table," the bully demanded. "Get out of here if you know what's good for you." Hurt and confused, we stepped aside.

I love to win any competition that life has to offer, to conquer the difficult challenges, and to achieve my goals.

It happened another time, and then again. At first, Li Huang and I gave in; we were afraid of the bully's threats. But after a while, I'd had enough. I felt it was really unfair, and I couldn't tolerate it anymore. I was ready to fight back.

The next time the big boy asked us to leave, I climbed on top of the table and stood there with my hands on my hips. I yelled, "Tough guy! You only bully girls. Shame on you! Why don't you try to push other boys around? You're scared, aren't you? You couldn't touch them. You're such a coward! You're chicken!"

The playground fell silent. Everyone was staring at us. The bully looked at me and then looked at the crowd. I didn't move. I maintained my straightforward gaze at him and kept my chin high.

Then suddenly the other girls, their anger stirred by my words, began shouting.

"Coward! Coward! Coward!"

The boy's face reddened, and he lowered his eyes. He tried

to pretend that this awkward situation didn't bother him, but I could tell that he was highly embarrassed.

"Who cares to deal with you silly girls?" he said sarcastically. Then he beckoned to his friends. "Let's go!"

Muttering and swaggering, he and his buddies gave up their mission and moved on. As I got down off the table, I felt vindicated and powerful.

This incident taught me to stand up for myself and for my group. I learned that strength is not measured by what size or age we are, but by our ability to speak our mind, to announce the deep beliefs in our heart. When we claim this strength, no one can take it away from us. It comes from our unbreakable spirit, and, when we honor it, it leads to our success and satisfaction. I didn't know it then, but I would put this lesson to good use in the future to challenge what I believed to be the unethical business conduct of a giant corporation.

* * *

Life in Lanzhou was vastly better than it had been in the coal-mining village, but we were still very poor. A lot of families had bicycles, but we didn't have one until my third year of junior high. We also had few clothes. Mama never wore skirts or dresses. She had a Red Guard–like jacket in green and just two pairs of black pants. Like the other professors, my father had two formal suits of the type called *zhongshan zhuang*, one gray and one navy blue. This sober-looking style with its tunic-like jacket was named after Sun Zhongshan, known in the West as Dr. Sun Yat-Sen, who helped to overthrow the Qing dynasty and establish the Republic of China.

Fashion wasn't an issue at all; everyone wore the same kind of clothes and made them last as long as they could. When we kids tore our shirts and pants, or when they developed little holes, Mama patched them using whatever leftover bit of fabric might be available, regardless of whether the color matched. We could count on having patched elbows, because that part of the sleeve always wore out fast. I hated wearing such obviously mended clothing. At least most of the other kids had to wear them too.

Strength is not measured by what size or age we are, but by our ability to speak our mind, to announce the deep beliefs in our heart.

Doing the laundry was a laborious process. We had to soak the dirty clothes, scrub them with soap or detergent on a wooden washboard, and then go to a place about half a mile away from home to get clean cold water for rinsing out the soap. Washing clothes could rip the skin off your hands. Mama's hands were always chapped and rough. In the winter they would become so dry that the skin would split.

We hung the sopping clothes outside on a steel rope we shared with four or five other families. Sometimes we had to fight for the space, squeezing our clothes among those of our neighbors. Everyone hung their laundry outside, even their underwear, bras, and socks. Balconies all over the city—in fact, everywhere in China—were colorfully decorated with drying clothes. In the winter the clothes would completely freeze, like ice cubes, and the frozen pants and shirts were pretty in their icy sheath. My sister and brother and I always fought for the privilege of smashing the ice. Thieves often stole clothing or sheets that were hanging outside, so another job Mama gave to me was to keep an eye on the laundry as it dried. I liked this job because I was allowed to read novels while I watched our clothes.

We didn't have an iron or ironing board. My parents folded their clothes carefully and placed them underneath their pillows, and the next day their pants and shirts looked neat and unwrinkled. I found that fascinating. Later on I used the same method to put crisp creases down the legs of my pants.

Wintertime meant we had to wear *mianku*—heavy, bulky cotton pants that were handmade by my mother. I hated them and the thick, clumsy shoes that went with them because they looked so ugly and made it hard to move. To avoid having to wear them, I would pretend I wasn't cold, even though my teeth were chattering. One year I came down with a dreadful cold, and after that Mama forced me to wear *mianku* the whole winter.

I counted the days until winter was gone and prayed for an early spring so I could get rid of those pants that much sooner. I looked forward so much to wearing thinner pants and slimmer shoes and being able to dance and play *jian zi*, which is a traditional game like badminton or shuttlecock that girls played by kicking a little feathered birdie.

Every day, even on the coldest days, we heard a tired, husky voice from the street: "Collecting empty toothpaste tubes, rusty metal, and wasted copper!" The cry came from one of the street garbage collectors, sometimes an ugly woman carrying a wooden crate, and at other times a dirty, wrinkly old man with shabby clothes and a stinky smell. My sister would immediately run to find stuff to give them; almost every family tried to give them something. These pathetic people earned their living from our discarded metal items. When they had accumulated a large enough quantity of scrap metal and aluminum, they could take it to a garbage station and exchange it for money. Sometimes these garbage collectors would bring a surplus of eggs, to exchange them for clothes, white flour, and other necessities of daily life.

Whenever they came, Mama lectured to us. "You should feel lucky. We have jobs, we have a home to stay in, and we have food and clothes. We should appreciate what we have and be grateful we're not like the garbage collectors."

* * *

When I was in my second year of junior high, my family finally bought a fourteen-inch black-and-white TV, but Mama restricted the time when we could watch it. On weekdays, I was allowed to watch *Follow Me* at six o'clock, and the whole family gathered for the news broadcast at seven. Sometimes on a weekend we'd view a soap opera with Mama. We loved these entertaining, touching, and dramatic stories.

On weekends we could go to the movies, either at the public movie theaters that were opening or at the big university auditorium, where we didn't need to fight for tickets. Most of the films shown came from Europe, Japan, North Korea, and Mexico. They didn't play American movies, though, due to the poor relationship between the two countries.

My friends and I especially liked the love stories. Although they were very chaste, showing nothing more intimate than a little kissing and hugging, we giggled with embarrassment at those scenes. The government maintained strict controls over what could be shown. Nudity and explicit lovemaking scenes were forbidden, and any foreign movie could be subjected to quite a bit of cutting and editing to make it suitable for Chinese audiences. The films were given new Chinese-language soundtracks by an organization called the Shanghai Dubbed Films Factory, and the best of the dubbing artists, such as Ding Jianhua and Tong Zirong, became huge stars. Their distinguished voices, like the images of the films, became imprinted in our minds and hearts.

Listening to the radio we laughed at *xiangsheng*, or crosstalk, a popular form of comedy dialogue that involved telling intricate stories with lots of humorous wordplay and tricks of language. Another special series featured long works of fiction in a serial style; some of the stories took years to finish. The series was broadcast nationally every day at noon, and it had many fans. It seemed as if every family spent their lunchtimes listening to the same story; no one wanted to miss a single episode.

The lunch break for most people lasted from noon until two o'clock, and they went home to cook and eat their meal. After lunch, the whole country took its regulated lunch nap for one hour. This nap was extremely important to Mama; without it she couldn't function very well for the rest of the day. The habit became ingrained in me also; a nap is part of my routine today wherever I am.

* * *

In the early 1980s, we could see that life in China was improving gradually, but most Chinese people still lived on government-issued food cards and oil cards. Meat was not as limited as it used to be, and every family was entitled to have two bottles of milk a day, although you had to sign up by the month to get it. It was my chore to pick up the milk and buy our supply of vinegar and soy sauce. Every morning we would all have a small amount of boiled milk to drink. I didn't like it because to me it smelled awful, but Mama would watch me until I finished the last drop. I had to hold my nose and drink quickly so I wouldn't taste it so much. At least she let me skim off the thin oily skin created by the boiling. When I got to college, I was finally able to get away with not drinking milk. What a relief.

In the summer we enjoyed having a variety of vegetables. Sometimes we got a chance to buy green chili peppers or spinach or tomatoes. Even in the winter, we had more choices than just the cabbages and potatoes available to us in Shandan Meikuang. Not that we disdained potatoes. Every day the three of us fought for our share of sliced sour-and-spicy potatoes, which is one of the most popular homemade dishes in China. I still cook it once or twice a week, and I serve it at dinner parties for my friends. Most of my Western friends can't tell that it's just potatoes. For me, this dish is more than food—it contains so much history, so many memories with laughter and tears, and so many intimate moments with my family and friends. And of course it tastes delicious.

Mama was right: we were lucky. My family had jobs, a

home, clothes to wear, and food to eat. We had so much to be grateful for, especially when we compared our lot in life to the days of my early childhood. But as I moved into my teenage years, dark clouds were gathering on the horizon. Our home was about to become a stormy place.

Diana's Stepping-Stones on the Journey to Success

Look to your early sources of joy. We may discover and discard many interests in the course of our life, but what gives us great pleasure as children is often a manifestation of our true self. When we are trying to discover our talents and passions, a good place to begin is to recall what we loved as a child. Our early passions are original, pure, strong, and unbreakable forces buried in our heart.

Believe in yourself and what you are doing. Confidence leads to persistence, which leads to success. When we are confident that what we want to accomplish is worthwhile and that we have the ability to achieve the goal, we can muster the drive to see the effort through to the end.

Cultivate your skills as a leader and as a team player. Few of us achieve success entirely on our own. We must call upon the skills, the efforts, and the encouragement of other people to assist us as we make progress toward our goals. The ability to inspire, motivate, and work with others is an invaluable asset.

Stand up for what you know is right. The principles of fairness and justice are always worth fighting for.

Reunion with high school friends at the Yellow River bridge in Lanzhou after the first semester of college. Bai Tai Mountain is in the background.

考试和恐惧

Three Tests and Tribulations, 1981–1986

During one of my summer breaks from junior high, my father surprised us. Without consulting Mama, he brought his mother from Hubei province to live with us. This caused a huge fight. Our apartment was already cramped with the five of us, and Mama was constantly exhausted with the effort of raising three children, taking care of Baba, and keeping up her great performance at work. Now she would have the added responsibility of my grandmother—a woman who detested her. I can imagine how angry and frustrated she must have felt.

I didn't like the idea either, nor did my sister. We remembered the prejudice with which our grandmother had treated us after our brother was born. But my father was her youngest and most spoiled son, and of course he would do anything for his own mother. So no one else had a vote in the matter.

By now my grandmother was in her early eighties, and when she arrived we were shocked to see how shrunken and bony and wrinkled she had become. But her sour personality and her prejudice against girls were still the same.

During her stay with us in the coal-mining village when I

was a little girl, I had never noticed her feet, but this time there was no way not to be aware of them—the infamous bound feet that I had only read about in novels. At one time the practice of binding girls' feet was fairly commonplace in China. Lily feet, as they were called, were considered delicate and dainty and were a mark of gentility and respectability. Women who had them walked with mincing steps and a swaying gait that was seen as very attractive. The binding process began when a girl was still a small child, and it was intended to stop the foot from growing.

I could not imagine how anyone could think that such a deformity was beautiful, and I was glad that I'd been born after the custom was abandoned. My grandmother's feet were little stubs, scarcely more than three inches in length, and each one was completely wrapped in a long, thick, and very smelly cotton bandage that seemed to be one hundred years old. The bandaged feet fit into tiny handmade shoes that were decorated with silk flowers. Every day Mama rewrapped the long bandage, and its horrible smell would spread through the room. We had to open the window to let in some fresh air.

Having three generations squeezed together into the tiny apartment made life chaotic for all of us, especially Mama. Because of her advanced age, my grandmother could barely talk, move, or think straight. She had her cane to support her, but she didn't move around much. Most of the time she was half asleep in her comfortable bamboo chair with the big cushion that Mama made for her. Poor Mama had to feed her and clean her and help her go to the toilet.

We didn't have an extra space where my grandmother could sleep, so she shared our bed with us. All three of us kids were uncomfortable having her there, with her shrunken body and her weird feet with their unpleasant smell, and we squashed ourselves together as tight as we could in order to stay away from this tiny ancient countrywoman who had invaded our bed.

Home was crowded, smelly, and filled with sounds of arguments. It was so bad that I spent as little time there as I could, hanging out with my friends instead. When I told Li Huang about my grandmother, she was surprised that such strong prejudice against girls still existed, especially in the university. My exaggerations about my grandmother's evils scared her so much she wouldn't even come to visit my home.

* * *

In my last year of junior high school, my life became difficult. My changing body, my sudden awareness of boys, my constant battles with my mother—all of these things contributed to my rebelliousness and misery.

For the most part, school continued to go well. I received a lot of prizes for my studies and sports. My parents showered me with praise for these achievements, and my headmasters gave me positive evaluations. I become too proud and a bit spoiled. I admit I was a little bully to my younger sister because I got better grades.

Even at school, though, there were problems. I couldn't

stand my Chinese literature teacher. She bored me to tears, and she treated me badly. Once she made me read an essay I had written out loud to the class, offering it up as a bad example. My writing was too creative and original for her. In Lanzhou we had frequent sandstorms, and in my essay I had described the pretty coral-colored light that occurred when the sun shined through the veil of wind-borne sand. The teacher insisted I was wrong—there was no beauty to be found in sandstorms; I had to say they made everything dark and dirty. Standing before the class in humiliation, I held my paper close to my face and mumbled the words. All the kids laughed. I felt mortified.

My body was changing, which was quite a shock. I had always been petite, and I liked that because I thought a beautiful girl should be slim and flat. Now, all of a sudden, I was growing. I became just a few inches taller—from under five feet to a little bit over—but I gained what felt like a lot of weight. I now tipped the scale at nearly a hundred pounds. Even worse, my breasts were getting bigger, becoming more and more obvious. I hated them.

I know now that these were normal signs of the transition from little girl to young woman, but at the time I was convinced I was becoming fat and ugly. I dressed in big, baggy clothes to hide what I thought of as my disgusting body, and underneath I wore a tight band that pressed my breasts close to my body so they would be less noticeable. When Mama gave me my first bra, I was ashamed to wear it, as I thought only fat girls wore bras.

My self-esteem plummeted, and I became even more shy and

quiet as I struggled with these physical changes. Whenever my mother wasn't around, I gazed at myself in the mirror, unhappy with what I saw. I tried on my old clothes, hoping to see myself skinny again, but they no longer fit. My girlfriends were still pretty, staying slender even as they grew taller than me. I felt awkward around them, so I distanced myself, going home alone or spending time with the more plain-looking girls. I was in a constant state of turmoil.

At the same time, I began to notice boys. I found myself distracted by the cute boys in my classroom. I didn't understand the surge of strange feelings that came over me in their presence. There was one boy in particular to whom I felt very close. Whenever I could, I tried to sit right next to him, though I didn't dare let anyone know about the maneuvering I did to make this happen. I did my best to hide my affection for him and my attraction to the others—oh, how shameful these feelings were.

The turbulence that was churning within me made it hard to focus on my studies. When my mother caught me not concentrating on my homework and asked me why, I was too embarrassed to tell her the truth.

Fortunately, despite all this inner turmoil, I managed to pass the entrance examinations for high school without too much difficulty. During the summer break, my mother assigned me extra homework: reading some European novels. This was the only time she gave me homework I loved, for those books brought me much joy. They transported me into brand-new worlds, far away from my own troubled life. I became completely absorbed in them; I could read for hours without moving. Over the summer I devoured a bookshelf's worth of novels like *Jane Eyre*, *Les Misérables*, *The Hunchback of Notre Dame*, and *War and Peace*, all in Chinese translations. It was the beginning of an attraction to foreign literature that continues to this day.

Once I was so intently focused on a book that my mother decided to take the opportunity and cut my long hair. I didn't even realize she was there until I felt the tug of the scissors as they sliced through my locks.

"Mama!" I yelped. "What are you doing?"

I was furious; I didn't want to give up my long hair, and I didn't want her making decisions about my appearance without consulting me. But now I think the sacrifice of my hair was worth it, because that was the only summer break when my mother let me read foreign novels.

Sometimes I'd get completely lost in one of the characters— especially Jane Eyre. I was deeply and emotionally attached to her. Sometimes I pretended that I was Jane Eyre. I struggled with her, laughed with her, and cried with her. It was the first time I noticed emotions welling like this inside me. I didn't understand them at all, but they fascinated me.

My mother, being a good teacher and parent, quizzed me about what I had learned from the novels. I couldn't give her satisfactory answers because I didn't really grasp what I understood about them. I had no words to describe the strong emotions and dramatic feelings the stories engendered in me; I just knew that I was drawn to them. But even if I could have expressed what I felt, I would have been afraid to tell her. Confessing would have simply inspired her to harsher criticism, and I felt she already criticized me more than enough.

"What are you thinking, Jing-Jing?" she asked me constantly.

I always replied the same way: "I don't think anything." The answer only made her angry.

* * *

When I got to senior high school, the university authority rewarded my father's career progress by giving us a better apartment. We moved to Professor Building 15, located in one of the best residential complexes in the university. Three apartment buildings, three to five stories high, shared a big public lawn. One of the buildings was specially designed for the highest-ranking university officials. Some of them were provided with cars and maids by the government because of their titles and authority. To us, they were like royal families with superpowers. My girlfriend Liang Yian's family was one of them.

Mama was a little happier after our move. We had more space—325 square feet instead of 160—and my grandmother was no longer with us, having been sent back to her hometown. The new apartment had three rooms, a separate kitchen, and our very own bathroom. One room did triple duty as my parents' bedroom, our living room, and my dad's reading room. Yan-Yan and I shared one tiny bedroom, and our brother slept in the other, which was also a family room where we ate, watched TV, and did homework together. No longer did the three of us have to share the same bed.

We celebrated our new home by getting some new furniture. We bought our first small sofa, which we placed in my parents' room, and an armoire with a large mirror in the middle; I spent a lot of time looking at myself in the mirror when Mama wasn't there to make me do homework. Of course, my father needed bookshelves for his books, and he also got his very first desk, where he could write his books and prepare for his classes. We brought our dining table and all the small wooden chairs from the other apartment.

We often saw Western visitors and scholars in this new neighborhood, and we even had chances to meet them. These exotic strangers intrigued me, and I was always curious to find out more about them. They looked so different from the Chinese people I saw every day, with their big noses, blond hair, green eyes, and tall physiques, and I loved their unique and colorful clothing. Well, most of the clothing—as I watched the foreign women walk across the frozen, windy lawn in the wintertime, I couldn't help but wonder how they could bear to wear skirts when their legs must have been turning into icicles.

Life was getting better not only for my family but for many people in China, due in part to the economic reforms led by Deng Xiaoping. The northwest of China was still one of the poorest regions of China, far behind Shanghai and Beijing and other southern cities. But even in Lanzhou, large private markets were opening to sell clothes and food. We gradually began to see people wearing clothes that were more colorful and more fashionable—not only those pretty if impractical skirts, but also high-heeled shoes and trendy pants with wide legs that swept the floor that were made popular by the Japanese movie *Zhuipu*, whose title means *Chasing and Capturing*. Women, including my mother, had their hair permed in chic styles.

We could now choose among a variety of foods, including

different kinds of deli items that we could purchase without a meat card. In the summertime, we were able to buy many types of fruit, but watermelon and the luscious *bai lan gua*, the honeydew melon that was a specialty export to overseas markets, continued to be favorites. My parents bought huge bags of melons and kept them beneath my brother's bed. Mama kept careful count to make sure none of us kids ate one alone without permission. In the summertime, after lunch, we all had watermelon for dessert, and Mama would rub her face with the rinds. This treatment made her skin look really clean and smooth; maybe that is one of the reasons she still looks so young today.

My mother had another unique way of staying healthy. Once, when she was coughing a lot, she consulted a doctor of traditional Chinese medicine, who recommended that she take cold-water baths. After that, no matter how cold the weather was, even if it was snowing, she would bathe in cold water. She kept up the practice for more than ten years. Watching her do that every day was inspiring to me, and I really admired her strength and endurance.

Best of all, our improved circumstances meant less struggle and frustration for my parents. Now that their long battle against poverty and hardship was behind them, they were in better moods, and they looked younger and happier.

* * *

One benefit of our rise in prosperity was that the Spring Festival celebrations we enjoyed now for the Chinese New Year were much more fun and exciting than the modest revels we'd known in the coal-mining village, or even those of our early years in Lanzhou. Feasting, fireworks, games, and gifts—how eagerly we looked forward to the occasion!

My parents bought a variety of fireworks for the big event. One year they gave some small firecrackers to Hui-Hui. My adventurous little brother, who enjoyed practical jokes, tried to scare the younger boys in the neighborhood by throwing lit firecrackers at them. When his firecrackers burned holes in the kids' new clothes, he laughed hard at first, but his glee turned to dismay when their angry mothers came to Mama and demanded that he be supervised.

Mama, shocked and embarrassed by Hui-Hui's behavior, forbade him to play outside. But she couldn't really mind him because she was preoccupied in the kitchen, getting ready for the big New Year's Eve banquet. "You will have to keep an eye on him, Jing-Jing," she told me.

This became my major task for the New Year preparations. I watched my brother so closely he began to twitch under my gaze. His restlessness quickly turned to boredom, and he fell asleep. What a relief for Mama and me.

The banquet was well worth all the effort Mama put into it. These days we enjoyed greater abundance at our Spring Festival table. The main feast usually included twelve dishes or more. We savored meat, fish, vegetables, cakes, different kinds of dumplings, candies, cookies, peanuts, walnuts, sunflower seeds, and the special black watermelon seeds. My parents bought expensive hard liquors to take as gifts when visiting their colleagues. It seemed that we had everything we wanted. My sister, brother, and I didn't have to fight for the food anymore. There was too much for us to finish for the entire month of Spring Festival. Every year, after the big banquet, I would get a stomachache from eating more than I could digest.

One special dish was the dried, preserved Wuchang fish my aunt made. Each year she sent us some. The first time a package of fish arrived we were still living in the old apartment. At that time, fish was still a precious and rare food, and we were eager to eat it right away. "No," Mama insisted. "We will save it for the Spring Festival." Since we had no refrigerator, she hung the dried fish outside her bedroom window. The neighbor who lived underneath us had a dog that bothered us by barking constantly. When the time came for Mama to cook the precious dried fish, we were dismayed to discover why the dog was so noisy. Only a tiny piece of fish was still hanging there; the rest of it was gone, gobbled up by the dog. Mama complained to the neighbor, but of course that didn't bring back the fish. Never again did she store the Wuchang fish that way.

As the New Year clock ticked toward midnight and we were enjoying our big banquet, Mama always performed her own ceremony, giving thanks to our family's ancestors and grandparents and entreating the heaven and earth to bless our family with joy, happiness, harmony, and prosperity. It was always fun to watch her. (She still does this ceremony at each spring festival.) She murmured the words as she lifted cups of hard Chinese liquor with both hands up to her eyebrows, then poured the liquor to the floor. Then she touched every dish on the table with chopsticks, symbolically inviting our grandparents to share the food with us. Once she had finished all that, we knew it was our happy time—time to eat the delicious feast and watch the CCTV New Year celebration program.

All of a sudden we would hear a huge noise—*pili-pa-la!*—as the midnight sky exploded with color and light. Hundreds of kinds of fireworks shot up to the heavens and exploded into sparks, swirls, and showers of stars. The show lasted more than an hour. Through the first three days of the year, people would continue to play with their firecrackers. It was so lively; the air was full of laughter, enthusiasm, and energy.

We stayed up all night long to greet the New Year, a custom called *shou ye*. We passed the time playing Chinese poker games with family and friends. A lot of families played mahjongg—a classic Chinese game that is similar to some Western card games, though it uses small wood or ivory tiles rather than cards. However, Mama didn't allow it in our home because she didn't approve of gambling. As a result, even today I don't know how to play mah-jongg.

The first morning of Chinese New Year, our family observed the tradition of *bai nian*—the offering of season's greetings. The three of us had to kowtow to our parents, kneeling before them and bowing low, and wish them Happy New Year. We did this every year, even when we were little in Shandan Meikuang. This ritual continues today as my nephew kowtows to his own parents, my brother and me, and our mother and father. I have always treasured this harmonious, good-spirited family custom.

When we finished giving them our tribute of respect, our

parents offered us their blessing and encouragement. Then they gave us our gifts of brand-new clothes, either store-bought or made by my aunt. We would go out proudly to see our friends, wearing our new outfits to show them off and compete with the other kids to see who had received nicer clothes and who looked prettier.

Our parents also handed out red envelopes containing our long awaited *ya sui qian*—our annual good-luck pocket money. The amount was small—five *mao* (half a *yuan*) to one *yuan*, which is equal to about one-eighth of a U.S. dollar—but it was enough to buy us a treat, like a sugar ice stick, which is a frozen confection of sugar and water. Sometimes milk was added; in that case it cost twice as much but it was the most delicious snack a child could wish for.

The first time my sister received five *mao* for her New Year bonus, she spent it all for five pieces of spicy barbecued lamb meat as soon as she woke up in the morning. Another year she saved enough to buy a big bowl of beef noodle all by herself. The time I remember most vividly was an occasion when Yan-Yan had four *fen* (a *fen* is like a Chinese penny), which was one *fen* short of what she needed to buy an ice cream.

"Can you lend me one *fen*, Jing-Jing?" she asked. "If you do, I'll share the ice cream with you."

I gave her the coin, and she generously let me have the first bite. She took a bite of her own. "My turn," I said, eager for the next taste.

Yan-Yan turned aside. "You've had your one-*fen* share." She walked away, licking her ice cream, leaving me filled with disappointment.

* * *

As I started senior high school, the conflicts escalated between my mother and me; our quarrels grew louder and more frequent. My grades started to drop, to Mama's great disappointment. It seemed as though she spoke to me only to berate me for my lack of achievement and nag me to focus on my studies. I hated it. She took after my sister in the same way. Yan-Yan's grades were worse than mine, and she was even more troubled and rebellious. Only my brother, who always made excellent grades, could please our mother.

My father was doing well at the university. He had written a book, and he was well regarded by his students. A group of them often gathered at our home in the evenings, and I enjoyed taking part in their discussions. The move to a larger apartment was a sign of my father's success.

Mama, though, felt stymied in her career. She had left her teaching post at the grammar school after the first year to take a position in the administrative office of Lanzhou University, but the new job had failed to satisfy her ambitions. She had to deal with political in-fighting among the professors and between the professors and the administration, which made her work environment very unpleasant. She brought all her disappointment and dissatisfaction home with her, and it expanded to fill our little apartment.

I never quite understood my parents' relationship. They could love each other so much, but they also could fight like cats and dogs. My mother and father both were sensitive, cultured, artistic, and intellectual people. They enjoyed taking long walks along the Yellow River, whether in summer heat or winter snow. They loved nature, and sometimes Mama wrote poetry describing the beautiful snow scenes and or the green plants around our home. Early in the morning they went jogging together, and after dinner every day they strolled around the campus holding hands. Occasionally I would walk in on them by accident as they watched TV together, Mama lying in my dad's arms, my dad stroking her hair. It was a romantic side of our parents that we kids rarely saw. It made me happy when I got to see them like that, instead of witnessing another of their constant arguments.

As a matter of fact, my parents' marriage was probably one of the best relationships in China. Most people of their generation married in response to parental or societal pressure, with little expectation of happiness. Often the new husband and wife were barely acquainted. They may not even have liked each other, let alone felt love. A bad marriage was a life-long trap. The couple would swallow their pain and endure their suffering, because a divorce would create a ruinous scandal, costing them their social status and their professional careers. Even today, when divorce is more common, it is considered shameful. In the inland provinces, a divorced woman in her thirties or older is often a social outcast, the object of unpleasant gossip and ill treatment.

I recognized the enduring affection my parents had for each other, and perhaps that should have helped me forge my own peace with my mother. But it didn't. I defied her whenever I could. If she told me to move to the right, I'd move to the left. If she berated me, I'd yell at her, or turn my back in sullen silence.

I began spending more and more time with my friend Liang

Yian, the daughter of the head of Lanzhou University, and Li Huang, the friend I'd made years ago when I broke her thermos bottles. Both of them were kind and caring. My mother didn't mind when I went to study with Li Huang in her family's apartment because she was smart and her grades were much better than mine. Mama hoped her good study habits would rub off on me. Most nights I stayed at Li Huang's very late, until my mother had to come and fetch me. I returned reluctantly to what I felt was a cold and unsupportive environment. I felt as if I was becoming more and more isolated from everyone who was supposed to be my family. It was strange not to want to be home, but life at home was becoming unendurable.

* * *

The first time I ran away I was actually hiding in Li Huang's home. That night I refused to go home because I hated the way my mother nagged everyone. Li Huang's parents kindly let me spend the night. The next day I returned to a home that felt just like hell—the atmosphere was tense and I felt terribly rejected.

My mother demanded that I admit I was wrong. I answered her with silence, which only made her more angry. She yelled at me and spanked me hard with a wooden stick. I bit my lips; tears streamed down my face as I tried to avoid her blows, but I refused to speak. She was distressed and insulted to think that I didn't like our home. More unforgivably, I had made her lose face in front of others, so that she became the target of gossip within the university community. It was an ungraceful and ungrateful thing for me to do.

But I was much too defiant and headstrong to concede I was wrong. For days I did not speak a word to my mother, and my unrelenting silence eventually wore her out. She finally stopped criticizing me and left me alone. I hadn't realized before what powerful results I could achieve by being strong, stubborn, and persistent. Later I would learn to use persistence in more positive ways; it would become a hallmark of my personality and one of my secret weapons for achieving success.

The second time I ran away I hid in a classroom overnight. My mother was frightened at first because no one knew where to find me. Eventually I was discovered. For a brief while my little adventure was the talk of the senior high school.

Once again, my mother punished me for my escapade by slapping and spanking me. I punished her in return by refusing to speak to her, and even refusing to eat and drink under her roof, for days at a time.

I stayed away from home more and more, usually spending the time with Liang Yian. She was a true friend, nurturing and sympathetic. Her home was always harmonious and quiet. I became especially fond of her grandmother, who was extremely loving. She made us special snacks to eat while we did our homework. I wished that she was my grandmother and that Liang Yian's home was my own.

One time I asked Liang Yian and her mother if they would allow me to sleep at their home just for one night. But later that evening Mama arrived to fetch me back home. She felt intense shame on account of her wayward daughter—so much so that while she was there she burst into tears. She was mortified to be weeping in front of the head of the university, but that didn't bother me at all.

My world had grown cold, desolate, and lonely. I was lost and couldn't find a way out. I'd always been proud of being competitive, earning top grades, excelling at sports, and meeting people and making friends. Now I felt worthless; I felt as though I were nothing.

In my second year of senior high, there was one bright light: my physics teacher, Miss Ma. Just as the Miss Ma I met in fourth grade changed my life by introducing me to English, this Miss Ma changed it by giving me the warmth and acceptance my mother couldn't give. I felt as if she were my mother and I was like a daughter to her. She encouraged me to study hard, but she did it in a positive way that made me want to please her.

I thought my mother was the harshest mother in the world. Gradually, though, I noticed that many other kids received even worse treatment and less encouragement from their parents. Today I understand that actually I was lucky. My mother loved me and wanted what was best for me, even though she did not always know how to show that in a way I could appreciate. I've realized that much of our conflict came from the fact that in many ways my mother and I are alike. We both are strong willed and stubborn; we both fight hard to get what we want. The difference is that my mother tends to view the world through a lens of negativity, while I have learned to focus on the positive. Where she sees difficulties and limitations, I look instead at boundless possibilities.

I'm glad that my mother and I still communicate regularly and maintain a good relationship. The important thing, I believe, is to accept my parents for who they are and not let myself be restricted by the circumstances of their lives, by their successes or failures, or by their expectations for me.

* * *

During high school I developed a problem, one that all my teachers noticed—I became extremely anxious about taking tests. In classroom discussions and homework, I caught on quickly. I understood the questions and was good at coming up with the correct answers ahead of other students. But faced with a test, I panicked. I didn't understand why I was so terrified, but I did know that this sudden, profound fear could hurt me terribly when it came time to take the university entrance examinations.

I wasn't alone in dreading these exams. All students graduating from high school dreaded them. Taking them was a grueling three-day ordeal, and if you wanted to attend a university, how you did on the exams determined your fate. Your grades counted little toward university admission, even though the pressure to make good ones was very strong, and there was no such thing as an athletic scholarship.

> *The important thing is to accept my parents for who they are and not let myself be restricted by the circumstances of their lives, by their successes or failures, or by their expectations for me.*

As our senior year began, so did our intense preparation for the exams. I roused myself from my deep depression to notice that I would actually have to study if I wanted to pass them. I had my sights set on attending Beijing University, and being admitted there would require a high score.

I still hated myself, yet I was sure I could do well on the exams. I'd been a high achiever in the past, and if I focused hard on my studies I could be one again. Besides, even though I felt nothing I did was good enough for my mother, I had her good example to follow. With her children all in high school, she'd decided to become a student at Lanzhou University. It was a very courageous and ambitious move for her. She wanted not only to expand her career prospects but also to be able to help us with our homework. She couldn't bear the disadvantage she felt compared to our friends' parents, who had college educations. Mama had studied hard to pass the examinations, and now, in her late thirties, she was in college studying history and Chinese literature. Her courage, determination, and ambition made her an inspiring role model.

As I began to study harder, I noticed that my relationship with my parents changed a bit for the better.

Luckily, during this year I had several excellent teachers. Cao Qing Zhong, a young teacher who had just come to my school, brought us a fresh teaching style. Energetic and open-minded, Mr. Cao respected us and encouraged us. He guided us to sophisticated adult thinking and challenged us to discover there was more to life than just grades. He became involved in our leisure activities and tried to discover our goals and dreams. Mr. Cao introduced us to a famous novel called

Wei Cheng, usually translated as *Fortress Besieged*. Written by one of China's most notable writers, Qian Zhongshu, this profound book depicts the life of a young intellectual in the thirties, using his experiences to tell the real story of interpersonal relationships in China. It remains one of my favorite books. Through his mentoring and his encouragement, 95 percent of our class of fifty-plus students made it to college, one of the best records of the entire high school.

Another teacher who influenced me deeply was my English teacher, Mr. Xu. He wouldn't strike anyone as an attractive man. He was short and bony with a hunched back, and he was constantly coughing. His eyeglasses always sat crookedly on his face, so that you felt they were about to drop off. Yet he was one of the most honorable, most knowledgeable teachers I ever had. He had graduated as a journalist from one of China's, and the world's, most prominent universities—the University of Shanghai, also called Fudan University—and he brought fierce intelligence and great kindness into the classroom.

When Chinese students learned English, they were typically taught to recite phrases in a singsong rhythm and monotonous tone. To my ear, that version of the language sounded weird and boring. I much preferred the lively lilt and cadence I'd learned from *Follow Me* on television, and I'd speak that way when my classmates and I read aloud together from the English textbook. At first no one noticed because my voice was just one of many. Then one day Mr. Xu pointed out a paragraph about the American writer Jack London. "Lu Jing-Jing," he said, "would you read this passage to the class?"

I did, exposing my secret to him and the other students. I sounded more like a native speaker.

"Your pronunciation and intonation are very good," Mr. Xu told me. "You sound as though you have spent time in England. Where did you learn your accent?"

"From television." I explained how I loved to watch *Follow Me* and other English-language programs, and I described how I would practice my English by speaking to foreign visitors and by murmuring the words over and over to myself. "I'm lucky—I never have to study or memorize words the way other kids do. For some reason I'm good at imitating the sounds of foreign words. When I read a word a few times, the meaning and spelling get filed in my head." I described some rules and tricks I'd discovered to help me master new vocabulary. "Of course," I finished, "the best way to learn English is to find ways to speak it in real life."

He peered at me through those crooked glasses. "Have you ever thought about focusing on a foreign language when you go to university?"

"I . . . I don't know." I would have loved doing that, but I knew that my choices for my higher education would depend on my family's opinions. In the last year of high school, the program was divided into two curricula: one concentrated on the sciences and one on the arts. I was drawn to the arts— I loved words and music and all forms of creativity. But my mother had pushed me into the sciences. Science students were considered smarter and they garnered more respect. Their future seemed brighter, too, with more abundant job opportunities. All of these things were important to Mama.

Mr. Xu invited me to come to his office as part of my English studies. We worked together to improve my pronunciation, and he taught me how to read with greater expression and emotion. He also gave me books in English to read, by Jack London and other authors.

The best way to learn English is to find ways to speak it in real life.

I was devastated when Mr. Xu was diagnosed with liver cancer. He died before the school year was over. Along with the teachers and other students from our school, I attended his funeral. We paid respects to him as he lay in his coffin, looking shrunken, his face yellow. Then we offered condolences to his wife, who kept her arm around their little son. I knew her because she was a janitor at our school, a position to which she had originally been assigned as part of the Cultural Revolution. It grieved us to see her all dressed in white, the color of mourning. For a long time afterward I felt lonely and sad. I had lost not only an excellent teacher but also a good friend.

Miss Cheng An Li took over as our English teacher right after Mr. Xu's death. She immediately gave us a fresh start. A tall, thin woman in her thirties, she wasn't like the other teachers, who seemed old-fashioned next to her. I admired her straightforward and outspoken manner, her graceful style, and her exquisite taste. One reason my classmates and I were always eager to go to her class was so we could see what she was wearing that day. We thought she must be wealthy because she wore different clothes every day. I particularly remember how elegant she looked in one outfit: a jade green sweater that she wore with a tailored, cream-colored suit.

Like Mr. Xu, she recognized my English skills, which made me very happy. When she wanted a quick answer, she always directed the question to me, and she often had me read to the class. I was the only student who could speak with an accent that sounded authentically British, and she was impatient with the kids who made no effort to learn the proper enunciation. I learned a lot from her, because her own English was excellent. She knew exactly how to pronounce the words, how to use them properly, and how to connect them into grammatical sentences. I enjoyed the class, and I missed it quite a bit after graduating from senior high.

My English grade would always be the best of all my grades.

     * * *

Mama started to worry about my sister. Yan-Yan was not doing at all well in her studies. She had not been able to enter my senior high school, which was one of the best in the province, ending up instead at a school with lower scholastic standards.

One day Mama found a little love note in the bathroom. We were shocked to discover that my sister was secretly dating a boy in the school—a total breach of societal standards and school rules. For a young girl like Yan-Yan to be dating was absolutely forbidden; it was the kind of shameful, immoral, disgusting behavior that could bring down shame upon the whole family, making the parents as well as the child the targets of gossip and ridicule. It was particularly disgraceful for such a thing to happen in a professor's home.

Mama was furious. She dragged Yan-Yan into her room, locked the door, and spanked her so hard that her backside became swollen.

Yan-Yan was deeply hurt. To her, the relationship was innocent, merely the exchange of sweet little notes. I sympathized with her a lot. Being penalized so severely, not just by the family but by society, had a profoundly negative effect on her self-esteem. She began coming home late, making excuses for her behavior and poor grades, and lying to avoid punishment. Naturally those tactics didn't work; they only subjected her to further punishment, harsh criticism, and disrespect from our parents.

Her experiences and mine were not unusual. Millions of people who grew up in China in our generation, including some of my close friends, are still paying the painful price for deep emotional injuries they suffered as a result of the way their parents dealt with them as teenagers. In those days, the competition to survive was brutal, and many parents treated their children in the same way my mother did, and often much worse. Compared to those families, we were actually very lucky.

Unlike my sister and me, my younger brother was my parents' pride. Hui-Hui was extremely bright and well behaved. He earned top grades, and he was attending a high school that was even more academically distinguished than mine. When his time for college came around, he would go to a prestigious university. Being a boy and the youngest child, he enjoyed a special status. Mama rarely criticized him; the truth is, our parents spoiled him. Yan-Yan and I were jealous of him because he seemed to have a much easier childhood than we did.

* * *

As graduation approached, every student's attention and energy were focused on one thing: the university entrance examinations that loomed ahead. All year the preparations had been intense because so much was at stake. A high score guaranteed you entrance into a first-tier university. A lower one relegated you to a lesser school. If you didn't pass, you would not be admitted to college at all, and your future would basically be ruined.

It was possible to repeat your final year of high school and take the exam again next July, but to get the privilege of the extra year you would have to make use of special relationships and pay extra money, whether you stayed in the same high school or transferred to a different one. Moreover, everyone would know about your failure. You would be a year older than the other seniors, and no one would respect you; the other students wouldn't even bother to talk to you. The teachers would treat you as if you were mentally slow. One or two students like that were in my class. I always had huge sympathy for them, but most of the time we all avoided talking to them for fear it would make us look stupid. They always sat at the very back of the class regardless of whether they were tall or short. Their parents never stopped criticizing them and reminding them how bad they were. What a miserable life. I could not imagine how I would survive if I failed the exam.

During the intense preparations we'd had to pass many smaller exams. When we took the midterm exam, one student was caught cheating. The next day we were shocked to learn that he had hanged himself at home. He could not endure being responsible for his parents' humiliation and punishment, and he was too mortified to face all of the students and teachers. That horrible incident made the entire student body even more frightened and nervous. Driven by the fear of failure, the other kids and I studied hard day and night to prepare for the big exams.

* * *

In July 1986, after months of preparation and practice, the days of reckoning came for me and every other student who graduated from high school in China that year. Hundreds of thousands of us, all across the country, shared the agony at the same time as we sat down to take the university entrance examinations.

The ordeal lasted three full days, from morning to evening, with breaks only for lunch. We struggled to answer questions about a wide variety of subjects—Chinese literature, politics, English, physics, chemistry, and two types of mathematics. Proctors monitored our movements to make sure we didn't cheat; security guards were posted at the doors leading into the room. Outside, our anxious parents hovered, lending support through their presence.

For the entire time, my heart was thumping, my palms were sweating, and my stomach was tied into knots. I was eager to do well so I could go to Beijing University. I knew I was good at academic subjects, so I felt hopeful, but I could tell that the old familiar test panic was fogging up my brain. My fellow students were jittery, too; the smell of their nervous sweat permeated the hot, stuffy room.

At the end of day three, exhausted and bleary-eyed, we turned in our exams and began two weeks of anxious waiting. The classroom teachers and university professors who were hired to grade the exams were locked into special rooms so that no one could interfere with them while they worked. My dad was one of the professors chosen to grade the exams.

Finally I received my scores. My English grade was outstanding. I had earned one of the two top scores in Gansu province. My politics score was high, and I did alright in physics, too. But what was this? Poor marks in math and chemistry? How could this happen? It turned out that I had skipped over several pages of questions, thinking that they were for extra credit. But they were part of the regular exam, and leaving them blank cost me dearly.

I felt so ashamed. When I visited my mathematics teacher, I could tell she was very disappointed in me. I was one of the students who had made her most proud.

Going to Beijing University was out of the question. Where could I go instead? My parents and I discussed various options, but it was very clear which one my mother favored.

"You'll enroll at Lanzhou Medical University," she insisted.

"A medical school?" I was dumbfounded. Surely I had heard her wrong.

"It is the best solution. You will be guaranteed a good job." As far as she was concerned, the discussion was closed.

Lanzhou Medical University was not far from Lanzhou University, although not affiliated with it. While not as prestigious as its neighbor, it was considered the leading medical school in northwestern China, and it would prepare me for a high-paying and respected career. From Mama's point of view, that made it an excellent choice. She was happy; while her daughter might not be going to a top-tier university, medical school held a certain esteem.

Becoming a doctor had never occurred to me. I couldn't say that I was enthusiastic about the idea. I had been looking forward to going far away to an entirely different city. Now that dream was thwarted, but at least I'd be leaving home and living on my own. A whole new world was out there waiting for me.

Diana's Stepping-Stones on the Journey to Success

Understand that you are a worthy person. Sometimes negative emotions overwhelm us. When we feel sad and scared, we can begin to feel we are worthless. But that is never true. Every one of us is a valuable individual who deserves the best that life can offer. When you develop a sense of self-worth, you give yourself a priceless asset.

Strive to understand others, even when you disagree with them. When we find ourselves in conflict with people we care about, it helps to view the situation from their point of view. If we understand how their own experiences, knowledge, and perceptions have shaped their actions and attitudes, we can find the way to harmony.

Find supporters. It is important to search out the person who has faith in us. Our loved ones are not always our best supporters and cheerleaders, but each of us has someone out there who believes in us and encourages us. When even one person's voice joins in chorus with the inner voice that guides our dreams, it can expand our hope, strength, confidence, and determination by many magnitudes.

Be flexible when things don't go as planned. We may not always get what we want or expect, but that doesn't mean we can't proceed anyway.

Singers, dancers, and military hospital officials after a musical show in
1990 at Lanzhou Army general hospital, where Diana was an intern.
She is in the second row, fifth from the left, holding a fan.

医学院

Four Good and Bad Medicine, 1986–1991

With reluctance, I prepared to begin my studies at Lanzhou Medical University. I had serious doubts that this was the right place for me.

My original goal had been to go to Beijing University. When that fizzled, I should have pushed to go to Lanzhou University instead. Most of my high school friends were going there. Since I lived in the campus housing with my family, I knew from personal experience that the school would be a good fit for me. I enjoyed its sophistication and its vigorous energy. The students and teachers were intelligent and open-minded, and the dynamic environment of the campus supported a diversity of views and opinions.

Lanzhou Medical University was a different kind of place, even though it had a similar name and was located right across an alley from the larger school. It was a good place for someone who wanted to be a doctor, but I felt as if taking all those science courses would be like building a cage around my spirit. I craved chances to be creative and explore new ideas. I wanted to study languages, art, music, and subjects that would expose me to the wide world beyond China. But when I fumbled the entrance exam, I'd blown my chance to get the kind of education I'd dreamed about.

As the beginning of the academic year approached, I did my best to resign myself to my fate. Over and over I repeated my mother's words: *Doctors are valued members of society. Doctors enjoy good salaries, status, and privileges. Doctors get satisfaction from helping people.* All of that was true, but not for me. Still, I was excited about my new life. It was going to be an adventure living away from my family for the first time.

My dad spent a lot of time getting me ready for college. One of his requirements was that I get a nice canopy of netting to put over the bed to protect me from mosquito bites. Every student had a designated dormitory; he found mine, selected a suitable bed for me, made all the arrangements, and accompanied me when I moved in. I was really looking forward to spending my first night there.

Fifteen girls lived in the room where I would be staying, one of the large rooms on the third floor. We each had a bunk bed and a small table where we could study. The whole floor shared one big washroom where we could wash our faces and dishes and clothes, and a small restroom that spread its stench into the hallway. We would keep our clothes in suitcases under our beds.

I began to feel uneasy as I met my roommates. Nearly all of them were from the countryside; I could tell by their rough hands, their wind-burned red faces, and their strong rural accents, which I barely understood. They struck me as loud and unsophisticated compared to my high school friends. I felt outnumbered by them. When my dad left, I was lonely.

My greatest fears were confirmed that night. I was kept wide awake by all the snoring and grinding of teeth. In the darkest part of the night, when I had almost talked myself into going to sleep, I heard a creepy screeching noise. It freaked me out—so much so that I spent the rest of the night standing up on my bed, ready to defend myself. I never did learn what made that awful sound.

In the morning, we were roused early to go jogging. Everyone in the dormitory was required to go, and I hated it to death. When we had to use the restroom, we were directed to the large public one located in the track-and-field grounds. It was filthy and disgusting, with a stink so unbearable I couldn't even breathe. Holding my nose I rushed back outside. How could people endure such inhumane conditions? I couldn't bring myself to use that restroom. Instead, I ran back to my parents' home to use the familiar facilities there.

My parents were surprised to see me. "Jing-Jing!" my dad said. "What are you doing here? Has something terrible happened?"

I began to cry. "I hate that university. I'm going to quit and start the search over again. I want to find a school I will love."

"What is the problem with this one?"

I explained all of the things that had gone wrong. My mother frowned. I could tell I had made her extremely unhappy. "How can you possibly want to drop out of school because of such petty discomforts? Suppose you do quit and start over again—what if you can't pass the examination again? You will lose your chance for an education."

"I can pass the exam. I can get in somewhere else. I know I can."

"You won't become a doctor. You have a chance to become someone important. We can't let you throw that away."

"But, Mama, I don't even want to be a doctor."

"You must go back. If you give up now, we cannot support you any longer."

So another battle between us began. For two weeks I couldn't stop crying. My stomach ached the whole time. I was at a loss about what to do. I knew that this school was wrong for me, but nothing could change my mother's mind.

Though I desperately wished I had another choice, I knew what I had to do. With my heart sinking, I swallowed my tears and dragged my unwilling feet back to that depressing school.

* * *

Lanzhou Medical University had a few thousand students. In addition to the school of clinical medicine in which I was enrolled, there were schools of dentistry, pharmacology, nursing, and public health. Though most universities took four years to complete, as a medical student I faced five years before I could graduate; on top of the regular academic schedule, there was a yearlong internship program.

Five long years. It felt like forever.

Over my mother's objections, I spent a lot of time in the comforting familiarity of my parents' home. But gradually, if grudgingly, I got into the routine of a medical student.

Each morning the loudspeaker awakened us, and we pulled ourselves out of bed for the mandatory jog. After our exercise, we would all squeeze, hot and sweaty, into the small wash-room to freshen up, splashing our faces with cold water; hot water was not available.

Then it was time for class. We met in large lecture halls that held two hundred students. The first-year classes in-cluded chemistry, physiology, physics, geometry, politics, English, computer science, and physical education. In subse-quent years we focused even more intently on medical subjects like pharmacology, anatomy, gynecology, pediatrics, surgery, biochemistry, histology, microbiology, and genetics. The sched-ule didn't allow for electives. The university was strongly oriented toward Western medicine, although courses in traditional Chinese medicine were scheduled for the third year.

At lunch breaks we went to the auditorium, where the uni-versity canteen was set up. We brought our bowl and spoon and stood in long lines to be served terrible food. It was al-ways crowded. One time as I stood in line I was jostled and squeezed so hard by other students that when I started to eat I discovered my spoon was bent. Another time someone rush-ing by made me bump into a tall male student who was stand-ing behind me. I thought nothing of it until I got back to the dormitory with my food. My roommates pointed at my hair and laughed to tears.

"Hey, Lu Jing-Jing, where did you just get your new hair style? That is pretty unique!"

"It definitely stands out."

"Haa-haaa!"

I didn't understand. Peering into my tiny mirror, I saw two

pens hanging in my hair. They must have hooked onto my head when the tall student and I collided.

"Hey, that's why people shouldn't push me," I joked back to my roommates. "It was their loss. I got new pens!"

During lunch, tables were set up, but it was rare to find one that had any available space, so often my friends and I carried our food back to the dorm to eat it there. It was a five-minute walk, and when the wind blew hard off the desert, a layer of dust would settle on the food container by the time we got to the dorm.

After lunch we returned to our classes, which dragged on until six o'clock. Most lab classes were scheduled for the afternoon. When we had to sit through more lectures, it was often hard to keep from falling asleep. That was especially a problem for me in pharmacology because the professor was so boring. To keep awake, I chattered with my neighbors, letting her droning fade to background noise in my mind. One day, though, all of a sudden the hum of instruction stopped.

"Ladies and gentlemen, I cannot continue," the professor announced. "There is a student dressed in red who is talking to everyone around her, front and back, back and front, left and right, right and left. Watching her is making me so dizzy that I cannot focus on teaching."

Her speech made the students laugh, and they all turned to stare at me. I was so embarrassed that my face burned brighter than my red sweater.

A worse incident occurred in my anatomy class the first time a dead body was brought in for us to study. I was so repulsed by its creepy look and terrible odor that I ran out of the room and down an endless corridor to get outside, where I vomited in the bushes. Later on, to prepare for my exam, I had to spend a whole day with a dead body. That awful experience bothers me to this day.

Once we were released from classes for the day, our time was still not free. After dinner most students returned to the classrooms to study. Whenever I could, I did my studying at my parents' home. Or, even better, I'd go over to Lanzhou University. The classrooms were more pleasant, and the boys were cuter. A number of my high school friends were enrolled there. I sought out their company, and through them I made more friends. Compared to my medical school classmates, the Lanzhou University students were fun and fascinating. I learned to play competitive badminton with them. We cooked and laughed and danced together and flirted with the boys over the weekends. I was so grateful for my wonderful, supportive Lanzhou University friends.

Curfew was at eleven o'clock, and I had to get back before the dormitories were locked. In my own dorm, I immediately felt the contrast between my roommates and the friends I'd just left. I had little in common with the medical school students, and their rural ways struck me as strange and unsophisticated. So I avoided their company and rarely attended group activities. I admit it: I was a snob. I must have seemed arrogant and superior to those kind, humble, innocent students, but in truth I felt uncomfortable and lonely around them. Perhaps I was seeing in them the small, scared child I used to be and what I might have become if I'd stayed in the coal-mining village.

* * *

In my first semester, in my first English class at the university, I had a surprise beyond my wildest dream: my teacher was a native speaker! Wow! What could be better? Because of my high English score on the entrance exam, I had the good fortune to be selected to attend the advanced class. The teacher's name was Karina Zabehe, and she was from Yorkshire, England. Her mother was Persian, her grandmother French, and her father English. She had black hair, olive skin, long legs, and a slender and curvy figure. I thought she was the most beautiful foreign woman I'd ever met.

The first thing she did was to call the roll. We were to answer with a "yes." When my turn came, my "yes" rang out through the room. Everyone laughed because I didn't sound like they did. My pronunciation sounded natural, much closer to the way an English person would speak. Karina noticed that right away.

Karina and I became close friends. This was the first time I'd had an extended acquaintanceship with a foreigner, and she was my idol for a long time. A talented and artistic teacher, she spoke seven languages: English, French, Russian, Arabic, Spanish, Italian, and German. She loved music and dancing and was particularly fond of the theater. My mind craved exposure to her kind of creative energy, and I spent a lot of time after school with Karina and her foreign colleagues on the faculty, learning about foreign languages, foreign cultures, and foreign arts and theater.

A highlight of the year for me was a production of William Shakespeare's great play *Romeo and Juliet*. Karina wrote an adaptation of the script, adding music, and produced and directed the show. We performed it in the university auditorium. Most of the actors were graduate students, but Karina found two roles for me: I danced in the chorus and I was the announcer for the play. This was my introduction to Western theater. I didn't understand the whole play, but I was thrilled to be part of the production.

I told my parents all about Karina, and I was excited when they warmly invited her to dinner at their home. This was quite an event for my family, and I even invited my brother and his best friend to join us. My mother made special vegetarian dumplings in Karina's honor, which she must have enjoyed very much, as she ate a lot of them.

My friendship with Karina was a breath of fresh air in a stifling atmosphere.

* * *

We did not have to pay any tuition for the school, and every student was provided with a food card. Women's cards entitled them to thirty-two pounds of bread or other flour foods per month. The men were entitled to thirty-four pounds, which wasn't enough food to keep many of the male students from going hungry.

Beyond that, we were responsible for our own living expenses. My parents' financial situation had improved, so they gave me an allowance of seven dollars a month to buy food, snacks, and incidentals. This was a little more than the average student received, and it meant I didn't need to rely on my food card; I used only part of my ration and gave the rest to students who desperately needed it. Since I had a little money, I could go out to eat. The big alley between Lanzhou University and Lanzhou Medical University had an open market and many restaurants. Usually I ordered my favorite dish, the spicy Lanzhou beef noodle.

With my little bit of pocket money I was also able to buy clothes of my own choosing, so I stopped wearing the clothes Mama had picked for me. My mother's younger sister still sent us beautiful clothes on occasion. Every time one of her packages arrived, it was like a festival. My sister Yan-Yan and I spent hours in front of the mirror, trying on the clothes and modeling them for each other.

Boys were beginning to notice me. I dated casually, but none of my relationships with men developed into a serious romance. My dating experiences were innocent and pure, characterized by holding hands, warm hugs, and a simple kiss on the lips.

Physical intimacy between students was strictly prohibited. If you got caught, you would be expelled from the school, for such behavior was considered immoral and shameful. Girls were expected to be virgins when they got married. If a girl had sexual relations, it was assumed that she would never be able to find a good husband. When a couple fell in love, they expressed their affection in more acceptable ways —he would buy her food, while she would cook for him or do his laundry.

When a boy visited a girl in the dorm, he had to register and sign in. By eleven o'clock, all the lights were off, the big entrance door would be closed, and boys were not allowed to stay in there. The men's apartments had no such restrictions.

Because of the strict, complicated rules and procedures for visiting girls, our dorm was called the "panda" house, indicating how precious and valuable the girls were.

My sister had run afoul of the strict social mores when she'd begun dating while she was still in high school. I didn't violate those rules, but Mama became upset with me for a different reason. I was bored to tears by medical school. When I was in class, I felt as if I were in prison. I spent more and more time with my friends at Lanzhou University. My poor attitude about my studies resulted in sloppy grades, which disappointed my mother terribly.

Despite our physical disadvantage, our hard-working enthusiasm and focused spirit led us to victory.

My brother, however, made up for my sister and me. He was attending the top high school in the city and continued making outstanding grades. At least Mama had one child of whom to feel proud.

* * *

During my freshman year I became involved again in competitive sports, which I'd loved since junior high school. I was chosen to be a member of the volleyball team. We played in provincial college tournaments and did well. I was still small, and my team members weren't all that tall either. Despite our physical disadvantage, our hard-working enthusiasm and focused spirit led us to victory.

Early in the second semester of my second year, I began to

experience extreme fatigue and swollen ankles after volley-ball games. One day I noticed that my urine was very dark. When I told Mama, she was shocked. She insisted I see a doc-tor the next day. I did, and to our relief he pronounced me fine.

But I wasn't fine. About a month later my fatigue grew much worse. My urine became darker and darker, and I grew more and more scared. One day, to my distress, I could not even take my pants off because my ankles were so swollen. This time Mama took me straight to the medical university hospital. The doctors there ran a series of tests and found blood in my urine. But what was causing it? Despite my symp-toms, I looked normal and healthy. No one could figure out what was wrong.

My mother was terrified I had kidney cancer. She was so worried that she was constantly in tears; she would weep while washing clothes and dishes. Finally, the doctors de-cided I should return to the hospital for treatment, observa-tion, and further diagnostic testing. I was admitted as a pa-tient for an extended stay.

My classmates visited often and did their best to encourage me. Though I'd felt so different from them at first and had held myself apart, they now showed me great compassion. I was moved by their concern and felt myself getting closer to them. The walls that had separated them from me in my heart were coming down.

Karina made a special meal for me and brought it to the hospital.

"Eat this, Jing-Jing," she urged, handing me a bowl filled with a white-and-orange mixture. "It will help you get well."

"What is it?" I asked.

"A blend of milk, boiled cauliflower, carrots, and bananas. It's very nutritious."

That didn't sound at all appealing, but I dutifully took a bite. The dish had no seasoning, and it was mushy and flavorless. I ate it anyhow, forcing spoonfuls into my mouth to show my appreciation. Karina was very happy. After she left, I asked my roommates to taste it. When they did, they all grimaced and shook their heads. "Could this be typical Western food?" I asked. If so, I didn't want to try any more of it.

The true beauty of a human being is the beauty of the mind, and the tenderness of the heart is eternal.

I got along well with the five other patients in the ward, especially "Aunt" Wan. A pretty woman in her forties with an oval face and large dark round eyes, she was the manager of a large manufacturing plant. She was in the hospital to be treated for a kidney infection. I took to her at once. When I spoke to her, I felt like I could talk to her forever.

Aunt Wan acted like a mother to me, the first time I felt such love and acceptance from a really intelligent and educated woman who was not my blood relative. She recognized my talents, my passions, and my unique personality. She taught me that the true beauty of a human being is the beauty of the mind, and that the tenderness of the heart is eternal.

"Do you have boyfriends?" she asked me.

"Well, sometimes," I told her. "There are boys who think I'm pretty."

"Are you in love?"

"In love? I don't understand that."

"When I was your age, I was in college. That's when I met my husband. He thought I was pretty, but what I loved about him was that he saw my inner beauty."

"What do you mean, inner beauty?"

"Physical beauty can only last a short time," she explained. "But a woman who is not pretty will still be seen as beautiful and sexy if she expresses her personality and lets all of the good qualities she has within her shine forth."

"In other words," I said, "real beauty is more than skin deep."

She smiled. "Exactly. My husband gave me a great gift by helping me bring forth the beauty I have inside."

I was touched and comforted by her love story, and I have carried her principles with me and lived by them my whole life. When Aunt Wan left the hospital, I felt a deep sense of loss. I cried like a baby I missed her so much. It is too bad we did not stay in touch, but my love for her remains in my heart. I have dreamed about her for many years. If she is still alive and is reading this book, I pray that we will meet again. If not, let her message be shared with my readers, and in that way, let our friendship live on.

* * *

I remained in the hospital for three months. In a way I was grateful for a reprieve from my studies.

My diagnosis still eluded the doctors of Western-style medicine at the hospital. None of their techniques or medications was working to stop the bleeding. Finally my mom got fed up and took me to a well-known practitioner of Chinese medicine. He prescribed a traditional herbal remedy, which my mother prepared and baked every day based on his instructions. My father brought it to me at the hospital.

The concoction of herbs tasted so bitter and smelled so bad that swallowing it was almost unbearable. But I had to take it, and I did. After several weeks of this regimen, there was no more indication of blood in my urine.

Soon I was strong enough again to leave the hospital during the day to attend some of my classes, but I had to return every evening. Because I didn't really look ill, the doorman refused at first to let me back in; he wouldn't believe I belonged there until I showed him the badge that identified me as a patient.

My tests had been sent to an expert in Beijing, who eventually sent back a report that led to my diagnosis. A close examination of a chest X-ray revealed a tiny scar on my lung. That, combined with other test results and symptoms, led to a conclusion that I had been suffering from kidney tuberculosis. By this time I was nearly well, thanks to those foul-tasting herbs. I've been told that traditional Chinese medicine sometimes works miracles with serious illnesses that Western medicine cannot cure. That proved true for me. I think it's a pity that traditional Chinese medicine has not been well promoted in the rest of the world.

* * *

I had missed nearly a semester of school, and now I was facing tremendous pressure. Final exams were only a month away, and it seemed almost impossible that I could pass them with so little time to prepare. I was taking six major subjects, but I was still barely able to attend classes, and I knew next to nothing about what had been taught. According to university policy, if you failed two exams you'd be expelled.

My mom begged me not to take the finals. "Take some time off, Jing-Jing. Next year, with your health better, you can take this whole semester over again."

I shuddered at the suggestion. No way could I stand to stay in this university an extra year. It would be torture, a waste of my life. If I could not pass the exams, I would rather be expelled.

"I'm going to take the exams. Give me the chance, I can pass them," I swore to her. "If I don't pass, they can ask me to drop out of their school. I don't care if I lose my diploma."

I was fortunate to have the help of my fellow student Guo Shuang Ping. We had met in Karina's English class and become good friends. I had even gone to visit her family, who lived on a farm in the country nearly three hours from Lanzhou. She didn't want me to drop out of school, so she offered to help me catch up on my studies. A down-to-earth, caring woman, Guo Shuang Ping had tremendous strength and more than enough love to help others even when she was stressed about preparing for her own exams. She was also very bright and eventually earned her PhD. I want to take this opportunity to acknowledge my appreciation of her loving and generous friendship. Without her, this would have been a disastrous year, one that could have negatively altered the course of my life.

Thanks to Guo Shuang Ping's help, I passed all my exams.

On a few of them I scored in the top ten in my class. My mom was astonished by my success and determination. She was starting to believe I had more potential and capability than she had been giving me credit for. I'd earned poor grades in earlier semesters because I simply had no interest in studying medicine. In fact, I hated it.

When we choose something we love, we will always do well; if we pursue something we don't enjoy, it only stops our growth and troubles our parents.

Even more amazing was the English test. While I was in the hospital I found out there was going to be a test for fourth-level English, the highest and most difficult English exam you could take for a bachelor's degree. To keep my mind off my medical problems and relieve the boredom of being a hospital patient, I took the exam, even though I wasn't studying English that semester. I was shocked when I learned that out of the whole university I was the only one who passed it. In contrast to my medical subjects, I loved studying English. I was beginning to understand that when we choose something we love, we will always do well; if we pursue something we don't enjoy, it only stops our growth and troubles our parents.

When I told my mother about the English test results, she thought I was joking. She refused to believe me until the dean, who was a friend of my parents, convinced her it was true. I found out that the faculty had held a ceremony at one of their meetings to honor my achievement. To my regret I was at home at the time, locked up with my studies. I didn't know this tribute had taken place until afterward.

Because I was considered to be a talented and valuable student, I was told that the head of the university made me a promise: the university would keep me in the school as a teacher after I graduated. It was an honor to be offered this opportunity, and I was thrilled. Having a career as a teacher, and eventually becoming a professor like my parents, appealed to me far more than becoming a doctor did.

                    * * *

In the spring of my third year of college, a powerful political spirit swept over China. I heard the trigger was the death on April 15, 1989, of Hu Yaobang, the former General Secretary of the Communist Party of China, who had been ousted from his post two years earlier for being too sympathetic to prodemocracy demonstrators. The movement began with calls for his good reputation to be reinstated and grew to encompass a widespread protest against government corruption and demands for political and economic reforms.

In Beijing, hundreds of thousands of students and their supporters—intellectuals and workers alike—gathered in the large public plaza known as Tiananmen Square. For several weeks they staged hunger strikes, marches, and peaceful demonstrations.

Universities all over the country joined in the protests, and mine was no exception. Students rose up to support the fight against corruption, although most of our students literally knew nothing about actual experiences of corruption. We were just fascinated by the idea—at least I was. The whole school stopped working. There was no more routine, no studying. Students refused to attend classes. It seemed as though the world had ceased to move.

Along with most of my classmates, I joined a huge parade in Lanzhou that drew students from the entire province of Gansu. All of the local colleges held rallies on their own campuses, and then the participants marched to a large boulevard that ran through the downtown. There the marches flowed together into a vast river of people, many of them carrying flags and banners bearing political slogans. Residents came to watch the spectacle and handed out food and water. The parade lasted all day and all night.

One of my roommates and her boyfriend felt so strongly about the cause that they jumped on the train and went to Beijing. But I felt a little bit isolated from the political uproar. Other than the parade, I didn't protest or take part in hunger strikes. Like my fellow students, I hated corruption, and I sympathized with all their intentions. Even so, I just didn't feel right about the chaos the demonstrations were causing. Many students were sincere in their beliefs and took part in the protests out of strong principles and a pure moral conviction. But I could see clearly that political opportunists and false leaders were at work, encouraging the protesters and fueling their anger. They would order their followers to go on hunger strikes, yet secretly seek out food for themselves. They manipulated and misused people while maintaining their charade of moral commitment. I was disgusted by their hypocrisy.

When I went home, I got into passionate and vigorous debates with my parents. My mom was very angry about the chaotic situation that was being created. Nobody was working, and the transportation system was crippled. The streets were filthy, with garbage everywhere. All of the classrooms were empty, and the professors were simply staying home doing nothing. Government officials couldn't function because their buildings were surrounded by protesters. While she sympathized with their cause, she felt that their methods were no different from the Red Guard's abusive tactics during the Cultural Revolution.

"Our country cannot afford another disastrous political movement like the Cultural Revolution," she said. "China has suffered for two decades. It is extremely critical that we have stability now, after all that our country has been through."

"But the protestors' cause is just, Mama. Corruption *does* exist in the government. Change *is* needed."

She shook her head. "Creating turmoil and dissension won't improve anything. If we want to make our country better, we must find positive ways to do it."

"What should the students do then?"

"What's best is that they focus on their studies. If they take advantage of their time at school, they will learn more about society, learn more about other people. With a good foundation of academic knowledge, they won't be misled by politicians. They will be able to create change that is meaningful yet not disruptive."

My mother had strong principles, and she would fight for them with her life. From her I learned about the strength and power that come from honesty, decency, and justice. In my mind and heart, my mother is a most noble and forceful spirit, and I feel fortunate to have been guided by her wisdom.

She was a strong supporter of Deng Xiaoping, believing that his open-mindedness and farsighted political decisions benefited the whole country. She was pleased when he chose to manage the protests with a firm hand. In late May the government cracked down on the demonstrations in Beijing by declaring martial law. When that didn't end them, the military was sent in to forcibly clear Tiananmen Square, and I heard from other students, who'd learned the news from unofficial sources, that this move had resulted in many casualties. Fortunately, the government was able to quell the demonstrators more peaceably in other cities, including Lanzhou. The protest leaders in our city suffered political black marks. They were closely supervised from then on and punished by being relegated to unfavorable jobs.

Creating turmoil and dissension won't improve anything. If we want to make our country better, we must find positive ways to do it.

From an academic standpoint, a big part of the school year had been wasted. I lost out on the training I was supposed to have in traditional Chinese medicine, which had been scheduled for the squandered semester. But I was glad to have life return to normal.

* * *

In the fourth year I auditioned for the university's dancing group. The group would be our school's official representative in a province-wide musical competition that would be staged in the Lanzhou University auditorium. More than twenty colleges would be taking part.

To my delight, I was one of the seven girls selected. A choreographer who was famous in China created the dance we would perform and supervised our instruction and rehearsals. It was a privilege to work with such a talented person, and a welcome break from all of the hours spent on dull science.

No one had to push me or press me; my love for what I was doing generated all the drive and strength I needed.

I was surprised when my mother frowned on my dancing. I had thought she would support and encourage me. Having been a professional performer, she knew firsthand about the joy and excitement of being on a stage, of honoring her creative passion and reveling in the audience's appreciation and applause. But she insisted that I was wasting my time; I should concentrate on my studies. As a result, I found myself growing detached from her. I loved dancing far too much to quit.

In our performance we portrayed the seven flying goddesses who play musical instruments in heaven. In Chinese legends, the goddesses visit the earth to bless people and bring them happiness. The dance we were learning was beautiful but technically difficult. At first our movements were clumsy, but gradually they became fluid and smooth. Fortunately all seven of us worked hard, and we enjoyed working together. We practiced for months and followed a strict diet so that we would fit into our costumes. They were gorgeous—tight-fitting bodysuits topped with filmy layers of color: pink, coral, and cream.

For the competition we wore special makeup that enlarged our eyes, transforming us into seven beautiful goddesses with enchanting smiles. We were so nervous that our smiles froze on our faces. But as we danced through the clouds (a fog created by dry ice), our audience was captivated. To our surprise, we won the highest score, beating Lanzhou University by two-tenths of a point.

This was one of the most memorable and thrilling moments of my college life, and it's a great example of a time when my passion led to success. I enjoyed the experience and was gratified by the result—not only winning the competition but also achieving something based on my genuine passion and true talent. No one had to push me or press me; my love for what I was doing generated all the drive and strength I needed. Even though hard work and discipline were demanded, it never felt like work, because I loved what I was doing. The process was full of fun and joy.

That's what life is about. We should always choose what we love, and enjoy what we do. That is the best plan for achieving our goals.

That's what life is about. We should always choose what we love, and enjoy what we do. That is the best plan for achieving our goals.

* * *

After four years of class work, it was time for my internship. I was lucky to be one of two dozen students selected to go to the general hospital of the army of Lanzhou, which was well equipped and had talented and capable doctors. We rotated from one department to another, working closely with doctors in various specialties to gain direct experience in treating patients.

I received some extraordinary training from great doctors in the hospital. I particularly remember Dr. Hung, the director of the ear, nose, and throat department, who was an inspirational teacher and a great humanitarian. His exquisite skill and medical knowledge were respected by all his patients and fellow doctors, and his compassionate, affectionate heart warmed everyone. He showed us what it means to have the highest standard of professionalism and a strong sense of responsibility as a doctor. I always think doctors should be like him.

Another standout was Dr. Zhou, my instructor in the general surgical department, who was funny, kind, and talented. I enjoyed this rotation and proved adept at assignments like closing the stomach incisions of ulcer surgery patients. Making neat, tight, and quick stitches was part of my expertise.

But many of my experiences that year were painful and discouraging. One of the most disheartening was my gynecology/obstetrics rotation, where I helped to deliver three babies. Though the birth of a child is usually seen as a happy occasion, I witnessed the weeping, wailing, and emotional anguish that occurred in that department every day. The process of birth was shocking and unpleasant. The women screamed as though they were getting slaughtered, and the newborn infants were distressingly wrinkled and bloody. One woman struggled for over twenty-four hours to deliver her child. No medications were provided to reduce her pain, and we stood by helplessly, unable to find a way to ease her suffering. I could not understand why a woman would have a second and third child when the first time was so traumatic. I guess until the day I give birth to a child of my own, I will not resolve this puzzle.

An incident in the ophthalmology department was also dispiriting. A nineteen-year-old soldier was brought in for surgery. He had been hit by a drunk driver, and his right eye was severely injured. We had to remove the damaged eye and replace it with a fake one. Here was this young, handsome boy marred for life. It was painful to realize that as doctors we were often incapable of truly healing people.

When I rotated to neurology, I had a real problem, which became apparent the first time I saw surgery done on someone's brain. I watched the surgeon drill into the patient's skull, and the next second I did not see or hear anything. Finally the doctor found me passed out on the floor. This happened several times, until the neurology staff had to transfer me to another department. They could not have a fainting student in their surgery room. No one could understand what the problem was; I was stalwart and brave in other surgeries. I have no explanation, but I could not deal with the idea of drilling into a person's head. Whenever I watched it happen, I felt as though I were helping to kill someone.

My most agonizing experience occurred in pediatrics. I was on duty one night when a five-year-old boy was brought unconscious to the hospital. His father and grandfather claimed the boy had taken some drugs, but they did not know what the drugs were. I went to find the physician on duty and discovered him asleep. I had to wake him up twice before he slowly dragged his feet to the boy's bed. By then it was too late. I watched as this cute little boy closed his eyes and drew his last breath.

The father and grandfather looked ravaged with pain and guilt. In tears, I told them, "I am so sorry for your loss." My heart felt as if a knife had sliced through it.

I could not believe what had just happened. I felt so useless and helpless. As an intern, I was not allowed to issue direct instructions for treating a patient, and even though I tried very hard to get him there, by the time my instructor arrived it was too late to save the little boy. I was terrified to see how easy it was to destroy a person's life and how irresponsible and incompetent a doctor could be.

By now I was seriously questioning whether I wanted to pursue a career in medicine. Thank goodness the university would be giving me a teaching job.

* * *

The best times I had during my internship didn't take place in hospital wards or surgery clinics but on the stage. The chance to express my artistry and creativity was always a huge boost to my spirits.

The first opportunity that year came when the university asked me to take part in another provincial arts competition. This time I was a solo singer backed up by an orchestra. Costumed in an evening gown with a big bow, I performed two songs. One was a patriotic tune called "October Is Her Birthday—My China," and the other was a children's song, "My Little Backpack." I spent a lot of time preparing for my performance—so much time that I almost had my internship suspended because I was so often absent.

Even more exciting was a variety show featuring many musical numbers that was staged in the hospital theater in celebration of the army. Military personnel, including some of the highest-ranking officers, joined doctors, nurses, and students in the audience for this big event. As the only student selected in the auditions, I had a chance to perform with professional singers and dancers, who exposed me to much higher artistic standards than I'd experienced before.

Later that year, I produced, directed, and performed in a little musical for the hospital's New Year celebration. I selected folk dances, ballroom dances, and songs and wove them together to tell a love story.

For me the applause was more effective medicine than any Western pill or Chinese bitter herb.

* * *

When I finished my internship, I went back to school to prepare for the lengthy, comprehensive, and daunting final exams. I was afraid I might fail and not receive my degree. Nightmares about those exams haunted me for years afterward. It was such a relief to wake up each time and be able to say, "That was just a bad dream. I did it. I graduated."

In the summer of 1991, my five years of college life—full of tears, fear, disappointment, and occasional joy—finally were over. Still, I hated the choice that my parents made for me to study something I disliked, which proved later in my life to be a very wrong direction for me.

The next step for my fellow students and me was to receive our job assignments. It was the university's role to decide for its graduates where they would work and in what position. My friends were nervous; the manner in which jobs were assigned seemed arbitrary and often capricious, and most graduates had no clue about what fate awaited them. But I knew what was in store for me, and I was looking forward to my new job—the teaching position I had been promised by the former head of the university.

What a shock I had in store.

Diana's Stepping-Stones on the Journey to Success

Choose to do what you love. When we love what we are doing, it will bring us joy, inspire our creativity, and hold our interest. It will give us unlimited drive, strength, and energy to succeed.

Listen to others, but, above all, listen to your heart. What others have to tell us can provide valuable wisdom and insight that we should take into account. But when it comes to our education, our career, or other life decisions, we should base our choices on our own passions, goals, and needs—not theirs. Doing something only because it will satisfy others or gain us their approval does not benefit us in the long run.

Learn from your experiences. Even negative experiences can give us opportunities to acquire skills, understanding, and knowledge that will help us in the future.

Diana at her parents' home, summer 1991.

冒险和收获

Five Risks and Rewards, 1991–1993

I stood waiting in the municipal personnel office, one of many people in the long line of new college graduates. The room was stuffy with summer heat. In this drab, utilitarian place our future would begin. We were about to learn what our first job was to be and set off on our career paths.

The line inched forward. The nervousness that everyone felt was obvious in murmured conversations and restless shuffling of feet. I watched as people ahead of me reached the head of the line and were given their news. Some responded with a smile, others with a frown, still others with a resigned shrug of the shoulders.

At last it was my turn. A bored clerk handed me the envelope that held my future inside. I tore it open and pulled out my assignment notice. When I read what was written there, I screamed.

I'd been assigned to a position as a doctor in a clinical hospital on the other side of Lanzhou.

Impossible! It could not be. I was supposed to be an instructor at Lanzhou Medical University. I'd been counting on the commitment the school had made to me three years earlier.

"This can't be correct," I told the clerk, giving him back the notice. "Look at this. There has been a mistake."

He barely glanced at the paper before handing back to me. "No mistake, miss. Step aside."

Everyone was staring at me. I fled from the office and ran to my parents' home.

"Baba," I cried, "this is terrible. They have given me the wrong job."

My father agreed to visit the faculty dean at Lanzhou Medical University, who was a friend, and ask what had gone wrong. I kept hoping an error had been made, only to lose that hope when Baba reported back to me.

"The head administrator who told you about the job has retired," he explained. "The new one knows nothing about it. The job has been given to someone else."

"But . . . but why didn't anyone let me know? I thought the position was promised to me because of my English talent. The university made a commitment."

He put his hand on my shoulder. "I'm sorry you're disappointed, but look on the bright side. You've been offered a very good position. You should be glad."

I shook my head. "It's not a good position for me. I don't want to be a doctor."

"You ungrateful girl," my mother scolded. "You should jump to embrace your good fortune. A career with so many rewards—most people would treasure such a marvelous opportunity."

Mama was right. Being a doctor had a lot of advantages. I would be assured a good salary, high status in the society, and a comfortable standard of living. I would be doing good, important work, helping patients who were sick and in need. Against this long list of positives, there was only one negative: the thought of being a doctor turned my blood to ice.

The job I'd been given was indeed a marvelous opportunity—for someone else.

* * *

The day was approaching when I was to report to the hospital. And the closer it came, the more I dreaded it. Being a doctor was a huge responsibility. I'd learned a lesson from the little boy who had died from a drug overdose while I was on duty: a doctor could kill someone as easily as cure him. That possibility scared me to death.

Why couldn't I have a job that was in keeping with my talents and passions? Why was it up to the government, the university, or my parents to decide who I would become?

I wanted to work not with people's bodies but with their minds and hearts. The teaching job I had expected would have been perfect—a chance to express myself, to honor my creativity, to communicate with others and exchange ideas. Someone else might discover those rewards in medicine, but in my five years of medical training, I had never found them.

Most of my classmates had accepted their job offers. If they weren't pleased by their assignment, they took the attitude that this was what fate had arranged for them and so they would comply. Only a few turned down the position they'd been given, and they had the support of parents who had enough money and power to help them find something else.

After thinking long and hard, I made a fateful decision. I would not accept the hospital position. Instead I would take my chances to seek a job that I would enjoy.

It was with great trepidation that I told my parents my plans.

"Jing-Jing, are you crazy?" my mother cried. "How can you even think such ridiculous thoughts?"

"Taking a job I hate—that's what would be crazy. Whenever I think of working in that hospital, I feel like I'm choking."

"I can't believe you are being so foolish! You have a chance for a good life and you want to throw it away."

"I'll make a life that's even better."

"Ha! How will you do that? You're indulging in a fantasy."

"I'll find a good job somewhere else. You know I can do it."

"Where can you possibly find anything as good as this?"

"Please, Mama. Believe in me. Give me your support."

"How can I support such imprudent behavior? You have no idea what you're giving up. Take the job you were given, Jing-Jing—I insist you do that. It's the only sensible course."

I understood why she felt as she did. She and her family had experienced so many reversals of fortune. She had endured long periods of poverty, deprivation, and hardship. After a long struggle she had finally achieved a position of prominence and respect. She had graduated from college and was now the manager of the files department in the main administrative office of Lanzhou University. She wanted her children to have an easier life than hers had been. My brother was on the right track; he was in Wuhan, studying at Huazhong Technical University of Science and Technology, one of the top polytechnic schools in the country. My sister, though, had left school. After attending a short-term professional school, she was working in the Lanzhou University library. Yan-Yan had her own salary and a level of independence that I'd envied as I struggled with my own studies. But our mother was concerned that without a better university degree, Yan-Yan's opportunities would be seriously limited (although later this would prove not to be true). Mama had been pleased that my future would be secure, and now I was dropping this bombshell.

She urged and pleaded and commanded, but I refused to change my mind. My stubbornness led to a series of painful and exhausting arguments between us. My mother took a hard line against me, which made me very angry. I needed my parents' help and encouragement, but she would not bend. My father took her side, which dismayed me even more. He had always been my source of strength, an ally I could rely on.

Finally, Mama gave me a choice. "Either you will take this job, Jing-Jing, or you will leave home. If you insist on being stubborn, you are on your own."

It was a horrible dilemma. I didn't know where I would find a job or how long it would take. I had no money, no prospects, and no other place to stay. I didn't know if I had the strength, the will, and the courage to fight for myself. If I obeyed my mother, I would have my family's approval and affection and a job that paid well but made me feel dead inside. If I struck out on my own, I would have nothing but my dreams.

I could not believe how frightened and tense I felt. I pictured myself becoming a ragged beggar on the streets. But deep down in my soul I knew that I really had no option but to leave. There must be someone who would recognize my talents. There must be a job somewhere that I would enjoy, one that would reward not just my purse but also my spirit.

If my parents didn't believe in me, fine. I would believe in myself.

* * *

I left home with only seven dollars in my pocket.

I asked around for a place to stay, and one of my best friends from high school came through for me. Guo Jun Ming was in graduate school, living in a university dormitory, and his parents were in Guangzhou, where his father, who worked for a scientific research institute, had a temporary assignment. So for the time being their apartment was empty, and Guo Jun Ming kindly allowed me to stay in a room there. I want to take this opportunity to acknowledge the gifts that he gave me in a difficult time: his friendship, his generosity, and his assurances that I deserved a good job and would find one. His confidence in me had a tremendous impact, propelling me to move forward in pursuit of my goals.

As my job hunt proceeded, I truly needed his reassurance, because I met failure so many times.

In China at that time *guanxi* was the path to a better job. This was a system of backdoor relationships, in which individuals traded on their connections with people in positions of influence in order to get ahead. But I had no backdoor relationships to draw on. I wasn't on close terms with hospital officials who might have offered me a teaching job or found another way for me to use my medical training without being a doctor. Nor did I have connections with any of the personnel officers for the municipal institutions or government-run companies in Lanzhou. Even if my parents had been willing to help me, they were not plugged into the *guanxi* network. Their strong sense of pride and dignity meant it was beneath them to beg or flatter anyone to help get me a job.

Without *guanxi* connections to ease my way, I had to return to the municipal personnel office, give them back my file, and hope they could come up with a suitable placement. This large, centralized bureau handled the hiring and job assignments for all government jobs—which meant just about every job available, since in China the government owns and runs nearly every institution and business.

The office was a large room with row upon row of desks. The clerks kept themselves busy by chitchatting, reading newspapers, knitting, crunching on sunflower seeds, drinking tea—anything except helping the patrons. I went there day after day, waiting for hours at a time, but the clerks weren't interested in finding a job for me. After a while, they no longer even bothered to greet me when I arrived. Eventually they gave up on me. One of them told me, "I don't know why you keep coming back here. We have nothing for you."

I replied, "I come back because I need to find a job."

"We have nothing for you. You will have to go somewhere else."

"There is nowhere else. This is the only place that handles jobs for people with any education."

"So sorry, miss." But I could tell she had no concern for me at all.

Then I tried visiting the various hospitals in the city, hoping they might be willing to consider me for a teaching position or an administrative job. Everywhere I went, I reached a dead end.

One day I heard that the Gansu Health Department, the public health ministry for the province, might have openings in its Foreign Affairs Office. The ministry brought in health experts from other countries as advisors and consultants, and it also was responsible for health services for foreign workers employed by Lanzhou companies. With my English skills and medical training, I was sure a job there would be the perfect fit for me.

The new director of the ministry, Mr. Wong, had just come back from studies in the United States. Because of his experience abroad, I thought he might be more open-minded than other government officials and imaginative enough to recognize my abilities and talents. But how could I meet him? I asked around, trying to find a way that I could possibly meet such an important official. No one offered to help me or even gave me good advice, and I realized there was only way to get what I wanted—go directly to his office and ask.

I approached the receptionist. "If you please, I would like to arrange a meeting with Mr. Wong."

CLOCKWISE FROM ABOVE:

Diana, a few months old;
one year old, with Mom
and Dad; Beijing, 1969
(Chinese characters on the
left translate as "Always loyal
to Chairman Mao"); two years
old; eight or nine years old
in the coal-mining village.

In the coal-mining village, student performers in Tibetan, Uighur, Russian, and Hui Muslim costumes are gathered for a government official's visit. Diana is in the front row, far right. Diana's father is in the second row, third from the right. Miss Zhang Li is in the third row, third from the right.

ABOVE: Diana's high school graduation, 1986. Diana is in the third row, fourth from the left (with the glasses and braids); Mr. Cao Qing Zhong, her master teacher, is in the second row, fifth from the right; Ms. Cheng An Li, her English teacher, is in the second row, fourth from the left. Mr. Cao's big accomplishment was sending over 90 percent of the class to college.

BELOW LEFT: Hiking and dancing with college friends in Xing Long Mountain in Lanzhou, 1988.

BELOW RIGHT: Diana (front row, second from left), with high school friends in Lanzhou after finishing the first semester of college, spring 1987.

ABOVE: Diana's university volleyball team, fall 1986. Diana is in the first row, far right. Their coaches, Mr. Liu, Mr. Yang, and Mrs. Yao, are in the center.

RIGHT: With college friends at the Bridge of the Yellow River in Lanzhou, spring 1991.

BELOW: With other hospital interns in Lanzhou, summer 1991.

ABOVE: Graduates at the main teaching building on the Lanzhou Medical University campus, summer 1991.

LEFT: Singing at a music competition of the Gansu provincial universities, winter 1990.

BELOW LEFT: Diana as a university teacher, after cutting her hair at home, 1992.

BELOW RIGHT: Three of Diana's students, who are Uighur, Tibetan, and Hui Muslim, at Northwest Minorities University in Lanzhou.

姓　名	鲁京京
性　别	女
民　族	汉
出生时间	1967 年 10 月
籍　贯	湖北天门
工作单位	医学系
职　务	
职　称	
发证日期	1992 年元月 9 日

民院证字第0829号

Diana's teaching credential for Northwest Minorities University.

姓　名　鲁京京　性别　女

出生日期　1967　年　10月10日

原单位＿＿＿＿＿＿＿

原住址　兰州市城关区西北村1号

现单位　深圳香格里拉大酒店

现住址　女大街新阁1-7栋

—3—　　　　—4—

Diana's temporary Shenzhen resident card, issued through the Shangri-La Hotel.

February 13, 1993

Lanzhou University
78 Tian Shui Road
Lanzhou 730000
Gansu Province

To Whom It May Concern:

    This is a recommendation for 鲁京京 , whom I will refer to as Diana.

    It has been my pleasure to know Diana since my arrival to China in September of last year. As a foreigner, I had many needs as I tried to familiarize myself with, adjust and survive in my new environment. Diana smoothed this transition by acting as my translator, teacher, guide and friend.

    Being an English teacher in the Foreign Language Department of Lanzhou University, I am quite attentive to the English skill of the people I meet. I can confidently say that Diana's English speaking and comprehension level is extraordinarily high. She has the innate ability to obtain knowledge quickly and is very driven to excel in whatever she attempts. Diana is an honest, loyal, and very pleasant individual to be around. Furthermore, she can successfully interact in a variety of interpersonal and group situations.

    Taking all of this into consideration, I give her my highest recommendation. Due to her mastery of the English language, her high people skills, and her outstanding character, Diana would be nothing but an asset to your company.

    Please feel free to contact me for questions and verification.

Very Sincerely,

Ginger L. Onishi
English Lecturer
Lanzhou University

The reference letter provided by Ginger Onishi for Diana's job hunting in Shenzhen, February 1993.

February 13, 1993

Lanzhou University
78 Tian Shui Road
Lanzhou 730000
Gansu Province

To Whom It May Concern:

I would like to encourage you in your consideration of 鲁京来 for employment. I have known her for over six months as she has sat in on some of my classes for doctor students. She was by for the best student and would just come to class as a listener to perfect and improve her skills. She is hungry to learn even more and is very teachable. I heartily commend her to you not simply because she is a friend but because I believe she would be an excellent addition to your joint venture team. She has an excellent command of English, has a charismatic personality and is very competent in her field of expertise. I personally have found her a great help as a translator and was quite impressed with her polite manner. I do not think you can do any better and so I heartily give her my highest commendation.

Please feel free to contact me if you have any questions.

Sincerely,

David Godfrey

The reference letter from David Godfrey for Diana's job hunting in Shenzhen, February 1993.

Beihai Silver Beach, April 1993; working at China Securities; in a shopping mall during Diana's first business trip to Zhenzhou, summer 1993; a company social outing at a beach in Shenzhen, summer 1993; Diana's second business trip to Zhenzhou, 1993.

At Splendid China during Diana's mother's first visit to Shenzhen, January 1995.

LEFT: With a friend in Beihai, December 1994.
RIGHT: With Ginger Onishi at the Great Wall, summer 1993.

CLOCKWISE FROM ABOVE:
Working as a training officer, spring
1994; Diana's employee identification
card from the Shangri-La Hotel; with
co-workers; at a PPICA party, March
1995; at a PPICA party where Diana
was thrown into the pool, causing her
wig to fall off, May 1995.

Diana at the famous West Lake in Hangzhou for a business trip and vacation, fall 1995.

TOP: Diana with her parents and her brother at a karaoke restaurant during their first visit to Shenzhen, February 1996.

MIDDLE: Reunion with Xi Wei Hong, who lent Diana a bed in the Lanzhou University dorm, during a business trip to Shanghai, spring 1996.

BOTTOM: Visit with a former coworker in Shanghai, after Diana got her first U.S. visa, summer 1996.

ABOVE: At the "Window of the World" in Shenzhen, February 1996.

LEFT: At the Draxler office, summer 1996.

BELOW LEFT: With a Draxler client and a vendor, summer 1996.

BELOW RIGHT: At the Shangri-La for a business meeting, spring 1996.

ABOVE: With Draxler vendors at an exhibition booth, November 1996.
LEFT: Drinking tea at the teahouse of Laoshe in Beijing, spring 1997.
BELOW LEFT: With an Australian business associate at an exhibition booth, November 1996.
BELOW RIGHT: At a conference in Shanghai, 1996.

Diana at her first apartment in Shenzhen, with separate living room, dining room, and bedroom, which she rented on her own after working for Draxler International, March 1996.

Diana's father with Zhang Li's parents in Diana's parents' living room in Lanzhou, where Diana's family lived for more than fifteen years, February 1997.

"Who are you and what business do you have with him?"

"My name is Lu Jing-Jing. I want to see him about working for the ministry." I explained why I thought I could be of use to them.

She wasn't impressed. She looked at me and said in a condescending tone, "Director Wong doesn't have time for this kind of trivial thing. You are wasting his time. You should go somewhere else."

I felt insulted and crushed, but I didn't say a word. I just stood there.

She pointed to a sofa and told me to wait.

I sat on the stiff sofa for the rest of the afternoon. I didn't speak and neither did the receptionist. The silence was like a huge rock pressing on my chest to suffocate me. Two hours of waiting seemed like ten years.

Finally the workday ended, and I was sent home with no reason to be hopeful. I went away very disappointed.

The receptionist's arrogant attitude didn't stop me. I came back the next day to try again. Once more I sat for hours on the sofa, to no avail. After several days of this routine, the receptionist finally took pity on me.

"Come back on Thursday," she said. "Mr. Wong can see you at four o'clock."

"Oh, thank you, thank you. I'll be here." It was all I could do to keep from jumping for joy in the middle of the reception area.

When I told my friends about the scheduled meeting, they were delighted for me, and also amazed. They couldn't believe I'd actually managed to get an appointment with such a highly placed official.

I came back on the appointed day at precisely four o'clock, dressed in my professional best, my heart thumping with excitement. Once again the receptionist directed me to wait on the sofa. I felt so frustrated. After all this, was the director going to back out of our meeting?

I waited for more than three hours. It was well into the evening when at last I was ushered into the office of the elusive Mr. Wong. He was in his mid-forties, and his manner was stern. He greeted me without a smile. Folding his arms on his desk, he said, "How may I help you, Miss Lu?"

Today's another day; it's different; things will get better.

I tried my best to explain to him why I was there, how my talents and skills could be useful to the Foreign Affairs Office. I spoke to him in English, hoping to impress him, but he didn't seem interested. His blank facial expression told me he was no different from any other bureaucrat.

In just fifteen minutes my first interview in English was over. "We'll get back to you, Miss Lu," he told me with a poker face.

I never heard from him.

* * *

Autumn faded into winter—the longest and most depressing winter of my life. No hope. No help. No light. No support.

It seemed as if an unbreakable evil force was working against me. I felt powerless and alone. The weather was cold, and the city hunkered under a sky that was thick and dark with smoke from the heavy pollution.

I despaired of ever finding a job. Perhaps my mother was right—I'd thrown away the only good opportunity I'd ever have. My struggles with her grew more severe, and I felt I'd lost my dad's great friendship and support. I was hanging on by the thinnest thread. If my parents had had influence and money, my life would have been a lot easier. But those things were unimportant compared to their emotional support. If they had believed in me, that would have made all the difference.

My power springs from my indomitable belief in myself.

For a long time I avoided my friends. I couldn't bear to tell anyone I'd been through yet another disappointing day. In my room in Guo Jun Ming's apartment, I would wake up in the middle of the black night and start weeping. But I knew in my heart that I couldn't give up. In the morning I'd pull myself out of bed and make myself say, "Today's another day; it's different; things will get better."

Gradually I began to cheer up. I didn't know where my strength came from, but it was there. I've come to realize that I drew strength from my father's example, remembering how he always maintained a positive attitude, even during our family's grueling years of exile in the coal-mining village. He had overcome difficulties far greater than those I was facing.

I've also come to understand that my power springs from my indomitable belief in myself. It was present in the little girl in pigtails, in the innocent, competitive girl in high school, in the passionate and strong-willed college student, and in the confused and lonely woman in her early twenties. It still guides me today as a secure, independent, and visionary entrepreneur.

I played sports and attended social events with my friends. We went dancing, cooked together, and gathered at parties. All this distracted me from my depressing daily rounds of job hunting. When Guo Jun Ming's parents returned to Lanzhou, I had to leave the room where I'd been living, and I moved in with some graduate students, close friends of some of my high school classmates. Their joyful spirits warmed my heart; they made me feel hopeful again about living in the world.

"You'll find a good job, Jing-Jing," they kept telling me. "Just don't give up."

Those simple words inspired me. I had to give myself the chance to find my own way to fulfill my dreams. The important thing was to keep trying. Success was not guaranteed, but it could never come if I didn't take the risk.

* * *

One evening I happened to visit a classmate from Lanzhou Medical University. Her brother and sister-in-law were there. We were sitting in her tiny apartment, eating noodles and chatting, when one of them casually mentioned that another classmate had resigned from a teaching position at Northwest Minorities University.

All of a sudden I could see light at the end of my long, dark tunnel.

I set down my bowl and chopsticks. "Have they hired someone else?" I asked.

"No, I don't think so," said my friend. "Why don't you apply?"

The next day I rushed to see my parents. I asked them if they thought I could get an interview for that job.

They checked around and confirmed through their professor friends that the job was indeed available. I was so excited, and, best of all, my mother and father were excited with me. We contacted the faculty of the medical department of Northwest Minorities University and asked if I could be considered for the position.

I was invited to come in for an interview, a forty-five-minute session in which I would give a sample lesson just as if I were teaching a class. I had a week in which to prepare, and I threw myself into the effort, determined to be so good that they wouldn't be able to resist hiring me. Fortunately, I had two outstanding teachers to guide me. My father helped me select and summarize material from the textbook, and he showed me how to present it and what to emphasize. My mother advised me about what I should wear and how I should stand and hold myself so that I would look confident and professional. I rehearsed the lesson over and over, and they critiqued my performance to help me improve.

The important thing was to keep trying. Success was not guaranteed, but it could never come if I didn't take the risk.

"Keep your pace steady, but don't rush," my father would say.

"That's a key point for students to know. Don't forget to emphasize it," Mama would remind me.

On the day of the interview, I dressed carefully in a stylish outfit that my aunt had sent me: a long black skirt and a black-and-white sweater, with a black scarf at my neck. I combed my hair back and fastened it with clips to make myself look a little older. When I stepped into the classroom where I was to teach my sample lesson, I was dismayed to see thirty faculty members there. I hadn't anticipated that my audience would be that large.

Taking my place at the lectern, I inhaled deeply to quell my nervousness. Most of the professors smiled at me, which reassured me a little. I nodded to them and began speaking.

"Today we will have a class on . . ."

I managed to keep my voice steady, but as I reached for a stick of chalk to use on the blackboard, I realized my hands were trembling.

When I was finished, the faculty representatives thanked me, but no one said what I wanted to hear: "You're hired."

A week passed with no word, and I grew ever more anxious. Perhaps I had not done as well as I had thought. Maybe I had seemed too confident or not confident enough. Could I have made some terrible error without knowing it?

Finally my father went straight to the top. The head of Northwest Minorities University had formerly held the same post at Lanzhou University, and he was a neighbor of my parents. My dad called him to find out if a decision had been made.

When he told me about the call, he was wearing a big

smile. "Jing-Jing," he said, "allow me to congratulate the newest member of the faculty at Northwest Minorities University."

* * *

As a result of that miraculous forty-five minutes, my life changed from hell to heaven. I would be teaching pharmacology at a noted university, beginning with the spring semester.

The gamble had paid off. I had suffered for eight painful months from my family's anger and my own doubts, fears, and despair. At times I was in such a state of gloom and hopelessness that I lost sight of my objective, but I always made myself get back on track. I pushed and persevered, and now I had my reward—a job that I would love. I felt a huge sense of achievement.

This fateful choice convinced me for the first time that I could choose my own life. I didn't know it yet, but the persistence with which I had pursued my dream would become one of the solid foundations of my future adventures and successes.

* * *

Northwest Minorities University is an important institution. A separate university has been set up in each major region of China to serve students who belong to ethnic minorities. More than 90 percent of China's people are Han, which is considered to be a single ethnicity even though it encompasses a great deal of cultural and linguistic variation. But the country is also home to people who come from fifty-five officially recognized minority groups, and many of them live in the western provinces, including Gansu. While minority students can attend any college, attending a minority university gives them certain privileges and advantages. For one, all their expenses are paid. Tuition is free for all Chinese college students, but at other universities students must pay for textbooks and living expenses.

The persistence with which I pursued my dream became one of the solid foundations of my future adventures and success.

The university is located on the top of a hill in Lanzhou, close to a large national memorial cemetery for fallen soldiers. The campus is a beautiful, energetic, joyful place—the complete opposite of the medical college I'd attended. The students—who were Tibetan, Uighur, Tajik, Kazak, Russian, Hui, Hasak, and many other groups—bring their own rich cultures to the college. I was filled with excitement and gratitude as I arrived there on the first day of class.

My classroom was a large laboratory full of science equipment. When I walked in and called the class to order, none of the students believed at first that I was the teacher. There were more than forty of them, all sophomores, and I looked as young as they did. Soon we became comfortable with each other. We conversed with ease and they would sometimes tease me as if I were one of their peers.

I loved working with my students. They were warmhearted and intelligent, and I felt invigorated by their knowledge and their energy. They made my job rewarding in so many ways. One big way they helped was to bail me out of a dilemma. Every week as part of my lecture I used two rabbits to demonstrate how to do drug tests and identify the reactions. At the end of the class I was supposed to kill the animals. I only managed to do it once, and it was one of the most painful experiences I'd ever been through. After that, the students killed them for me. Later the rabbits would be cooked and eaten. Even though I ate rabbit, like any Chinese person does, I couldn't bear to kill them; I didn't even want to witness the act. My students made fun of me for my sensitive nature.

Most of the students were multilingual and spoke Mandarin, the official language of the classroom, with a slight accent. Among themselves, they spoke their own languages. Whenever I heard their conversations, I felt as if I were in a foreign country, especially when I was with the Russians and Uighurs and Hasaks, who looked Caucasian rather than Chinese. They had strong facial expressions and used their hands and bodies to emphasize what they were saying. Compared to the Han Chinese, their communication style was much more emotional and direct.

I felt very much at home in the culturally open atmosphere of the university. Any time I strolled across the campus, it was full of color and music. People were always playing musical instruments, singing, and dancing. I loved the beautiful sound of the *dobula*, a harplike stringed instrument, and the passionate rhythm of the Uighur drums, which are specially made for dancing. When I heard their unique sound, my body tingled and I could not resist the temptation to jump right in and dance along with everyone else.

I admired the minority students' looks and their distinctive styles of dress. To my eyes, they were extraordinarily attractive. They were tall with dark eyes and defined facial bone structures, unlike the Hans' flatter features. The women tended to have full, curvy figures, and they wore heavier makeup than the Han people. While most of the Hans wore plain clothes in simple styles, the minority women wore colorful and exotic dresses, skirts, boots, and accessories. I especially noticed their earrings, something that Han women usually don't wear. Each of the groups had its own individual style that made it stand out among the others. For example, the Uighur men wore bright and embroidered skullcaps called *doppas*, and the women wore dresses and scarves that were made out of patterned silk that had as many as fifty colors and motifs.

The enthusiasm, warmth, and hope of the students rubbed off on me. Every time that I went to the campus to teach was a wonderful experience.

* * *

My life fell into a pleasant routine. I had a nice dormitory room with a pleasant roommate, a teacher who worked in the university's administrative office. Our furnishings consisted of two twin beds, a table, and a tiny dresser; that is all. But at least in this simple place I no longer had to sleep in a bunk bed or share a room with seven other girls.

I ate in the huge university canteen. It was always crowded

with hungry students, who waited in long lines with their bowls to get their food. There were many different kinds of foods offered, but never any pork. Although pork is a popular meat in China, eating it is against the religious principles of many of the ethnic minorities. So the canteen usually served lamb instead. This was a problem for me, because the smell of lamb made me nauseated. If I fixed my own food with pork in it, I could not eat it in front of the minority students or use their cooking utensils because such rude behavior would have insulted them.

Though I was happy and comfortable in my new living situation, I began to stay less and less often in the dorm. It was a long way from my parents' home, and I frequently slept there instead. To my relief, my relationship with my parents was improving. My mother had come to accept my choice not to be a doctor, and she was pleased with my new life as a university teacher. One thing that helped to convince her I was doing well was the fact that I was making almost the same salary as my dad, because the pay rate at the minority colleges was higher than at the standard universities.

I had to go to campus only twice a week, on Tuesdays for faculty meetings and on Wednesdays to teach my two-hour class. Even with homework papers to grade, the schedule left me a lot of free time to do other things I enjoyed. I spent a great deal of that time at Lanzhou University because I wanted to stay close to my friends there who helped me through my dark weeks of joblessness. We played badminton, sometimes for four, five, or six hours a day, and enjoyed many meals together.

In China the graduate students' dormitory washrooms are

quite different from those in the West. They are set up so that students can wash not only themselves but also their dishes and clothes. When I ate with my friends, we'd wash our dishes together and I would sing. The washroom had great acoustics that made my voice sound beautiful. Soon I became famous around campus as the washroom soprano.

The graduate students decided to enter the chorus competition that was part of Lanzhou University's annual arts event. They needed a solo singer, and my reputation as the washroom soprano and the recommendations of my friends brought me to the attention of the director of the graduate team.

"You have a wonderful voice, Jing-Jing," she told me. "We'd like you to be our soloist."

"Oh, I'd love to!" I said. "But how can I? Don't you have to have someone who's a graduate student?"

"We can make an exception or two and not be disqualified. Besides, you may not attend classes here but you do your singing in our washrooms. I think that makes you one of us."

I was delighted to take part. What made it even more fun was that my close friend Xi Wei Hong was selected to be a member of the chorus.

We became busy with rehearsals, and I stayed in a dorm with friends so I'd be close by and ready. The chorus conductor, Ms. Yao, was a dynamic leader who did a fantastic job preparing us for our performance. Finally the big day for the competition arrived. When our turn came, I sang my heart out. As always I loved being onstage; it is one of the places where I truly feel at home. At the end of our performance the music didn't stop; we were treated to the beautiful sound of the audience applauding without stopping. To add to the thrill for all of us, we were awarded first prize.

* * *

One of the students in the chorus was a handsome and interesting man named Liu Tong. He was from Wuhan and was in his last semester of his graduate studies in chemistry at Lanzhou University. The time we spent together at rehearsals blossomed into a close friendship. We went to the movies, went dancing at nightclubs, and played sports together. We enjoyed each other's company very much. Slowly and tentatively we began to talk about a future together.

After Liu Tong graduated, he took me to Wuhan to visit his family. While I was there it became clear to me that they didn't support our relationship. Why not? As far as I could tell, they objected to me simply because I was from Lanzhou, which in their mind was a poor and unsophisticated city.

At the end of my five-day stay, I returned alone to Lanzhou, while Liu Tong went to hunt for a job in the city of Shenzhen. His brother was working there and had described it as a land of opportunity. Liu Tong wrote to me during the summer, and what I learned about Shenzhen from his letters fascinated me. I got the impression of a dynamic and vigorous city where the economy was booming and people were becoming wealthy.

By autumn I'd decided to go there and see Shenzhen for myself. I felt challenged by the snobbish attitude of Liu Tong's family, and I wanted to find out if I could make my way in such a wondrous place. Of course the fact that Liu Tong himself was there only added to its allure.

When I told my mother what I was planning, our fragile relationship shattered all over again.

"What an outrageous idea!" She could barely keep herself from yelling. "How could you give up such a wonderful job? I thought you liked teaching at the minority school."

"I love it. I love all the cultures, their energy, the different ways they do things. Knowing my students has made me understand that I need to experience the big world beyond Lanzhou."

"It is a great privilege for a young woman like you to have such a job. You will probably never do so well again."

"Shenzhen is probably the best city for jobs in all of China, Mama."

"And how will you find one, crazy girl? Shenzhen is a highly competitive commercial city. Tell me what can you do there? You have no experience in business or industry. Your father and I have no way to help you, and you have no powerful *guanxi* relationship to smooth your way. Remember how long it took you to find this job? Remember how difficult it was, how you suffered?"

"But I did it, Mama," I reminded her. "I took the risk and it paid off."

"Well, speaking of payments, how could you afford Shenzhen? It is a very expensive city to live in; neither you nor we could afford that kind of life. Can you imagine how hard life would be for you? You know very well that we have no extra money; we can't support you to go and live in that city."

"I'm not asking for you to pay my way."

"Shenzhen is not like Lanzhou. Here you have friends and family; there you have no one. Who will you turn to if you are in trouble?"

"I'm learning to rely on myself, Mama. And I'm sure there are good, helpful people in Shenzhen, just like Lanzhou."

"You have lost your mind! This is an absurd idea, absolutely not acceptable. You are daydreaming."

She was right in a way. I had no resources beyond my wits and talents to help me make my way in a new city. As she saw it, she was being loving and protective; she couldn't bear for her precious daughter to go through more hardship and disappointment. But the challenge of a new society and the excitement of a new life enticed me. I couldn't get the thought of an adventure in Shenzhen out of my mind.

Shenzhen is in the southeastern corner of the country; it sits right on top of Hong Kong. Like many Chinese cities, it has roots that reach deep into antiquity. What sets Shenzhen apart is the way it looks to the future and not the past.

In 1979 the central government chose this small fishing port to be China's first Special Economic Zone. The purpose was to encourage greater foreign investment, international trade, and economic development through tax incentives and market-oriented policies. As a result, Shenzhen was transformed into a major city and an economic miracle, so successful that the government quickly designated several more Special Economic Zones. Shenzhen became a center for foreign companies that desired to penetrate the Chinese market, and its residents prospered. Soon they boasted the highest level of personal income in the country.

This city differed from most of China in a very significant

way: it was a place where daring and initiative and ingenuity were rewarded instead of quashed. That was its big appeal to me. I could not get my mind off it. The more I thought about the city, the more curious I was, and the more determined. I had to go there and at least see what it looked like and what was happening there.

* * *

One day in the fall of 1992, I was at the post office to mail a letter when an exotic-looking young woman walked right up to me and paid me a compliment: "What a beautiful dress you're wearing."

I had just heard her speak to someone in English so I replied in the same language. She was visibly surprised. "I'm Ginger Onishi," she told me. I introduced myself, and that is how one of my best, most enduring friendships began.

Ginger was an American, the first American I'd met. She was the daughter of a Japanese-Caucasian marriage, which accounted for her striking attractiveness. She and another woman, Kathy Flynn, had been invited to Lanzhou University as English language experts to teach graduate students. That fall, the three of us spent a lot of time together. They found it a little difficult to pronounce my Chinese name, so with their inspiration I picked my English name: Diana. The name came from one of my favorite English novels, *Jane Eyre*, in which the priest's sister was called Diana. That character and I had many traits in common.

We went to the food court in the alley to eat my favorite beef noodle with plenty of chili pepper and vinegar to spice it up. They invited me to their dormitory, where we danced, laughed, talked about our different cultures, and even prayed together. Ginger taught me about her religion. A devout Christian, she was accepting and nonjudgmental, and sincere and pure in her beliefs. She opened my eyes to a different way of looking at the world.

Several times I took Ginger with me to Northwest Minorities University. My students there continued to give me joy, and I wanted to share it with her. She was astounded by the huge difference between Lanzhou University, a Han majority institution, and the minority school. She made friends there and loved learning how to do their dances. Because of her mixed blood, she was often mistaken for one of the students until she spoke in her native tongue. I felt proud to introduce her to a place where the atmosphere was so full of life and the varied cultures so stimulating.

Later on I met another American, David Godfrey, who joined Ginger and Kathy at Lanzhou University as an English language expert. When he first heard me speak, he asked, "Where did you get your American accent?"

The question surprised me. I didn't realize I had one. I'd always understood that my accent was British.

"I don't know," I told him. "Maybe it's from hanging out with some Americans here, Ginger and Kathy."

"Oh, I know them," he said with pleasure.

David became like my big brother, always looking after me. He told me a lot about New York—I liked its nickname, the Big Apple—and other cities in America.

Knowing Ginger, Kathy, and David made me curious about the United States and its people. I was struck by the contrast between the rigid attitudes and culture of the Chinese people and the natural, relaxed attitude my American friends had about their lives. I was overwhelmed by their friendliness, kindness, honesty, and openness. Perhaps in time I could study in the United States. It sounded like a promising place, a dynamic country filled with wonderful people like my friends.

But America would have to wait. For now, I was concentrating on getting to Shenzhen.

* * *

I asked everyone I knew about Shenzhen. How could I find a job? What kind of skills would I need? I spent a lot of time in the library, reading about Shenzhen in newspapers and magazines. I wanted to learn as much as I could about the city and its job market. It seemed that newcomers who arrived in Shenzhen with a good education and a lot of skills and talents were very likely to be hired. Gradually I pulled together the relevant information, and then I made a checklist of all the things I would do to prepare for a successful transition.

*Number One: Practice and study more English, and
learn other languages, like French and Japanese.*

Individuals who were fluent in foreign languages were in especially high demand. Once I heard that, I checked into the night classes for gradate students at Lanzhou University. They were perfect; I could join them without any restriction. So almost every night from seven to nine o'clock, I attended a foreign language class. Sometimes my friends joined me. I had always been fascinated by foreign languages, so although it was a demanding routine and a lot of material to learn, I didn't feel overwhelmed. I enjoyed what I was doing. Whenever the effort began to feel too difficult, I reminded myself of my goal.

Number Two: Have education qualification certificates.

The more education, the merrier, I learned. I had only my diploma from Lanzhou Medical University and a special English qualification level certificate. There was nothing I could do at this point to acquire more, but these were good credentials.

Number Three: Have reference letters that show my qualifications.

Obviously I had no reference letters yet attesting to my great success in a job or an academic field. So how could I put a checkmark by this item on my list? One day as I was reading an English educational book, I saw a comment that a reference letter regarding your talents and personality could help too. So I immediately asked Ginger and David if they would help me. They both were enthusiastic about my planned adventure, so without hesitation they wrote letters describing who I was and how good my English communication skills were, based on their experience.

Number Four: Prepare a resume.

A resume—what was that? I had never heard of such a thing. Not only would I need one in Chinese, I had to write one in English too. I asked around, but I found no one who knew how to write a resume, regardless of whether it was in Chinese or English. I was at a loss what to do.

While I was trying to figure out my English resume, I showed my first draft to Ginger and Kathy. I was so embarrassed when they burst into laughter reading my broken English out loud.

"Diana, I'm so sorry. I can't help it," Ginger said. "This is not English at all. Maybe it's hippie Ch-English. It sounds so funny and it makes no sense. But at least you were brave enough to try. Why don't you go to the library to get some samples, and write it again?"

The next day I rushed to the Lanzhou University library to search in English reference books. To my frustration I found almost nothing. But the following day at the city library, I discovered some English books that had great resume samples. How exciting! I copied each of them by hand. Then I went home and spent day and night studying resumes on my own.

From the samples I noticed that a person's educational background, skills, and working experience were all very important. I was disappointed because my own qualifications in these areas seemed so limited and inadequate. To make up for my shortcomings, I created a new category to highlight my strengths—my personality, my ambition, and my goals. I was excited by this idea—it was a way for recruiters to know about me beyond those paper qualifications.

I poured my whole heart into writing the resume. A month later, after revising and editing it more than fifty times, I showed the English version to Ginger and David and anxiously waited for their comments.

David patted my shoulder and winked at me. "Well, Diana, I am sorry to say this . . ."

My heart slipped down to the vicinity of my knees.

". . . but you don't have to change it any more. Well done!"

"Really? No, David, you are pulling my leg! Please, I am dying to know the truth!"

"Go ahead, ask Ginger," David said with a big laugh.

"Congratulations! Silly girl," Ginger added.

David explained that I had expressed a vivid image of a creative young woman with talents, energy, and passion, one who was eager to learn and ready to jump to work on anything new.

I could not believe it—they actually liked my resume! I felt so relieved and happy that I could not help reading my resume all day. I looked so silly that my friends who saw me thought I had received a love letter.

Number Five: Find financial resources.

This was the most difficult item for me to address. I made a plan that by the time I was fully prepared, with a checkmark beside everything else on my list, I would have the solution to this figured out. I didn't have much time to worry about money while I was preoccupied with all the other hard work.

Number Six: Develop a time line for my new adventure.

What deadline should I impose on myself to stop my risky plan if I failed to find a job? A deadline was important, because I had to face the reality of earning a living. If I didn't have some income within a reasonable time, I'd have to end my quest for a new life in Shenzhen. Two months, I told myself. Two months was the maximum trial time. If things didn't work out by then, I would come back and resume my teaching job at Northwest Minorities University. It might not reflect well on me if that happened, but it would not be the end of the world.

Number Seven: Do systematic self-checking.

Why was I going to Shenzhen? How passionate was I to do this? How determined was I? How confident did I feel in myself and the future? What was the worst-case scenario, and could I handle it if it happened?

These questions haunted my mind day and night as I prepared for my departure. They bothered me a lot and were distracting me from my studies and my teaching. After two months I was fed up with my worries, and I decided I would have to deal with them head on. The checklist was helping me deal with the practical aspects of my preparations, but I also needed a way to do self-checking—to look at how I was feeling so I could steer my feelings away from fear, and to find answers to the questions so they would cease their constant clamoring.

The checklist helped me deal with the practical aspects of my preparations.

Interestingly enough, the more I answered myself, the more clear I felt about what I wanted to do, and the more confidence I felt in my unknown future. I began to realize that the fear was not that big a deal.

At first I had a lot of fear, but I developed a system for touching my fear every day. I had always had a habit of talking to myself when no one was around, especially when I wanted to practice my English. Now I found that I was murmuring a lot about my fears, repeating all of the negative things they whispered to me. Eventually I decided that it made more sense to murmur to my fears, telling them what I would do to overcome them. I wrote down these messages, too—seeing my positive ideas on paper helped me believe that what I was murmuring was true.

Then I began humming and singing to my fears, making a little song out of them. It was a way to tease the fears, and to tease myself for being silly enough to believe them. It was like when my parents would threaten to punish me; if I could tease them into smiling, then they would let me go.

I could tease my fears and tease myself for being silly enough to believe them.

I put on music and danced as I sang. Music always changed my mood for the better. This daily routine of murmuring, writing, singing, and dancing about my fears helped me understand them and face up to them. They began to diminish, and I knew I could handle the consequences. I was feeling much more confident in my new adventure. Over time I have refined these basic techniques, and they have guided me to take on even bigger risks and achieve greater success. Today, with longtime practice, my unique system for handling risk and fear has made my life happier and more free.

Either I take the chance or I lose it. That was one of the messages I murmured to myself every night in the dormitory. One evening Xi Wei Hong and two of her friends came by and accidentally heard my murmuring. They plied me with questions.

"Where do you get your confidence from?" Xi Wei Hong asked me. "You seem so fearless."

"What really drives you to take such a risk?" asked one of the friends. "What makes you so sure it will work?"

"Have you thought about consequences?" asked the other.

I paused before I replied. I was not 100 percent sure about my adventure, so I didn't know what the right answer was. Finally I winked at them.

You will never know until you try!

"Hey, girls, you'll never know what can happen until you try. There's really nothing about it to be scared of, and having fear won't help me to get a job. Besides, I'm only going there for two months to see what's going on. How can I get hurt?"

But they knew I was determined to get a job and would never want to come back.

I was answering them, but deep down I was also answering myself. The response I gave them unconsciously helped me to become clear about my goal and confirmed my decision. I felt even more confident about going to Shenzhen.

"You will never know until you try!" has become my lifelong motto.

*   *   *

As soon as I started planning in earnest for a trip to Shenzhen, my battles with my mother escalated. We argued constantly and fiercely. Finally she refused to let me come back home again.

This created a tremendous difficulty. Winter would soon be approaching, and evenings were growing cold and dark. My language classes didn't let out until nine-thirty PM, and my dorm at Northwest Minorities University was a long distance away along a crime-ridden route. It was too dangerous to return there late at night. If I couldn't stay with my parents, I had no place to go.

Eventually I sneaked back home to ask Baba for help. My beloved father had always supported me. I knew I could count on him.

"I cannot overrule your mother's order and let you sleep here," he told me. "That would not be fair to her."

"I understand," I said, swallowing my disappointment.

"So we shall find another way. You have friends in the dorms here at Lanzhou University. If you stay there, you won't have to travel anywhere after your class is finished. There is sure to be extra space for you."

He gave me a set of sheets and a comforter so I could stay with my friends without creating extra effort for them. At that time the dorms were full. Each night I carried my bedclothes from one room to another to see if any student might be out for the night, leaving an unoccupied bed I could use. If there wasn't one, I slept on the floor.

I lived that way for nearly seven months. I have no idea how many bedrooms I slept in. It proved to be an exhausting existence, and it was hard and embarrassing to constantly ask people for help. But it was worth it if it would help me to achieve the desire that burned in my heart.

* * *

While I was getting to know my new American friends, I was also growing close to one of my colleagues at Northwest Minorities University. Ms. Mo Hui Xing was in her late forties, a sophisticated and open-minded Beijing woman and an inspiring lecturer. I told her about my boyfriend in Shenzhen and my plan to go there.

"Here is a book you should read," she told me one day, handing me a volume from her library. "It's called *A Chinese Woman in Manhattan*. It is a memoir, a true account of how the author journeyed to America and made a successful life there. She reminds me of you, especially the way you both pursue life so passionately."

I read that book over and over; it became like a bible to me. The author had gone to the United States to study. Though she had no money, she was able to use her communications skills to make fruitful connections and establish an international trading business. In a short time, she went from penniless student to wealthy entrepreneur. The story made me believe that if a person is really determined, he or she can achieve anything.

Mo Hui Xing and I spent a lot of time discussing my wished-for adventure in Shenzhen. She shared my hopes and fears, listening sympathetically to my struggles with my family. She recognized my strengths and talents and was proud of my pursuit of my dreams.

Best of all, she proved she believed in me by making it financially feasible for me to go forward. Shenzhen was an expensive city, and even under the most optimistic scenario it would take me a while to get established. I had no savings; my salary, though a good one, was only RMB200, equivalent to around thirty dollars a month. I knew I'd receive no monetary help from my family. Mo Hui Xing and another great lady friend from Lanzhou University were my lifesavers—they lent me a total of RMB2000. I want to acknowledge my appreciation and gratitude for their trust, love, support, and generosity. I am especially thankful to Ms. Mo for having faith in me, which is the kind of precious support we all need in life. She extended her spirit to me, and she helped me understand that life is hopeful. I always try to incorporate her spirit in myself, reaching out to give support to the people who need love and encouragement.

Her confidence in me was especially valuable because it countered my mother's rejection. In the seven hard months I'd spent so far in preparing to go to Shenzhen, she had not spoken to me once. Several times when I'd met her on the street, she had pretended to not know me. That really hurt; I felt spurned and abandoned as she looked the other way and crossed the road to avoid me.

I came to understand that this was her idea of "tough love." She was trying to prevent me from going to Shenzhen, to protect me from making what she saw as a bad mistake. But the more she tried to stop me, the more the rebel in me insisted I should go. I was determined to prove to my mother that I could do it—I could find my own way and make a better life for myself. I would not allow her to choose my path for me anymore. This is my life; I would live it in my way.

* * *

Something amazing happened in early 1993. My friend Jiangshan had told me about her fiancé, who'd studied foreign languages at Lanzhou University. Now he was working for a foreign trading company in Shenzhen. He was coming to visit her, and she invited me to meet him. I couldn't wait. It would be my first encounter with someone who actually had been to the city I was dreaming about.

Our first encounter was an informal get-together at Jiang-shan's dormitory. As soon as she introduced her fiancé to me, we began speaking English. I was surprised at how easy it was to carry on the conversation. My English had improved more than I'd realized during my seven months of extra studies.

Of course I asked him lots of questions about Shenzhen, and his answers made me even more eager to go there. I was concerned, though, that I wasn't well enough prepared to make my way in such a totally different world.

"Don't worry," he said when I told him this. "You are very ready for Shenzhen."

I could hardly believe what I'd heard. "But I don't know anyone there," I protested. "I don't have any contacts, or any network I can tap into."

"You don't need them," he assured me. "You speak English so well, and you pick up languages quickly. You're comfortable with foreigners. You're smart, passionate, ambitious, and determined. You have a lot of drive, and a cheerful and sunny personality. What's especially important, you are very good with people. Those are the things you need to succeed in Shenzhen."

"You're kind to give me all these compliments, but I don't want flattery. Please tell me the truth."

He patted his chest and said, "I am telling the truth. You can count on my word."

I was inspired by his vote of confidence.

Several more times during his visit, I met him and Jiangshan for dinner, and I continued to pepper him with questions. Thanks to what I was learning, I was already beginning to feel at home in this city I'd never seen.

* * *

At last it was time for me to leave for Shenzhen. I had arranged a two-month leave of absence from the university so I could return to my teaching position if things didn't work out. But as much as I enjoyed the job, I hoped I was done with it forever. I'd contacted a high school friend who lived and worked in Shenzhen so I'd have a place to stay when I got there.

As I was packing my things, my mother invited me home for Spring Festival. After all the months of bitterness, I was glad to be joining the family celebration.

During the festive meal, she said to me, "Jing-Jing, I know you have decided to go to Shenzhen, and I cannot stop you. What I want for you, my daughter, is happiness in your life. If this journey will bring you that, so be it. So that you will know you go with my blessing, I am buying your train ticket as my gift to you."

A few days later, on the cold, gray morning of February 18, 1993, my family came to see me off at the train station. All through college, I had gone there to see off friends who were leaving for distant places. It had always been my fantasy to be the person on the train to whom everyone was saying good-bye. Now it was my reality.

My dad patted my shoulder and told me to take care of my-self. My sister squeezed me, too, and her new husband shook my hand. When it was my mother's turn, I could see that she was worried to death about me. I held her hands tightly and said, "I'll be fine, Mama. Don't worry, I will write to you or call you once I get there."

Then I boarded the train. I looked back and smiled and waved at everybody.

My adventure was beginning. Nobody, especially me, knew what the future held in store for me.

Diana's Stepping-Stones on the Journey to Success

Expect surprises. What happens in our lives is never totally under our control, no matter how carefully we have planned or what promises have been made to us by ourselves or others. Life will deal unexpected blows and also will grant unex-pected favors. If we are willing to accept the surprise and deal with the new situation, we will develop our inner strength.

Be willing to take risks. When we perceive a risk, it is often a signpost pointing toward an open door or a new path—an opportunity that is worth exploring, as it may lead us to our goal.

Use obstacles as teachers. We are all beset at times by barriers, stresses, and confusion. They challenge us to test our poten-tials and discover and develop our talents and strengths.

Be persistent. When we believe that something is worth achieving, one sure-fire way to attain it is to be persistent. Persistence gives us power. It can overcome unbearable obstacles, sustain our progress toward what we want in life, and validate us with great rewards.

Set a goal. The more specific we are in naming what we want, the more likely we are to achieve it.

Make a plan. When we set a goal, the best approach is to make a step-by-step written plan for how to achieve it. As soon as we see it on paper, it begins to become real. A plan focuses our thinking, increases our belief that the goal can be accomplished, keeps us on track, and helps us chart our progress.

Understand your fears and learn to control them. Fears whisper to us all the time, telling us lies, and we hear them even when we think we're not listening. We can't ignore them, because that increases their power. The only way to control them is to look them in the eye and talk back to them. Sing to them, dance with them, tease them, have fun with them, and then take a positive step to achieve your goal. That way, they can never stop us.

Keep this motto in mind: "You never know until you try." Human beings have tremendous potential, which we can fulfill if we are willing to stretch ourselves. We never know what will happen—what miracles we are capable of—until we try.

Diana at the Beihai government civic center on her first business trip, spring 1993.

商海畅游

Six   Business Education, 1993–1995

After twenty-eight long, tiring hours on the train, I arrived in the city of Guangzhou, my first stop on my journey to Shenzhen. As soon as I arrived, I pulled off my knee-length leather boots, required footwear for Lanzhou's frigid winter, took a long hard look at them, and threw them away. "That's right, I am not going back," I told myself. I would not need heavy boots in the subtropical climate of Shenzhen.

The Guangzhou station was mobbed with hundreds of people, laborers from the poorer provinces, especially Sichuan, who had come in hope of finding work in one of China's major economic centers. Soon I spotted a familiar and welcome face—my high school friend Che Biao, who had come to take me to his home for a visit. He and his family used to live in Lanzhou; his parents had worked with mine and his sister had been a student of my mother's when she taught in the grammar school. Now they all lived in Guangzhou, where his parents were affiliated with Zhongshan University. Che Biao had earned a degree in chemistry and was working with Colgate.

I spent two enjoyable days with them. The family was very curious about my adventure. "I cannot believe you are doing such a brave thing," Che Biao's mother told me.

I could scarcely believe it myself.

* * *

I boarded the train again, and two hours later I was in Shenzhen at last.

The city was warm and bright. In late February it felt just like summer in Lanzhou. I was glad to have on sandals and not to be burdened by my boots. As I walked along the street, everybody looked modern and stylish and very, very busy. People were rushing everywhere. The conversations I overheard were all about business: new enterprises, new products, new clients, new opportunities to make money. Tall, sleek buildings crowded the skyline, and construction cranes showed that more skyscrapers were on the way. The landscape was decorated with palm trees, their fringed fronds rustling in the light wind. The breeze carried a scent unfamiliar to me—the salt tang of the ocean. Shenzhen, I knew, was one of the world's major ports.

Bustle, activity, energy, excitement—this was my kind of place. I was ecstatic to be here.

The first thing I did was to try to get in touch with two people. The first was Liu Tong, the boyfriend whose move to Shenzhen had sparked my desire to come here. Unfortunately I couldn't reach him. I had better luck with Lu Wen Zheng, the friend I'd contacted before leaving Lanzhou to ask about a place to live. He was newly married, and he had kindly arranged for me to stay in the dormitory where his wife had lived prior to their wedding. Six of us shared a room furnished with bunk beds. I was given a top bunk.

The girl in the bunk below immediately took me under her wing. Xiao Peng had a round, pretty face and large eyes that sparkled with enthusiasm. We discovered we had something in common—we were both from Lanzhou. She had been in Shenzhen for quite a while and freely shared many tips and ideas that would help me land a good job.

"Once they find out how well you speak English, you'll have no trouble getting hired," she told me. "But first you have to get them to notice you. You look like a girl from the country. That's all wrong for Shenzhen."

I nodded. I understood the tendency of people in China to judge you by what you're wearing when they first meet you. Each city has its own standard of dress. In just a couple of days I'd seen that Shenzhen women dressed with more color and flair than I was accustomed to.

"Let's go shopping," she said.

Although Shenzhen had many chic department stores, Xiao Peng took me to Badeng Street, which was lined with hundreds of small shops and booths selling clothes, shoes, jewelry, trinkets, electronic goods—merchandise of every conceivable description. I learned later that Badeng Street was famous for the prostitutes who frequented it in the evening. During the day, though, it was a huge bazaar thronged with shoppers seeking bargains.

With Xiao Peng's help, I picked out clothes that would

transform me into a stylish Shenzhen woman. I chose three short-skirted business suits in beautiful colors—one was red, one was white and ocean blue, and one was a pretty shade of tangerine. I also bought a navy blue dress with an ankle-length skirt and a crisp white collar.

When I tried on my new clothes, I made a surprising discovery—I had a good figure.

"That's a point in your favor," Xiao Peng said approvingly. "Shenzhen appreciates women with curves." As soon as we got back to the dormitory, I threw away all of the drab, old-fashioned clothes I'd brought from Lanzhou.

* * *

With my new clothes and the haircut and perm I'd gotten right before I left Lanzhou, I looked sharp and professional. Now all I needed was a job.

Before leaving Lanzhou, I had carefully prepared resumes in Chinese and English. David and Kathy checked the grammar and sentence structure in the English one and formatted it to look like a real English resume. My mom helped me make dozens of copies of both versions. The resumes detailed my academic history, my job history, my passions, my dreams, and my skills. I wish I still had copies of them just for the sake of the memories they'd hold.

Resumes in hand, I set out for the talent market. In China, this institution is unique to Shenzhen, although I later discovered that it's similar to an American job fair. Every day, recruiters for companies large and small set up booths where they talk to job seekers. Employers come and go, depending on whether they have openings, though some of the biggest firms maintain permanent booths.

The first morning I arrived at seven o'clock. Someone had told me it was important to get there early, because companies would leave as soon as they'd filled the available positions. As I entered the huge, warehouse-like space, I was amazed at how crowded and noisy and bustling it was. Thousands of people—students, laborers, business managers, teachers, clerks—were lined up in long queues at the various tables, waiting for a chance to hand the recruiter a resume and answer a few quick questions. Then they would move to another line, hoping that someone would be impressed enough to invite them back for a second, more in-depth interview. Standing in line myself, I had plenty of time to watch the dramas playing out in my fellow job hunters' lives. I witnessed hardship, hope, sadness, excitement, fear, courage, disappointment, acceptance, frustration, and joy.

Every day for a week I went through round after round of these interviews—long, boring waits in line followed by brief, fruitless encounters. When my turn finally came to face a recruiter, I tried to come across as sunny and enthusiastic, despite the fact that by then my feet ached constantly. In the evenings I read the local business papers and talked to people, trying to research the companies so that I wouldn't waste too much time standing in line for unsuitable jobs.

Then came a great moment—I was invited back for a second interview for a public relations job. I didn't expect much to come of it, because so many talented people had applied. I couldn't believe it when I was one of the three people hired. I was so proud and happy that I burst into tears. I rushed to a telephone booth and called my mother.

"Mama, guess what! I have a job. I'm a public relations officer for an international trading firm."

"But what about your position here, at the university? Does this mean you are staying in Shenzhen after all?"

"This is so much better than my teaching job, Mama. Can you believe it—my salary is RMB1200 a month."

There was stunned silence on the line. This was an unbelievable sum—the equivalent of about $180, compared to the $30 a month I earned as a teacher.

Finally my mom said, "That cannot be possible. You are only saying that so I will not worry."

"It's true. I promise you. The firm has even given me my own apartment. No more dormitories for me." It took awhile to convince my skeptical mother that I was telling the truth.

*   *   *

Now that I was getting settled in Shenzhen, I tried several more times to contact Liu Tong. I was eager to see him and share with him all my discoveries about this amazing city. Finally I heard from one of his relatives, who told me Liu Tong was having a difficult time launching his career in Shenzhen, and he was in no mood to see any of his old friends. So he and I never got together. I figured out that even the small success I was having could be making him uncomfortable.

I had already found what I was looking for when I moved

here—a good job and a new life in a place where prospects seemed to be unlimited for anyone willing to work hard and seize an opportunity.

When I'd been on the job at the trading company for about a month I received an unexpected phone call. The caller represented a real estate development firm based in Hong Kong, and she had interviewed me one day at the talent market. At the time the firm had no suitable openings for me, but she'd mentioned that a promising position might become available soon. Now she was calling to invite me to come for an interview. The Shenzhen office needed an assistant in the development department.

Okay, I thought, why not? I was enjoying my job, but it made sense not to turn down an opportunity without even learning what it was.

I was hired the next day. I couldn't believe it—in only a month I'd moved to a better position as an assistant manager at a high salary. I called my parents again; by now my mom was cheering me on.

My new job involved researching properties in which the firm might want to invest. I was inspired by the work, and I immersed myself in studying the real estate industry. I quickly learned how to spot the kind of good opportunities that would interest my boss, who appreciated my energy and creative ideas.

One place I thought had potential was a newly developed coastal area on the Gulf of Tonkin, near the city of Beihai. I gathered as much information as I could from newspapers and official data sources, and I discovered I knew someone there—

Wenjun, Liu Tong's best friend, was now in Beihai working as a secretary to the mayor. Everything I found suggested that Beihai would be a great place to invest in real estate.

When I suggested this idea to my boss, he said, "That's a great recommendation, Jing-Jing. I'd like you to go there, see your friend, and check out the real estate situation there."

What an honor! He was authorizing me to go on my first business trip—me, an inexperienced teacher, almost a complete stranger to the business world. I was thrilled by his trust in me, and by the encouragement he was offering.

On arriving in Beihai, I went to Wenjun's office to surprise him. When he was summoned to greet a visitor, he didn't recognize me at first. I no longer looked like a Lanzhou student. In my professional outfit I was the image of a Shenzhen businesswoman.

Beihai is a subtropical seaport in Guangxi province, close to the border with Vietnam, and it has beautiful holiday resort areas. Wenjun showed me around the famous Silver Beach, which extends for fifteen miles along the coast. Hotels, guesthouses, and restaurants lined the expanse of silvery sand. I watched people swimming, wind surfing, boating, playing volleyball, and building sandcastles in the warm sun. It was the first beach I'd ever been to, and it seemed like paradise.

Compared with Shenzhen, Beihai was still underdeveloped. Wenjun introduced me to people in Beihai business circles, and when I gave them my business card it was like a magic key. Realizing I'd come there to scout for real estate opportunities, they were eager to talk with me.

I carefully observed how Wenjun dealt with business clients and visitors. At first I thought all they were doing was drinking, dining, and reconnecting, but soon I realized that these activities were fundamental rituals of doing business. Ninety percent of the time, the conversation didn't seem on the surface to be relevant to any business goal. However, I noticed how people would slip business topics into the casual chatter and elicit the information they wanted in a subtle and indirect way. I learned to watch their facial expressions, which would silently reveal a lot of answers.

The best strategy is to pay attention to the unique qualities of everyone I encounter.

As I studied their interactions, I was fascinated to realize that having solid facts and figures was only a small part of negotiating a successful business deal. Before the deal could work, it was necessary to understand the psychological factors—people's titles, their political relationships, their instant reactions, their attitudes and personality and motivations. The best strategy was to pay attention to the unique qualities of everyone I encountered. It was exciting to put my people skills to work in what to me was a whole new arena. Soon the Beihai businesspeople and I were getting along like old friends. People were people, after all.

When I returned home from the three-day trip, I was on fire. I had gathered fruitful information for my boss and learned the basics of building business relationships. I even had a few nice photographs to send to my parents.

All night long I worked on my report. I could not wait to show it to my boss the next day. He was surprised but very pleased with the wealth of information I provided. Details about the city: the size of the real estate market, current and projected development, the competition, the overseas investor's privileged development policy. Profiles of the decision makers: their personalities, relationships, and connections. My own suggestions for a potential investment plan. The four-page report became a milestone in my career. I was discovering one of my best talents and one of my most productive niches—marketing research and analysis.

One week later, my boss sent me on another extended business trip to look at properties and spend time in the branch offices in Zhengzhou and Wuhan. I could not believe the opportunities that were falling into my hands. I was doing so many things I could never have dreamed of in Lanzhou. Fate was finally rewarding me for my persistent pursuit of my joy and my passion. All the battles with my family and the struggles I'd gone through in Lanzhou were paying off.

I flew from Shenzhen to Zhengzhou—my first airplane trip. I had brief discussions with the branch manager there, and then I took a cruise ship down the Yangtze River from Chongqing to Wuhan, investigating real estate opportunities along the route.

The Yangtze is the longest river in China and the third longest in the world (after the Nile and the Amazon), and it flows through one of China's most scenic regions. My breath was taken away by the splendor of the famous Three Gorges, where the narrow river is enclosed by the steep mountain precipices that rise on either side.

One of the stops on the cruise was Fengdu, also known as the Ghost City. My boss wanted me to check out a real estate project there, since the area was considered a prime site for tourist development. The Ghost City attracts many visitors, and seeing it for myself I understood why. Fengdu is filled with picturesque temples, pavilions, shrines, and statues—all honoring devils, departed spirits, and the gods of the underworld. The place instills fascination and fear; going there was like creeping up to the gates of hell, but with the promise of being able to safely retreat. As I wandered around the Ghost City, tourists all around me were screaming in delight and fear.

After I left the Ghost City a truly terrifying incident occurred—one that made me afraid I was about to become a ghost myself. I was sharing a taxi back to the ship with a fellow passenger, a middle-aged gentleman from Australia. Night was falling, and the road was narrow and isolated. About halfway into the fifteen-minute trip, two men flagged us down. One of them was supporting the other, and he waved to indicate that they desperately needed help. In the headlights it looked as though his companion had been badly injured. The taxi driver stopped, and we stepped out of the car to ask what had happened.

All of a sudden the two men jumped us. One of them overcame the Australian traveler and held him at knifepoint. The other thug grabbed me, and I felt the sting of his sharp-edged blade against my throat.

"Don't hurt her," the gallant Aussie beseeched them. "We'll give you everything."

"Please," I begged. "You may have it all. Just let me keep my ID card."

My resident card was my life. Without it, I couldn't survive; I would not be permitted to work. To replace it, I'd have to return to my old hometown of Lanzhou, where my card had been issued, yet I'd have no way to get there, because I'd need the card to board a train or a plane.

As frightened as I was, I managed not to panic. Perhaps my steady nerves appealed to these hoodlums. The thieves took our money and also my watch, my earrings, my necklace—all of it gold, the first good jewelry I'd ever owned. But they let us keep our identification documents.

As we got back into the taxi, we were shaking from fury as well as our fear. It was obvious that the driver knew the thieves and had set us up. I hated the idea of riding with him again, but we had no choice. There was no other way to get back.

As we boarded the ship, the Australian man said to me, "It's a good thing we are still alive."

"Yes," I agreed. "That's all that really counts. That, and having our ID."

* * *

The cruise took me to another two places where I'd arranged to meet with local real estate officials. Every city I visited wanted to develop large properties and had policies in place for granting privileges and offering incentives to encourage investors from overseas. I was becoming efficient at getting the right information and setting up the right connections for my firm's future business dealings. The local officials treated me exactly as if I were an experienced businessperson. I was quite happy about my progress.

I finally arrived safely in Wuhan, where I spent two months in my real estate firm's local office. Two things happened while I was there that made the trip worthwhile despite my horrifying experience at the Ghost City.

First, I had the opportunity to visit with my brother on the handsome, tree-lined campus of Huazhong University of Science and Technology. Hui-Hui was studying there, and our whole family was proud of his academic achievements. He and I had a good time together. It was a pleasure to spend time with him, and also to show off a bit. The last time he saw me, I was a struggling teacher in Lanzhou. Now I was a stylish and successful businesswoman.

Lee An's soothing, quiet strength and his belief in our abilities were a revelation to me.

The other great thing was meeting an incredible, intelligent architect named Lee An. A manager in my firm's Wuhan office, he became my first mentor. He walked me through every step of the real estate business, helped me formulate goals for the company and myself, and taught me how to interact with the clients and government officials. He knew the business thoroughly, but he also had broad interests, which extended into music and the arts.

I admired Lee An because he didn't assume that he deserved his team's high regard simply because of his title. He earned our respect and trust by treating us well and inspiring us to do our best work. He was proud of his parents even though they did not have positions of high status, and he told me how his father had impressed on him the importance of being respectful, honest, and encouraging in dealing with people.

The leaders I was used to typically used anger, criticism, and intimidation as tools to exert power and control people. Lee An's soothing, quiet strength and his belief in our abilities were a revelation to me. I embraced the spirit of his leadership and always try to emulate it in my own business experience.

* * *

In the summer of 1993, my friend Ginger finished her teaching term at Lanzhou University. She was ready to return to the United States to get married. Earlier in the year, right before I left for Shenzhen, her boyfriend, Craig, had come all the way from Texas to propose to his sweetheart. When Ginger showed me her big engagement ring, I was very happy for her. Most of her students had no clue about the significance of the diamond; they simply said, "Oh, what a pretty ring." Ginger and I laughed about the differences in the way our cultures approached relationships between men and women. In China, unlike in the West, there is really no such thing as a formal engagement. When a Chinese couple decides to get married, they go ahead and do it right away.

Ginger and I had kept in close touch, and I couldn't let my dear friend leave China without saying good-bye. So I took a few days off from my job and met her in Beijing so we could spend a little time together—my first visit to Beijing since I was a tiny girl about to journey with my frightened family to our new home in the coal-mining village.

This visit was more pleasant. The two of us went sightseeing at the Great Wall and toured the Forbidden City, the huge and lavish palace complex that was home to China's emperors for more than five centuries. This was a place I remembered from my family's photograph of me as a child with perky pigtails and a watermelon-covered face. Ginger and I were disappointed that everything had become so commercialized, but we had a wonderful time in each other's company.

All too soon, Ginger had to leave me and go home to her fiancé. The departure of this beautiful, affectionate, and sincere Christian woman affected me greatly. For a long time not being able to hear her voice left me feeling lonely and lost. Her cheerful love remains in my mind and in my heart.

* * *

When I returned to Shenzhen the weather had turned oppressively hot and muggy. I was sharing an apartment with three coworkers, and while it was a large place in a nice residential area, it had no air conditioning. The trapped heat inside made it stuffy and uncomfortable. It was a real misery for someone like me who had been raised in a much cooler climate.

To make things worse, the real estate business in Shenzhen had fallen flat. I had little work to do, which made my time on the job tedious. People in the office were sitting around chatting and reading the newspaper, reminding me of the lackadaisical clerks I'd had to deal with in the municipal personnel office in Lanzhou. What a waste of time—to sit in the office and watch myself and others do nothing.

I waited impatiently for new assignments, but none were forthcoming. Without a chance to make progress and learn more at work every day, I felt frustrated. My guts told me I had more energy and talent to be developed. I decided it was time to think again about making some changes in my business life.

As I started to explore alternatives, I discovered that it would be a great help for me to learn Cantonese. Like most Chinese people I spoke Mandarin, but Cantonese is the common language of people here in the southeastern part of the country. The writing system is shared by both languages, so something written in Cantonese can be read in Mandarin. But spoken Cantonese is an entirely foreign language to the people outside of Guangdong and Guangxi provinces.

My coworkers spoke Cantonese as well as Mandarin, and some of them offered to help me learn it. The first sentence they taught me sounded like this: "Ni, fa hao ah?"

I repeated the words. "What does it mean?" I asked.

One of my helpful colleagues translated it for me. "It means, 'Are you hungry?' "

I practiced the phrase the way I used to practice English when I was a kid, repeating it over and over to myself. After a while, feeling confident, I approached one of the girls in the office and tried it out on her. "Ni, fa hao ah?"

She jerked up and glared at me, yelling in anger, "Are you out of your mind, crazy woman?"

Everyone else in the office burst into laughter. I was shocked. I didn't know what I'd done. I asked her in Mandarin why she was so angry.

She understood then that we'd both been fooled by the rest of them.

"Don't learn from these jerks," she warned me. "They always want to make dirty jokes. That phrase they taught you means, 'Are you horny?' "

"What?" I screamed at the top of my lungs. I could not believe what I'd just heard. I was so embarrassed. How could they?

This practical joke challenged me. I would learn Cantonese as soon as possible. So what if I sounded silly at the beginning. Go ahead, laugh, I don't care; soon the knowledge would be mine. I looked only at the convenience and benefit I'd gain once I grasped the language. I watched more Cantonese TV, and I practiced my Cantonese whenever I could, like I had done when I learned English. Three months later, I could understand Cantonese completely, and I could make basic conversation with no problem at all. No one could fool me now. I could even bargain in Cantonese when I went shopping, which saved me a lot of money. Hallelujah!

* * *

A month after returning from Beijing, I still had no work to do and little indication from my boss that things would get better. I had to leave this job before I wasted more time, but the drawback was that I would have to leave my apartment too. Where would I live? That was my biggest concern, and it made me hesitate to make a quick decision.

Fortunately Mr. Fu Jianming, my dad's best friend, invited me to stay with his family until I found a new situation. He had met Dad through his sister, a classmate of my father's. Formerly the head of Wuhan University, Mr. Fu was working with a startup educational company in Shenzhen. He had a real entrepreneurial spirit and a joyful sense of humor. I loved talking with him about business.

I started to make phone calls to inquire about jobs. During one of my conversations I tried speaking in English. The personnel director assumed I was a foreigner and treated me with much greater courtesy than I usually received. He apologized that he could not interview me because the company only had positions for locals. This happy accident surprised and inspired me. From then on I made all my inquiries in English. I found that this gave me a far better chance of getting an interview directly with the boss. I was glad I could skip going back to the loud, crowded, suffocating talent market.

Through the autumn I took several jobs and then left them as I tried to figure out what sort of work suited me best. It was a fascinating time for me because I was learning so much about the business world and about my own talents and goals.

The first of these short-term positions was with a branch office of a financial newspaper, the *Chinese Securities Daily*. I thought it would be a good way to learn more about the workings of the stock exchange. Though I was called a journalist, what I really did was comb through reports and studies and do analyses of the facts and figures. I found it too technical to appeal to me, and I quickly grew bored with dealing with numbers all day long. I much preferred working with people.

Next I was hired to work in the marketing section of a financial investment company, where I got to interact directly with the clients. I was enthusiastic about this job at first, but a problem quickly developed. My supervisor and his brother, who was the president of the company, began showing too much personal interest in me. I knew that some of the young professional women in Shenzhen advanced their careers by sleeping with their bosses or "entertaining" their company's clients, but I felt that it was a terrible way to live. I wanted my work relationships to be respectful and businesslike. Before long my time in the office became extremely awkward. I tried to get my work done while avoiding my boss and his brother. Being alone with either one made me very uncomfortable, and it was worse when they were together and caught me in the middle.

I loved that job and hated to leave, but there was no way I could stay. This was the first time I had to give up a good job to protect my dignity and stick to my principles.

Knowing that I was job hunting again, a friend introduced me to a company that marketed light industrial products. They wanted to hire me to work in their Hong Kong office. I was ecstatic at the notion of working in Hong Kong. Being a British protectorate situated as a gateway to China, it was truly an international city, even more cosmopolitan and sophisticated than Shenzhen. But to go back and forth I was required to have a Shenzhen resident card. In China everybody has a permanent resident card, and mine was from Lanzhou. Shenzhen resident cards were in high demand and hard to get.

I contacted everyone I could think of to see if anyone could help me get a card. A colleague from the real estate firm where I'd worked put me in touch with a businessman who claimed he could get me one within a month in exchange for RMB3000. This was around $400, as much as my salary for two months. What could I do? I didn't have nearly that much money to spare, but I desperately wanted that card. After much thought, I asked Mr. Fu if he could do me the kindness of lending me the amount I needed, and he graciously agreed.

I paid the businessman as arranged, and thirty days later, as promised, he gave me my Shenzhen resident card. I went right away to present it to my future supervisor at the Hong Kong company.

He examined it closely and handed it back, saying, "I am so sorry. This is a fake."

I was shocked. "Wh-what do you mean?" I stammered.

"The card is counterfeit. You cannot use it. I regret that without a valid Shenzhen resident card, we will not be able to employ you after all."

I was crushed by humiliation and disappointment. I'd lost my chance to work in Hong Kong. To make the pain worse, now I was in debt for RMB3000. I tried to track down the scoundrel who defrauded me, but he had disappeared.

Too embarrassed to continue staying in Mr. Fu's home, I looked for a new place to live. I found someone who was willing to let me use the extra space in his apartment, so I moved in and slept on the sofa for two months. It was a difficult time—I had no job, no money, and a large debt to repay.

I began a new round of hectic job hunting. Finally, through my new host's contacts, I landed a market development position with a Chinese trading company that did business with Western firms. For the first time I became involved with direct business negotiations. I learned about international trading business procedures and the ways in which the negotiating styles of the Chinese differed from those of the Westerners. Soon I was able to help my coworkers negotiate better prices and terms for their deals. I found the work fulfilling and fascinating.

Unfortunately, though, the company director found a different source of fascination: me. He already had a mistress—they seemed to be a status symbol for businessmen in Shenzhen—but wanted to do me the dubious favor of letting me sleep with him too. Soon I was embroiled in the same frustrating situation that had driven me out of my previous job. Again I had to leave a company with great regret. I loved the job, but I would not put up with the director's appalling behavior.

I was frustrated and disappointed by these experiences, more so because I was coming to realize that my boss's attitude was commonplace. The business world of China is a predominantly male domain. Women are still rare at the executive level, and they face a constant battle to overcome this kind of harassment. Many men assume that attractive women in a business environment are sexually available, and often they are right. Moreover, women who indulge men in this way often gain advantages as a result. But I believed strongly that both women and men should be respected and rewarded solely on the basis of the talents, skills, and knowledge they bring to their company and the hard work they do to improve the company's performance.

My parents instilled in me the importance of maintaining my honor and principles. I was willing to give up an otherwise good opportunity if accepting it meant jeopardizing my integrity.

So I was back on the interview circuit yet again. By now I

was adept at job interviews since I had been through so many of them. Thanks to Xiao Peng, my first roommate in Shenzhen,

> *People should be respected and rewarded on the basis of the talents, skills, and knowledge they bring to their company and the hard work they do.*

I knew how to dress to create an attractive yet professional appearance. I'd also learned how to field the interview questions. I took time to think through an answer and frame it well, keeping in mind the three Cs: calmness, confidence, and clarity. I tried to convey enthusiasm, warmth, energy, and ambition in order to convince the interviewer that I would add value to the company through my efforts and abilities.

It was discouraging, though, to have to keep traipsing from one recruiter to another, one personnel department to the next. Occasionally I was offered a job, but the position invariably was one that didn't suit my skills or would open me to further sexual harassment. I wanted more than that.

By the last month of 1993, my money had almost run out. I was getting worried.

* * *

One day in December 1993 I called the human resources department at the Shangri-La, one of the largest and grandest hotels in Shenzhen. Speaking in English, I asked if they had any openings. I was told that only the chain's headquarters in Hong Kong hired foreign experts, but the hotel would forward my resume if I sent it. Once again I was flattered to be mistaken for a foreigner, and I decided to keep trying for a job there.

A week later, I called again. Miraculously this time, the new director of human resources interviewed me for more than half an hour. Then she said, "Miss Lu, welcome to the staff of the Shangri-La."

I was hired! Immediately I called Lee An, my friend and mentor from the real estate company, and told him about my good fortune.

Right after this happy phone call, my luck turned sour. As I was riding the bus home, someone sliced my purse open and stole everything inside. The thief was so stealthy that I didn't notice what had happened until I got off the bus. I was devastated. All of my money was in my purse, and now I had nothing left. I had to make a second call to Lee An, this time to ask for help. This kind gentleman sent a check for RMB1000 to get me through the month until I would receive my first pay from the Shangri-La.

Despite that mishap, I began my new job with a high heart. The Shangri-La was a five-star hotel—elegant, glamorous, sophisticated. Not only would I be working in luxurious surroundings, I'd get to interact with an international clientele. The Shangri-La group operated some of Asia's most prestigious hotels. What intrigued me was that though the ownership was Asian, the company was managed in a completely Western style.

One Western touch was that everyone who worked there had to have an English name. So right away I was transformed from Jing-Jing into Diana—a pretty enough name, though to my ears Jing-Jing was far lovelier.

Although I had no clue what "Diana" symbolized when I picked this name with Ginger and Kathy back in Lanzhou in 1992, I later learned that Diana was the mythical Roman goddess of the moon, who is often portrayed as a huntress. That seemed fitting too, since I've never stopped hunting for a better life.

I was one of ten people working in the human resources department. Mine was considered a junior management job, which meant I wore a burgundy-colored uniform with a crisp white shirt set off with a bow at the neck. The color of all the staff uniforms indicated the wearer's rank.

I moved into the Shangri-La's residential village for management staff, sharing a four-bedroom suite with four roommates. The complex was a congenial place. After work we cooked together and watched television together and gossiped about staff members' romantic liaisons. Some of the staff became my lifelong friends. I've stayed close to people like Sally, Peggy, Jenny, Rebecca, and Fred, and I feel fortunate that we've been able to maintain our strong friendships over so much distance and time.

My first job was to conduct the orientation program for new employees, telling them about hotel policies and showing them how to perform their duties in a way that would satisfy the clients. There was a lot of staff turnover, so the program was an ongoing effort.

Since I was new myself, training other workers was like having a crash course in hotel management. I learned a lot very quickly: the history of the hotel group and its properties all over the world, the organizational structure and functioning of the Shenzhen hotel, the typical Western style and skills of management, and the importance of teamwork in working with colleagues. I was trained to uphold the high standards of professionalism and customer service that the Shangri-La provided its clients. I even had the chance to practice writing in English in the formal business style. This job gave me a wonderful chance to gain knowledge that would help me advance my career, and I still treasure the experience I gained there. Of all the Western companies I've worked with, I have to say that the Shangri-La provided employees the most comprehensive professional training.

I was honored when I was entrusted with another assignment that turned out to be really fun—organizing the Spring Festival celebration for the hotel staff. The Shangri-La had more than one thousand employees, and I had never put together an event on such a large scale. There was one catch. I had just a week in which to organize and stage the event.

Okay, Diana, I thought, you can rise to this challenge. I'd been on the job for only a couple of months, and this was a good chance to prove my worth. I worked quickly to produce a work plan and assemble a team. We decorated the hotel's employee canteen with balloons and lanterns and arranged to serve a feast of food. For this special occasion, I bought my first evening gown—a beautiful coffee-colored, ankle-length dress that I wore with crystal earrings.

On the evening of the party, I took the stage as the mistress of ceremonies, introducing the games and making jokes with the audience. For entertainment we played crazy games like three-legged races and musical chairs. Winners were awarded prizes, and losers had to pay a penalty, such as singing a song in front of the crowd.

The party was a huge success, even beyond my expectations. The guests had a wonderful time, and so did I. My boss praised me highly for a job well done. This was the kind of project I loved, and I was motivated to do more of them.

Unfortunately there was little chance of that. Human resources turned out to be a quiet place, and I had far too much tedious, repetitive paperwork. I began to realize that my perfect job was not in human resources but in more creative, people-focused areas like sales, marketing, and public relations. Before long I was thinking about requesting a transfer to one of those departments.

Another reason I wanted to move from human resources was the frustrating office politics. The Shangri-La was no different from any other large corporation when it came to office politics, but our department seemed to suffer from this affliction more than other departments did. It seemed to me that the director's management style was the source of much of the problem; she didn't bring out the best in the staff. By the fall of 1994, she was having such difficulty working with us that the hotel management had to replace her.

At the outset our new director seemed completely different from our former boss. A former Miss Philippines, she was an attractive woman in her late forties who adorned herself with heavy makeup, a lot of gold jewelry, and a pretty smile. She had more energy and better communication skills. She sounded like a very inspiring director.

With changes happening in the department, I thought it was the perfect time to request the transfer I wanted. I was hoping to use my creativity and the people skills I'd cultivated to serve the hotel in a client-oriented role.

When I made my case to the new director, she listened graciously to my request.

"I'm sorry, Diana," she said when I finished. "We need you here. A transfer to another department wouldn't be in anyone's best interest."

I knew in my heart that she would never permit me to move to a more suitable position. Why should she give up a capable employee? I was too valuable to her where I was.

I felt angry, disappointed, and powerless. I believed then and now that a good manager encourages her staff to pursue their own personal excellence.

A depressed, dissatisfied employee can never satisfy expectations.

I noticed that in China oftentimes, some managers forget something very important: a depressed, dissatisfied employee could never satisfy their expectations. There would be no benefit to this manager or to the hotel in keeping me stuck in human resources.

Her refusal to help me was the start of a pattern of behavior. I became sick of this unnecessary chaos—literally sick. The emotional stress was taking its toll on my body. My back hurt all the time, I felt constant nausea, and I couldn't shake my fatigue. The director finally realized my health problems were getting in the way of my normal work each day. She gave me a month off in which to get a complete medical checkup and recover.

I used the month to see a doctor and at the same time to reflect on my work and my future. It was time to hunt for a job that would challenge and stimulate me in a positive way. Although I loved the Shangri-La, I wish I could have been transferred to the sales department. I would have stayed much longer and learned more from this great organization. But, stuck in human resources, it seemed to me that, after a year there, being a training officer no longer provided that kind of satisfaction.

I had noticed that people often reached a point when their current job had become unsatisfying, but because an easy solution wasn't obvious, they would compromise their need to be happy and fulfilled and stick with the job far too long. It didn't seem to me that they were doing themselves any favor. Their inaction only undermined their confidence, reduced their drive, and destroyed their hope. The longer they waited, the less courage they had to seek a new path.

I didn't want to find myself in that position. To me, it was important to keep evaluating my long-term goals, and to be willing to undergo temporary suffering in exchange for a better future. My body and my instincts were telling me that I needed to make a change, and I decided to listen to their wisdom.

In December 1994 I resigned. My boss expressed her disappointment at my departure.

I didn't care. I felt so relieved, so free, so happy that I had left that job. I could breathe again. I knew I'd made the right decision.

* * *

A friend suggested that I look for work at a Western company in the Shekou industrial zone. This section of Shenzhen had been developed especially to serve the needs of large European and American firms and their managers. Built for the comfort of Westerners, Shekou was even more modern and sophisticated than other sections of Shenzhen, and it had better weather. I found an employment agent who specialized in placing workers in Shekou companies and began the rounds of interviews.

One of the appointments the agent lined up was with the American oil company Amoco. I was optimistic about receiving a job offer because the interview went well and the agent confirmed that the company was interested. A week later, though, the agent called with bad news.

"I'm sorry, Diana. They've decided not to hire you after all."

"What? Why not? You said it was a sure thing."

"That was before they ran a reference check with your previous employer. Apparently one of your old supervisors told them something that discouraged them."

I was furious. How dare someone undermine me that way. What on earth did anyone have to gain by destroying my chances now?

This incident only strengthened my determination to achieve my goals. I would not allow this spiteful person—or anyone else—to stop me. I would show them all one day that I was better than the narrow vision they had for me. I adopted as my motto Winston Churchill's remarkable words: "We shall not fail."

My former Shangri-La roommate, Peggy, had been promoted and now had a room to herself. Since I had nowhere to live, she generously let me stay with her. I couldn't afford any place on my own. In Shenzhen most people lived in dorms or apartments provided by their employer; if you lost your job, you had no place to go. Unfortunately, some of the Shangri-La staff didn't think I should be there since I was no longer an employee of Shangri-La and put pressure on Peggy. I didn't want to get her in trouble, so I found a friend of a friend of a friend who had spare space where I could stay.

When 1995 began, I had neither a job nor a real home. The year was not getting off to a good start.

In January I received news from my mom—she was coming to visit me. She had been invited to participate in an academic exchange with Zhongshan University. Since she would be so close by, she was planning to take two extra days and come to Shenzhen.

What a bind this put me in.

After two years apart I wanted so much to see her. Yet I didn't want her to know about my dire situation. My reports home were always upbeat; I shared all my good news but never told my family about the negative experiences or hardships. If my mother found out I wasn't even employed, she wouldn't offer sympathy or encouragement. No, she'd sink into worry and try to force me to go home to Lanzhou.

Luckily a friend of mine helped me out so I could put my mother up in a hotel. That way I didn't have to worry about her needing to stay in my living quarters. As for my job situation, I resolved to explain that I had found a new job that would be starting shortly. I hoped that very soon what I told her would be true.

When Mama arrived we greeted each other with joy. As it turned out, we had a marvelous visit. I took her to visit Shenzhen's three big theme parks: Splendid China, which replicates China's main sightseeing attractions in miniature on a one-to-fifteen scale; Windows on the World, which presents a similar chance to experience the natural and historic wonders of other countries; and the Chinese Folk Culture Village, which lets tourists experience the arts and culture of the country's ethnic groups, along with typical buildings, costumes, food, and performances. So in just two days we accomplished an excursion across China and a round-the-world tour. We talked and laughed and had a lot of fun. It was wonderful to be together.

Before Mama left she told me, "You are so strong, Jing-Jing. Whatever happens you don't show your pain. You persevere and accomplish what you want. I am proud of you." It was the first time I heard words like that from my mother, and it was extremely gratifying to have her say them.

* * *

In February I interviewed with Phillips Petroleum International Corporation Asia, a subsidiary of the big American oil company. After my Amoco experience I didn't expect anything, but a job offer came quickly. I was hired for a three-month trial period to work for the administrative director.

I could hardly believe my good fortune. I was going to work for an American firm; I would be paid much more than I received at Shangri-La; and I would have an apartment in Shekou with only two roommates and a bedroom to myself.

Right away I noticed a huge contrast between this American company and the Asian ones where I had worked. The atmosphere was more open and relaxed and my American coworkers were so much fun to work with. They reminded me of my friends Ginger and David—open-minded, enthusiastic, honest, and direct. They were full of humor yet highly professional when it came to their work. They had a free spirit that I loved.

Something else I loved was the new treat they introduced me to—American barbecue. This group enjoyed throwing parties, and barbecue was often the main feature on the menu. At one of these events I provided the entertainment without intending to. Wigs were fashionable in Shenzhen at the time, and ever since I'd started at Phillips I'd worn one to cover up a short haircut I didn't like. On this occasion someone tossed me into the swimming pool. Suddenly all the guests were laughing. To their great surprise, my hair had floated away from my head.

While I was working at Phillips, I was invited by a handsome American co-worker to go to the Shangri-La for dinner. I wore a black cocktail dress with copper-colored trim, and we dined in the revolving restaurant at the top of the hotel tower. "Just think," I said, "just a few months ago, I was wearing one of those burgundy uniforms. Now I'm here as a guest." Changing places like that gave me a great feeling of satisfaction.

Phillips gave me the chance to learn new computer skills and become more proficient at speaking and writing English, especially American English. However, as much as I loved the company and the people there, the job and I weren't a good match. I answered phones and typed forms—demanding and tedious work when I longed for something creative. When

the three-month trial period ended, my contract was not renewed. In the formal discussion I had with my boss, we both
agreed: "This employee's personality and skills do not fit the
job." By that time I was ready to leave. There were no hard
feelings on either side.

But it meant that once again I was without a job.

* * *

My employment agent assured me that new opportunities
were developing in Shekou and he'd surely find me a job soon.
Banking on his confidence, I decided to take a brief vacation.
I'd never been to Hong Kong, yet ever since my failed prospect
of a job there it had beckoned to me. It was so close by but
part of another world.

For ten days I wandered the streets, visited the shops, and
took in the sights, and I enjoyed every minute. Hong Kong
was bright and colorful; it hummed with energy. I loved its
cosmopolitan blend of flavors and styles, the British intermin-
gled with the Chinese. There were plenty of opportunities to
speak English, and I took full advantage of them. The stores
were fancier than those in Shenzhen, and for the first time I
became aware of the importance of brand identities. The service was better, too. The people I met treated me with respect and appreciated my good manners—such a pleasant contrast to the behavior I often encountered at home.

That trip changed my outlook on life. I went home determined to find a position with another company that did business internationally. My visit to Hong Kong crystallized my

awareness of the values that were important to me—courtesy, creativity, rewards for personal initiative—and I was more likely to find them in a firm that dealt in a bigger arena than China alone.

* * *

When I returned to Shekou I decided to find a more capable employment agent. The man I'd been working with wasn't offering me the best opportunities and I was concerned that he might be overcharging me. After a search I hired Ms. Wong.

Within a week she called to say, "I have an interview set up for you. I think this may be the chance you've been looking for."

My heart began to pound. "What is the company? What kind of job?"

"It's a British firm called Draxler International. They're looking for an office manager."

A British firm! "What does the company do?"

"They're in the fiber optics industry."

My silence must have told her that I had no idea what that meant.

"Optical fiber is a key component of the cables that make up telecommunications networks," Ms. Wong explained. "The fibers are the means by which electronic messages are transmitted. Draxler represents foreign manufacturers of optical fiber and sells their products to Chinese telecommunications companies."

"This interview," I said. "When and where should I show up?"

She gave me the information and said, "Good luck!"

My two years of on-the-job education in business was about to pay off. When I first arrived in Shenzhen, there was no way I could have been ready to take on the challenges of a position like this. But I had learned so much since then: how to dress in a stylish yet businesslike way, how to handle many kinds of situations, how to use the three Cs —calmness, confidence, and clarity—to present myself as a capable professional. I had acquired valuable knowledge and skills.

Use the three Cs— calmness, confidence, and clarity—to present yourself as a capable professional.

Most of all, I'd learned that it was important to grasp the chance. To me, genius is the accumulation of all the chances you've taken, all the risks you've dared. Even the ones that don't turn out as you hope are valuable if you use them as stepping-stones on a path that moves you toward work that you love, work that is authentic for you.

I arrived for the interview precisely on time. I had dressed carefully in a black skirt, a black top with white trim, and black high-heeled shoes. I felt calm, but I might have been more nervous if I'd realized that the next fifteen minutes were going to change my life.

The company's offices were on a high floor in a modern office tower in Shekou, right next to the bay. I entered into an expansive reception area. The receptionist sat within a circular desk made of wood and topped with black marble. Behind the desk, the entire wall, floor to ceiling, was surfaced with matching marble, which was emblazoned with letters of gold: DRAXLER INTERNATIONAL, PLC. The space was handsomely appointed with sand-colored carpet and blond wood furnishings. A wide window provided a vast view of water and sky.

Genius is the accumulation of all the chances you've taken, all the risks you've dared.

It looked spectacular—grander than any other office I'd ever been to. I could tell right away that these would be pleasant and comfortable surroundings in which to work.

The head of the company, whom I will call Henry Smith, came out to greet me in the Western style, with a handshake. His eyes immediately caught my attention; they were piercing and intense. He was a young man, not tall but well built with broad shoulders. He had curly brown hair and a nose that bent slightly.

He invited me into his office, where he took his seat at his desk and I sat across from him in a visitor's chair. It was an effort at first to concentrate on his face and not be distracted by the beautiful bay vista behind him. But as he began to speak in his intriguing British accent, he had my full attention. I liked his manner and attitude. The way he talked about his company revealed him to be a strategic thinker. He was friendly and courteous, yet he manifested an aura of power.

As I answered his questions, I tried to convey to him that I was a hard worker, that I liked to learn new things, that I worked well with people and strove to inspire them—most of all, that I would be a real asset for his company.

One of his questions was, "Suppose someone on the staff was not working diligently. What would you do?"

I replied, "I would give him two chances to correct his mistake. If it happened a third time, I would fire him. The company cannot afford to waste time and money on people who will not pull their weight."

I knew in my heart that this was the answer he was expecting. Apparently he was impressed by this combination of firmness and confidence and efficiency, because he hired me on the spot. I would begin work the following Monday.

When I was outside again, I raised my arms and shouted, "I did it!"

Who cared if passersby gave me strange looks? I was overjoyed. A new chapter in my life was beginning. It was like being reborn. The new me was full of strength and energy and passion and hope.

I shouted again, to the bay and to the sky and to anyone who could hear me: "Yahoo!"

Diana's Stepping-Stones on the Journey to Success

Show initiative and enthusiasm. These attitudes are among our most important resources. They help us to learn more, to generate opportunities, to outshine and outperform the competition, and to draw positive people and energy into our lives.

Take chances. When we can muster the courage to take a leap, we win no matter where we land. We always gain something that will benefit us, whether it's knowledge, experience, or a connection with someone we meet.

Know when to move on. Sometimes we find ourselves in circumstances that work against our best interests. When we no longer have the chance to grow or to perform to our capability, or when a situation is toxic to our emotions, body, mind, or spirit, then we should leave. It is important that we listen to our instinct, which is our best guide.

Do your homework and prepare. When we have defined a goal, the next important step is to collect information, do research, and learn everything we can about what we are trying to achieve—in other words, prepare for the achievement with 100 percent of our effort and our maximum passion. Preparation is one of the main ingredients in good luck.

Don't be afraid to make mistakes. A mistake is not really a mistake; it is a necessary step in the learning process. Our mistakes give us the knowledge and experience we need to make the right choices in the future. When we believe that we must do everything perfectly, we are letting our fears run the show for us. Not being afraid of mistakes is a sign of maturity and strength, and it brings us more opportunities in the long run.

Diana's first hot dog on her first visit to the United States, New York City, October 1996.

爱情

———

Seven   Two Loves, 1995–1996

———

In May 1995, I began my new job as the office manager of Draxler International. Right away I ran into trouble.

The company had relocated its offices from Beijing to Shenzhen two or three months earlier. The staff had moved, too, and some of them, while proud of their accomplishments and experience, were unsure and uncomfortable in the midst of so much change. They were not happy to see a young, local upstart join the company in a position of power.

A woman named June made a particular point of showing her displeasure. On my first morning, Henry Smith held a meeting to introduce me to the staff. June shot me a belittling glance. "Oh, *she's* the new office manager," she said, sarcasm making her voice sour.

"Yes," Henry said firmly. "Welcome her aboard."

June was big-boned and plain-faced. A few years older than I, she was Draxler's sales coordinator, responsible for supporting the clients and sales staff. Beijing residents are famous throughout China for their haughty arrogance, and June had packed this attitude in her luggage and carried it with her to

Shenzhen. Now she folded her arms and glared at me. At the end of the meeting, several of the staff made a point of leaving the room with her.

That's when I knew June was going to be a problem.

I settled into my office and began getting to know the company by reviewing all the policies, performance records, job descriptions, and personnel files. I consulted frequently with Henry, and he asked me for my opinions of the employees. All I could give him were quick impressions because I didn't really know them yet, but he seemed to respect my judgment. He was often on the road, and it was important to have the business function well in his absence. He was relying on me to operate the office smoothly and efficiently.

It was clear, though, that I'd be getting no cooperation from June and her Beijing gang. During my first week she came in late three days in a row. On the third day I went to her desk and asked her for a report she was supposed to have prepared. With a flip of her hand, she told me, "It's not finished yet," and went back to chatting with a couple of her cohorts.

"Come into my office please, June," I said. "We need to talk."

"No," she retorted. "If you have something to say, you can say it here at my desk."

"I'll be waiting for you in there." I turned on my heels and went back to my office. After a while she turned up at the door. "Sit down, please," I invited.

"No." It was her favorite word. "What do you want from me?"

"Two things. I would like you to treat me respectfully, and I would like you to do what you are supposed to do in this office. That means arriving when you're expected and not wasting time with chitchat when you haven't finished your work on time."

She stomped out of my office and slammed the door.

The next day I heard her yelling at a client on the phone—another violation of company policy. And when I asked again for the overdue report, she still didn't have it.

"I'm not talking to you," she said. "I deal directly with Mr. Smith."

"He's in Hong Kong. When he's not here, I'm in charge."

"You're not in charge of me."

"We'll see. Let's ask him."

"How can we do that if he's not here?" She glowered at me.

"I'll phone him. I'm permitted to make international phone calls." I didn't have to remind her that no one else in the office had permission to do this. I placed the call but he wasn't available, so I prepared a fax. As I was about to send it, June grabbed me and spun me around.

"I've had enough of you," she yelled. "You deserve to be punched." She took a swing at me. "You bitch, I'm going to punch you to death."

She landed a blow against my head, knocking my fancy longhaired wig to the floor. For a moment stars danced in front of my eyes.

A couple of our colleagues pulled her away from me. I wanted to fight back, but I knew that was a bad idea.

As soon as I could, I reached Henry and reported that June

had assaulted me for performing the duties I'd been hired to do. "I can't do my job if I'm under attack. Fire her or fire me—you'll have to choose."

A few minutes later he called June and told her she was through, and then he sent a fax to confirm it in writing. We had to bring in a security guard to escort her out of the office.

Unfortunately that didn't end my difficulties with the staff from Beijing. They worked slowly and kept their files in disorder. Worse, some of them were slapdash about integrity and confidentiality. One day a salesman whom I will call Mr. Fan set down a client contract in a public area of the office in plain view of other clients or anyone else who might walk in. I'd noticed before that he had a casual disregard for confidential files and paperwork, but this was a breach I couldn't overlook. When I asked him courteously to pick up the contract and file it away properly, he refused and walked away.

The second time it happened, I approached him with a smile and calmly but firmly gave him a warning: "If that contract isn't properly put away in five minutes, I'm going to tear it up."

He snorted. "You would never do that. It represents a huge sale. You're bluffing."

I looked at my watch. When four minutes and fifty-five seconds had passed, I picked up the contract from the table where it had been tossed and began to rip the first page in two. Mr. Fan grabbed the document out of my hands and stalked off to put it away. After that, the staff began to use the system I had set up for customer files.

Another difficult issue I faced was monitoring the sales staff to make sure that no one was soliciting kickbacks. Western companies like ours worked through trading companies that acted as middlemen, arranging for letters of credit and other documentation that both buyer and seller needed in order to conduct business in China. When I learned that certain Draxler salesmen were attempting to seek kickbacks by making clients work through particular trading companies, I began to work with the customers myself, helping them establish direct contacts with trading companies that sidestepped the kickbacks.

Some of the old Beijing staff still resented me, but they now realized I was serious about my job.

When I reported these incidents to my boss, he said, "It's natural that you're meeting some resistance. They prefer to have their jobs stay familiar and easy, but we can't stick to old ways if we're going to grow. If you don't have any problems with them, you're not doing your work. Your role is to help Draxler become bigger and stronger. You're moving us into the future."

* * *

I loved the idea of moving into the future with Draxler International. At last I had found my professional home. The external rewards were excellent—I was now the highest paid local professional working in a foreign company in Shekou, and I had moved into a nice one-bedroom apartment, the first place I had all to myself. But the real joy came from the work itself. I arrived at work at eight o'clock every morning, including weekends, and stayed as late as ten o'clock at night. I didn't even notice the day had ended.

One night Henry was working late and noticed that I was still at my desk. "You're really on fire, Diana," he said. "Why are you still here? You should be home getting some sleep."

"I'm just reading," I told him. "I want to learn everything I can."

I spent hours studying the industry, hungry to learn more about the products, the vendors and clients, the relationships, and the strategies that could help our company grow. Draxler International was the exclusive agent in China for Optical Fiber, a joint venture between Corning Incorporated, one of the world's top manufacturers of optical fiber, and the British firm BICC. We referred to the joint venture as English Corning. The firm represented other vendors as well, but Optical Fiber was the core of the business.

In the mid-1990s, China was poised for a telecommunications boom. An immense geographic territory needed to be cabled and wired in order for the country to take advantage of the new technologies that were changing the lives of businesses and individuals worldwide. To build its telecommunications infrastructure, China needed optical fiber, and foreign companies were the only sources of supply. So Draxler was well positioned to succeed.

I discovered that we were a vital link in a chain. The foreign vendors developed the optical fiber. Draxler, as Optical Fiber's agent, sold the fiber on their behalf to Chinese manufacturers, who used it to make cables. Our customers then sold their cables to the companies that were creating and expanding China's telecommunications backbone networks.

Every day was an adventure. There was so much to learn and do. Henry gave me the full freedom and trust to manage the daily operations of the business. I worked with the sales staff to ensure that they met their goals, analyzed the company's financial performance, and handled human resources and all the administrative functions. I served as a liaison between Draxler and its vendors and clients, developed customer profiles, and did market research, digging out the information we needed for sound business decisions. When Henry was overseas, in Hong Kong, or elsewhere in China, I sent him a summary report at the end of each day to let him know what was happening.

Henry also gave me special projects. He had me develop a new system for staff performance reviews and a manual to document company policies and procedures. When we came up with a good way to resolve a problem with a client, I revised the manual to reflect what we'd learned. It became clear to me that the basic principle of success was understanding and meeting the customers' needs.

"Your boss is lucky to have you," my friends told me.

"We're both lucky," I replied. "He lets me do so much."

* * *

Optical Fiber officials came regularly to visit customers, and other foreign companies sent managers to visit the Draxler operation, eager to learn how to do business in China. Henry asked me to help entertain and educate the visiting vendors, accompanying them as they made their rounds of Chinese cable companies.

Traveling around the country with my boss and our vendors gave me a top-notch education. I learned effective techniques for conducting negotiations, creating brand recognition, and generating sales, and I made valuable contacts in the major cable companies in China.

One of the most valuable lessons I learned was how to do business across cultures. The vendors we represented were often surprised by how dissimilar the Chinese business style is from that of the West. But while the differences could create barriers, they also were doorways to opportunities for any person or company that made the effort to recognize and respect the other side's customs, traditions, and methods.

My role was to facilitate the getting-acquainted process by translating the discussions and helping the vendors and clients understand each other's philosophies, practices, and expectations. I had to be very sensitive to deliver the right meaning in the right manner, so that both sides could fully understand what was happening and what was expected. Lastly I would help them build a bridge of mutual agreement that would lead to their goals—a successful business transaction now and a solid relationship for the future.

It could be a challenging task. I constantly found myself in awkward situations where the two sides had entirely different understandings of each other's needs and the terms of the agreements they were negotiating. Often conflicts arose when the business styles of the parties clashed, creating confusion, errors, and insults.

For instance, one frequent Western visitor was a blunt, stubborn man who grew impatient and angry when customers didn't understand his products and their quality. His technical knowledge of his products was outstanding, but he had no clue about how to deal with Chinese customers. When I served as an interpreter in his meetings with clients, I quickly realized that I didn't dare translate what he actually said. His remarks expressed his frustration, and while they made sense from the standpoint of Western logic, the Chinese would view them as unforgivably rude. An accurate interpretation would create problems rather than resolve them, and probably ruin any chance for a productive future relationship. I took the liberty of reframing his rudeness into more polite terms that conveyed his meaning in a way that the Chinese could accept.

I was fascinated by the divergence between the two business cultures, and I worked hard to become comfortable and capable in both worlds, so that I could move between them with ease. I found that the cultural differences fell into certain broad categories.

Westerners are straightforward;
Chinese prefer an indirect approach.

Westerners are direct, forthright, and logical, and they take an entrepreneurial "let's make it happen" approach. They expect to act quickly, and they state their expectations for a deal in unequivocal terms—"This is my price; this is my quality. Take it or leave it."

In China, on the other hand, unpredictability, subtlety, and flexibility are valued, and directness can be perceived as an affront. The Chinese do not often indulge in the kind of business planning and strategic thinking that are routine in the West. Rather than conduct a logical analysis of facts and figures or risks and benefits, they are more likely to make decisions based on their emotions, intuition, gut feelings, and relationships. To gain information about a company and discern its needs, an oblique approach works best.

Doing business with a traditional Chinese company can prove perplexing for Westerners. When discussing a deal, Chinese businesspeople usually wait for the other parties to announce what their company will do, although that doesn't mean that the Chinese negotiators will go along. The Chinese are elusive; they won't say yes or no. "Let's discuss it further" may indicate that there is a possibility of coming to terms. "I will think about it" often means there is no hope. Learning to understand the communication style is very helpful for a constructive business discussion and negotiation.

> *Business in the West is regulated, systematic,*
> *and transparent; business in China is not.*

In the West, there are regular procedures by which business is conducted. Work practices and performance expectations are clearly defined, which makes operating an enterprise much easier. Companies prepare proposals, submit invoices, and pay bills according to widely recognized norms and standards. The functions and accountabilities of corporate personnel tend to be clearly delineated. When an agreement is struck or a deal is made, the terms are documented in a contract that both parties recognize as binding.

Systems and laws exist to govern business transactions, protect individual and organizational rights, and help companies collect payments they are owed. Should a dispute arise, the parties involved can achieve redress or resolution through the courts. Corporations are legally required to file reports that make them more transparent to outsiders than a Chinese company would ever be.

China has few such guarantees or protections. Concepts that are important in the West, such as intellectual property, patents, trademarks, and copyrights, are far less relevant in China. A company that launches a successful product can expect copies to appear in the marketplace and has little recourse when they do.

In China, I noticed that businesspeople disregard the importance of contracts and legal commitments. In China, parties to a deal rely on their personal bonds and each other's sense of honor to ensure that the terms of an agreement are carried out. If you push for a contract too early in the process, before goodwill and confidence have been established, the client is likely to balk or become upset. This is one reason why trust is such a critical factor.

> In China, parties to a deal rely on their personal bonds and each other's sense of honor to ensure that the terms of an agreement are carried out.

Without sufficient and enforceable laws and regulations to fall back on, Westerners who want to do business in China would be well advised to first learn its business customs and figure out how to fit into its culture. No matter how big or small a Chinese company may be, its systems, procedures, and rationales are likely to seem arbitrary, inefficient, and manipulative—in other words, they make no sense at all to someone with a Western mentality.

Yet despite its apparent drawbacks, the Chinese way of

doing business has advantages. It can in fact be a more flexible, efficient, practical, and profitable way to operate—especially in a huge, rapidly developing country, where anything can happen and anything is possible. Firms operating under the Western system can be overly rigid and procedure-driven; to succeed in China, they need to be more nimble. Chinese companies can respond more quickly to new opportunities and changing situations, and they can more easily generate alternative plans and flexible solutions to deal with irregularities that arise. This is one reason China's economy is growing so fast.

Western companies take a long-term view of marketing;
Chinese companies take a short-term view.

Westerners appreciate the power of marketing, branding, and corporate identity. They know that these are the keys to an enterprise's profit, growth, and longevity. Therefore Western firms make it a top priority to establish a strong corporate identity and a positive image for the company's products and brand. They realize that marketing doesn't just mean advertising or sales but encompasses everything that influences a person's opinion of the company or a customer's decision to buy or not buy. They place a high value on customer satisfaction and goodwill, and they have well-established systems for customer service. Western companies take a long-term approach to marketing, developing strategies and investing resources with an eye to a substantial future payoff.

Chinese firms are less sophisticated when it comes to reaching out to the customer. They tend not to understand that effective marketing is a long-term investment but one that has a substantial payoff. Establishing a strong corporate identity and, even more important, creating customer goodwill are keys to longevity in the marketplace, but they require a level of creativity and farsightedness that many Chinese companies have not yet developed.

In China, relationships are paramount.

Personal relationships are the key to doing business in China. At every step, from negotiating the deal to getting paid, success depends on building the most reliable relationships you can within a company's power structure. When Western businesspeople approach a Chinese company, they often don't understand who the decision makers are. Nor do they grasp how crucial political influences can be in a country where the government owns most of the businesses and sponsors the development and delivery of most products and services. The power structure of a Chinese firm can be quite different than a Westerner, accustomed to meaningful job titles and organizational charts, might expect.

Western companies take a long-term approach to marketing, developing strategies and investing resources with an eye to a substantial future payoff.

To make a project work in China, you need to know the members of the customer's team—their history and background, their education, their politics, their managerial roles, the chain of their internal working relationships, their decision-making impact, and their status within the company and the industry. Only when you have this information will you be able to operate effectively in the Chinese market.

Westerners have to be prepared to spend extra time and money in China in the beginning while they put in the effort needed to build the solid, trusting relationships that are essential for success.

Your Chinese counterparts will want to understand your team in the same way. They prefer to work with persons and organizations they know and trust, and they make deals and honor them based on their regard for the other party. Because everything is based on one-on-one dealings, the Chinese will be reluctant to deal with you if an individual on your team has a poor reputation or an abrasive personality. And remember that the Chinese business world is a small place; word about a company's trustworthiness, its business style, or the quality of its products can spread quickly.

Any Western company seeking to penetrate the Chinese market would be well advised to engage the help of a "middle channel"—an expert who understands both cultures and can help the company navigate through the seeming absurdity of the Chinese business world. A good middle channel understands and respects the Western business mentality, is well connected in China, and has mastered the sophistication, flexibility, and unpredictability of Chinese business. By providing a bridge between the two worlds, the middle channel fosters trust and understanding, to the benefit of both parties.

Westerners have to be prepared to spend extra time and

money in China in the beginning while they put in the effort needed to build the solid, trusting relationships that are essential for success. Patience, understanding, tolerance and flexibility are absolutely required and appreciated. It takes time, energy, knowledge, and a lot of hands-on work to find and cultivate the right connections, the right decision makers, and the right chain of relationships. But once you assemble all the pieces, the door to the Chinese market will swing wide open.

* * *

I gradually built my own system for working effectively with Chinese clients and Western vendors. Using my ingenuity, powers of observation, and communication skills, I learned how to strike a balance between the logical mentality of the Westerners and the emotional approach of the Chinese and find the middle ground where they could reach agreement.

Before engaging in any business discussion, I would do my homework, conducting intensive background checks on both companies to learn as much as I could about each party's capabilities, needs, and business goals. I looked at such factors as the companies' financial status, banking relationships, internal politics, and relationship dynamics, as well as information about the individuals involved. In general, obtaining the information I needed about Western vendors was easy, but learning about the Chinese clients was much trickier. It took time, effort, experience, and a bit of intuition to discover the companies' backgrounds and the personalities and business styles of the key decision makers.

I came to understand the customers' and vendors' points of view, and soon I was able to make recommendations to both sides about the products, the industry, contract terms, and marketing strategies. I was no longer just a translator—I was a problem solver who could monitor the communication and direct the discussion toward a positive resolution that satisfied all concerned. I worked hard to create a harmonious business environment and change contentious negotiations into win-win discussions. My goal was to build relationships—these were far more important than any immediate sale. A short-term compromise would always generate a long-term benefit.

Protecting the client's best interests is the key to enduring success in business.

The more I learned about the customers, the better I was able to resolve their problems, satisfy their needs, and protect their best interests. It was becoming clear to me that protecting the client's best interests was the key to enduring success in business. I built a reputation I was proud of, based on trust and constructive communication. As I won their confidence and respect, clients began to ask that I be present when the vendors came to call.

As a result of my efforts, Draxler's business was becoming more organized, productivity was improving, relationships with clients were getting better, and sales and profits were increasing significantly. After three months Henry gave me a promotion. At first my title was to be vice president, but due to some confusion with the financial arrangements, I ended up with the dual titles of office manager and sales director. Whatever the label, I was officially Henry's second in command.

* * *

Whenever I returned to the office from a client visit, I took up my role of managing the office staff. It was frustrating at times, because I could see such a contrast between some of the staff members' attitude about work and my own. It made me understand more clearly why my boss gave me more opportunity.

The big difference was that I felt as if I were working primarily for myself. The company was a platform for my personal sense of accomplishment. I loved what I was doing, and I enjoyed what I achieved.

The company was a platform for my personal sense of accomplishment.

Far more than the income I earned or the titles I held or the routines of the job, I prized the experiences I was having and the opportunities I was being offered, and I wanted to take full advantage of them. That's why I was motivated to work so hard for such long hours.

I was surprised and saddened to realize that, with a few exceptions, oftentimes employees in a company regarded their jobs merely as a means of earning income, not as a potential source of personal success and satisfaction. Unfortunately, this attitude was and still is typical in Chinese workplaces. Too many Chinese people passively accepted their job as a matter of fact, an unchangeable reality, regardless of whether the job was suitable for them, or whether they enjoyed the work, or whether it gave them a chance to learn more and improve their skills. They saw their job as a necessity rather an opportunity. Most of them had no clue about how to position themselves, or how to take steps to find their right niche.

It became clear to me that such narrow and shortsighted thinking would tremendously limit the growth of a person's career, and I figured out a solution: to overcome this drawback, it's important to build a strong sense of ownership of your work—for yourself as well as for the company. This requires accomplishing two things. First, investing real effort in discovering your potential and developing skills, professionalism, and an I-can-do-it attitude. Second, creating a farsighted, long-range vision of how you will manage your career, achieve your goals, and improve your life.

Narrow and shortsighted thinking tremendously limits the growth of a person's career.

This, I resolved, was how I would direct my own life.

So, at the same time that I worked to make a real contribution to Draxler's success, I was also taking steps to learn about my capabilities, developing my talents, and finding my sources of joy. I was creating my own philosophy of how business can be conducted successfully. I always promoted and protected Draxler's reputation by being honest, loyal, and consistent, and by maintaining a customer-first orientation that our clients valued. As I did, I was establishing my own reputation in the industry for competence and diligence, and especially for integrity. Step by step, I was moving toward what would become my own best niche in life—entrepreneurship.

* * *

My travels with vendors took me all over China, giving me a fascinating look at my vast and varied homeland. To communicate better with clients, I learned the dialects of different regions. This skill paid off in another way every time I traveled with the vendors. Taxi drivers were constantly trying to rip us off, charging us high fares for short distances. When I began speaking to them in their own accent, there were fewer attempts to fleece us, and if one occurred I could confront the swindler and demand the correct fare. It was a small thing, but it made our trips easier and less costly for the company.

Build a strong sense of ownership of your work— for yourself as well as for the company. Invest real effort in discovering your potential and developing skills, professionalism, and an I-can-do-it attitude.

Every city we visited had its own character. Their food, their business practices, and their levels of courtesy were all different. Shanghai was modern, commercial, and sophisticated. In places like Xian in northwestern China and the coastal city of Dalian, people were less urbane and business methods more traditional. Their food was simpler than in other places yet more plentiful. In the provinces of Jiangsu and Zhejiang, which border on Shanghai, the people favored food with delicate flavors. They were more entrepreneurial than in some parts of China but trickier to deal with because they are detail-oriented and master negotiators.

Create a farsighted, long-range vision of how you will manage your career, achieve your goals, and improve your life.

Food was an important part of the experience in each city. A business meal in China is a lavish event with extravagant quantities of food and drink. Refusing to indulge was an insult. On one of the earliest trips I discovered, in highly embarrassing fashion, that I'm highly sensitive to alcohol. Unlike some of my companions, I hadn't been over-imbibing, but all at once I turned red. I began stumbling, and my words became incoherent. Then I got quite sick.

After that I avoided liquor. When we were entertaining clients, I had to appear to be drinking to avoid offending our guests, so I surreptitiously substituted water for the alcohol. As the clients were getting drunk, they teased me: "You don't smoke, you don't date, but you certainly can drink." Little did they know.

Thanks to my travels, people came to know that there was a capable, responsible, and stylish lady manager in the fiber optics industry. I was glad they recognized that I was not just a pretty woman, not a decoration in the office, but a valuable contributor to my company's success. Several Western companies asked me to work with them as a consultant, advising them about doing business in China. With Draxler's blessing, I accepted some of these opportunities.

I was crazy about my work. Finally I had discovered my

true role and purpose. I'd found an industry that offered the challenges I craved and that rewarded someone with creativity and initiative. Henry was right: I was on fire, blazing forward—an unstoppable force.

* * *

One day in September 1995, I was in the Shanghai airport awaiting my homebound flight. I lugged my two heavy suitcases through the crowded terminal, looking for a place to sit. Finally I spotted one.

"Excuse me, is this seat available?" I asked the man reading a book in the adjacent chair.

"Sure. Please sit down." He was a clean-cut Caucasian wearing sandals and jeans, probably in his late thirties.

"I'm Diana," I said, offering my hand. "I'm sorry to invade your privacy."

As we chatted, I learned that he was an American heading home from a vacation in China, his first trip here. After a few minutes, his flight was announced. We exchanged business cards, and he stood up to go to his plane. I was surprised to see how tall he was.

A month later, I received a mysterious letter. In a warm and courteous tone, the writer—someone named Jon—asked me a lot of curious questions about myself. How could I speak American English with almost no accent without having lived in America? How had such a young Chinese woman come to hold a powerful and prestigious position in a European company?

It was a beautiful letter, one of the most well-written letters in English I have ever read. But I met so many people when I was traveling that I had no recollection of who this Jon person was. When I received a second letter from Jon, I flipped through my business card collection and found his: senior engineer, Princeton, New Jersey. Now I remembered him—the American at the airport.

I picked up the phone and dialed the number on the card.

"Who?" he said when I reached him. "Diana who?"

"Diana from the airport in Shanghai. You've been sending me letters."

We talked for more than half an hour about our backgrounds, our different cultures, his impressions of China. We discussed our work, and I was intrigued by his creative and original business ideas.

Finally he said, "We'd better go. This is costing you a fortune. Next time, I'll make the call."

After that we talked frequently and got to know each other well. Jon was warm, intelligent, and open-minded, and his letters and calls included romantic gestures that revealed his passionate side. I found myself becoming attracted to him. Through the fall, winter, and spring, his phone calls were lovely company for me.

I still adored my job at Draxler, but I was beginning to think that if I wanted to rise in the business world, it might make sense to get an MBA, perhaps at Stanford or Harvard. Most of the successful Chinese executives I knew had been educated in the United States, and the clients and vendors I worked with often were surprised to realize that I had never left China. Li Huang, my best friend since the long-ago day when I broke her hot water thermoses in Lanzhou, was at Harvard working on her PhD in physics, and she encouraged me to come. So did Jon, who sent me application materials from the top American business schools.

He included some information about a side business he was working on, distributing a line of nutritional supplements. The next time we talked on the phone, he suggested, "Suppose we work together? You could help me bring these products to China."

"That's an intriguing idea," I told him. "China could be a great market."

"Here's a thought," he said. "Why don't you come for a visit so we can talk about working together as business partners? You could check out some business schools too."

For a moment I was speechless. A visit to the United States! I did my best to keep my voice calm as I said, "That's an excellent plan."

I arranged with Henry to take the time off, and soon I was busy with preparations for the trip. I could scarcely believe it. When I told my friends and colleagues that I was going to America, they either laughed or shook their heads. "You'll never get visas," said one friend, voicing their unanimous opinion. "You're young, single, female, and pretty, and you speak great English—the American officials will be afraid that once you arrive in their country, you'll never go back home. And the Chinese will think so too."

"Nonsense, " I retorted, though I was secretly afraid they might be right.

I had to travel to Beijing to apply for my passport and my U.S. visa. For my appointments at the American consulate, I dressed in my professional best. I impressed the consular officials with my proper professional manner and fluent English as I explained my business visit to the United States. I was excited when I returned to Shenzhen with the U.S. visa in hand.

Wow, I thought, this is really going to happen.

* * *

My departure day came at last. Early one morning I boarded a Northwest Airlines plane in Hong Kong to begin my American journey. I'd be flying halfway around the world and wouldn't arrive until the next day. It was the beginning of October 1996.

My first stop on American soil would be Seattle. There I would go through customs and board a plane for New York.

The flight wasn't full, and the steward offered me a seat at the back of the plane where I would have more room to stretch out. Partway through the trip a tall, dark-haired man came down the aisle. As he passed my row he smiled at me, then stopped to say, "Hi there, need some company?"

What was he talking about? The word *company* referred to a business firm. Then I realized what he meant.

He sat down next to me and we chatted the rest of the way. I will call him Tim—he was a flight attendant on vacation, an American of Italian ancestry. "I'm on my way to New York," he told me.

"I'm going there too."

"Great. Give me a call." And he wrote down his phone number for me.

When we arrived in Seattle, I collected my suitcases and dragged them to the customs line. Though I wore comfortable

CLOCKWISE FROM ABOVE:
Diana feeling overwhelmed at the
White Mountain Hotel on her first
visit with Jon; in Washington, D.C.,
with police officers; at the entrance
to Chinatown; with Ginger and
Craig, October 1996.

TOP LEFT: Chatting with a bagpipe player in Washington, D.C.

TOP RIGHT: Diana eating her first French fry in the United States on her way to New Hampshire, October 1996.

BELOW LEFT: At the botanical garden in Washington, D.C.

BELOW RIGHT: At the Empire State Building.

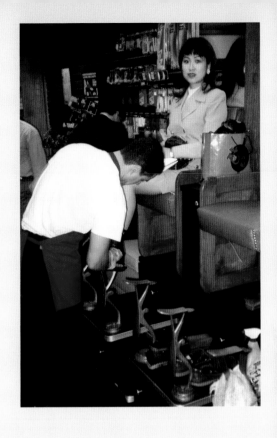

ABOVE: In New York, October 1996.

RIGHT: Getting a shoe shine in Penn Station, New York.

BELOW LEFT: In New Hampshire.

BELOW RIGHT: At the Princeton campus, New Jersey.

ABOVE LEFT AND RIGHT:
First visit to Hawaii, with newly met local people at a Halloween party, October 1996; having fun with entertainers at the Hawaii airport.

ABOVE LEFT: Learning about the hula dance.

ABOVE RIGHT: Dancing with a local Hawaiian.

RIGHT: With a Hawaiian salsa band after the first salsa dancing of her life.

A family reunion in Lanzhou, February 1997.
LEFT TO RIGHT: Diana's brother, Diana, her brother-in-law,
her sister, and her parents and nephew seated in front.

ABOVE AND LEFT: First reunion with college and high school friends in Lanzhou, spring 1997.

BELOW: Diana with her brother at the Kimpinsky Hotel during a business trip in Beijing, March 1997.

BOTTOM: Diana's family and Zhang Li's family at a Lanzhou karaoke restaurant, February 1997.

ABOVE: Diana and a friend on a Beijing street with the old emperor's walls, spring 1997.

RIGHT: A farewell brunch with Sally, her husband, and their daughter Meggy, May 1997.

BELOW LEFT: Diana and her nephew playing with chopsticks.

BELOW RIGHT: Diana's nephew in her 65-square-foot room in Lanzhou, which she shared with her sister through high school and part of college, February 1997.

TOP LEFT AND RIGHT: On her first business visit to Beijing after her move to the United States, Diana and her nephew visit Tiananmen Square, October 1997.
BELOW: Diana with her mother, sister, nephew, and father visiting the Forbidden City in Beijing.

TOP: With a client and his family at a Chengdu hotpot restaurant, fall 1997.

MIDDLE: Diana at her office in New Times Plaza.

BOTTOM: Diana and her mother, aunts, and nephew at her Shenzhen office, fall 1999.

CLOCKWISE FROM ABOVE:

A first visit to San Francisco, July 1997;
Diana with her nephew; putting on makeup
before the opera, July 2002; shopping at
Nieman Marcus, summer 2001; Christmas
in San Francisco, 2001.

ABOVE LEFT: In Venice, summer 1999.

ABOVE RIGHT: Windsurfing.

BELOW LEFT: After a meditation class in Kauai, fall 2002.

BELOW RIGHT: Posing for a pretend model photo shoot at a social networking event in San Francisco, 2002.

ABOVE LEFT: Visiting Gaudi architecture in Barcelona, 2003.

ABOVE RIGHT: Hiking in Maui, 2000.

LEFT: In Monaco, April 2003.

BELOW: On the beach at Cannes with some kids, April 2003.

clothes on the plane, I'd changed in the tiny lavatory shortly before we landed, putting on a black business suit. I was on a business trip, after all, and I like myself to look professional.

The officer checked my documents and asked me some questions. One of them was, "Is this your first time in the United States?"

"Yes, it is," I answered.

He looked surprised. "For real? You haven't been here before?"

"Why would I say it's my first time here if it wasn't?"

He pulled me out of the line and summoned another officer, a woman who was ABC—American-Born Chinese. She began to question me in Mandarin while her colleague examined the contents of my bag. I realized that because of my American-accented English, they didn't believe I was telling the truth about not having been in the United States before.

He asked me, "How can anyone in China who has never been to the U.S. speak American English like you do?"

That insult ignited my anger. Mustering as much dignity as I could, I told him, "Chinese people are not as stupid as you think. I have plenty of friends who are quite capable speakers of English."

He frowned; obviously he didn't like my answer. Without bothering to look at me again, he spoke in a low voice to the Chinese-American inspector. She asked me more questions— what was my job in China, how did I learn English—but her tone was courteous and calm.

"You must understand," she said, "most Chinese visitors don't dress professionally or stylishly, and if they do speak

English, they usually have a much stronger Chinese accent." Her patient manner pacified me. I could tell she understood Chinese people and was giving me the benefit of the doubt.

While they were searching my luggage, they found a packet of love letters in Chinese in my packet—not from Jon but from another man. Although that relationship was long since over, I carried the letters as a sort of good-luck charm. The letters seemed to help the lady officer convince the male officer. It proved that I was a traditional Chinese woman who had never been to the United States before.

Finally they let me go. By now several hours had passed and I had missed my flight to New York. The best that the customs people could do was to put me on a plane to Newark, New Jersey. This unpleasant experience had made me angry and upset, but I was flattered too. I hadn't realized that my English had improved to such a level.

I was afraid I would never connect with Jon. He was supposed to meet my plane in New York—what had he thought when I wasn't on it? But when I arrived at the gate in Newark, there he was. The customs people had phoned him about the change in my itinerary. He had waited for me for hours and with such patience. I was so happy to see him—and nervous too. He opened his big arms and I jumped into his embrace.

* * *

Jon brought me to his townhouse in Princeton—my first experience of an American home. I was amazed by its size and comfort. By Shenzhen standards I had a large apartment, but Jon's place was probably two thousand square feet in size—

four times as big as mine. The living room had a wall of shelves filled with books, and there was a fireplace. I'd never seen such a thing. It was certainly a far cry from the smoky, sooty stove we'd had in the coal-mining village. Imagine using a fire for decoration.

As he hauled my suitcase up to the guestroom on the second floor, Jon said, his breath puffing, "Oh, my God, this is so huge and heavy. Did you bring your whole house?"

"Of course not," I said. "Only what I'll be needing. I'm going to be here a whole month."

I was jet-lagged and exhausted, and he made me a cup of tea that helped me relax. My first night in America, I thought as I settled into my bed. Despite my fatigue, I was too excited to sleep.

The next day Jon took me to Princeton University, which was close to his house. The campus, with its gray stone buildings and broad lawns, was beautiful. I was reminded of my parents' university, where I'd lived for such a long time, and I felt peaceful and comfortable. It was early autumn, so many of the trees were still green, while the leaves of some were turning red, yellow, orange, as brilliant as flames. The sun was strong, the air fresh, the sky clear and blue—so different from smoggy China.

Jon and I strolled hand in hand on the grounds, talking about our lives, our beliefs, and our dreams. We exchanged business ideas, and we laughed and joked a lot. He was such wonderful company. I could scarcely believe that until yesterday we'd been in each other's presence for a total of only five minutes, when we met last year at the airport in Shanghai.

* * *

Now that I was in America, I was ready for adventure. I told Jon that I wanted to take the train into New York by myself. To me, New York seemed like the essence of America. I didn't know what that meant exactly, but I wanted to find out. I had impressions of skyscrapers and the Statue of Liberty, and I had heard in David's class years ago that New York was called the Big Apple. What did a big apple look like?

Jon tried to dissuade me. "That isn't a good idea. New York is not a safe place."

"I'll be fine. I've traveled all over China by myself. I'll call you if I get into trouble."

"How long will you be gone?"

"A day or two maybe. I'll let you know."

Though he wasn't happy about my plan, I could tell he admired my courage. Early in the morning he took me to the station. In less than an hour I arrived at Penn Station ready to see the Big Apple for myself.

The station was huge and crowded. People were rushing all around me, going in a thousand different directions. I had no idea where to go. I asked a policeman for directions, but what he told me made no sense to me. At last I made my way out onto the street.

My first impression of New York was noise and bustle. Horns honked, brakes screeched. People hurried along the sidewalk with their elbows extended to shove you out of their way. The towering buildings and flashing signs reminded me of Hong Kong. There were ads everywhere—

signs and billboards and moving displays: *See this. Buy that. Go there.* I began to feel dizzy.

After strolling for a while I grew thirsty, so I stopped in a little corner market and bought a can of Coca-Cola. When I opened my purse to get out my money, I noticed a slip of paper hidden in the corner. It bore the name Tim and a phone number. Oh, that flight attendant I'd met on the plane to Seattle—I had almost forgotten about him. Right away I found a phone and called him. By a miracle I reached him. "Great to hear from you," Tim said. "I'm going to be with some friends in Central Park. Come meet us there."

"Okay," I agreed. I stopped passersby to ask how to get to Central Park, but everyone was too busy, too impatient, or too rude to help me. Finally I found a hotel and got directions from the staff at the front desk.

My destination was some twenty-five blocks to the north, so I began hiking up an avenue. I window-shopped along the way, impressed by displays of beautiful clothes and amazing shoes. But much of what I saw was less attractive. I was surprised by the mess and garbage on the street, the run-down look of the old buildings, the unpleasant smells from sources I didn't even want to think about. Some men whistled at me, and I stopped, wondering what was wrong. Then I saw in their faces what they meant. Feeling myself redden with embarrassment, I walked faster to get away from them.

After a while I began thinking that perhaps it had been a mistake to wear my high heels. In China people made a point of dressing well in the city, and I'd wanted to look proper for my visit to New York. But from what I could tell, proper dress was not a meaningful concept in the Big Apple. I saw people in business suits with briefcases, but I also saw jeans everywhere, and they were often tattered or torn. A tall black woman caught my eye. I'd never seen a woman with such dark skin. She looked so elegant in her short, tight suit and stiletto heels that I figured she must be a fashion model.

I was hungry by now, so when I saw a cart selling food, I stopped. But the items for sale were all unfamiliar. I couldn't figure out what to ask for.

"Ya wanna pretzel?" the vendor asked.

"What's that?" I asked.

"Eh, I'll just give ya a hot dog."

He presented me with a sausage in a tube of bread and directed me to put yellow mustard on it. I paid him and took a bite. Delicious!

I felt odd eating on the street, so I took my lunch into a nearby hotel lobby and finished it there. I asked someone, "Why is it called a hot dog?" which got me a strange look but no answer.

Finally I reached Central Park, where I actually managed to find Tim and his friends, another guy and a girl. I told them about my walk from the train station.

"How come you speak English almost without any accent?" the young lady asked.

"It's not so great," Tim teased. "You didn't pronounce the name of that gourmet treat correctly, Diana. The right way to say it is *hot dawg*."

"Yeah," said the other guy, laughing. "And you wash down your *hot dawg* with a *cuppa cawfee*."

We all went to a restaurant, and they suggested that I place the order. So I told the waitress, "We'd each like a hot dawg and a cuppa cawfee."

"How do ya take it?" she asked. Huh? I had no idea what she meant. My companions explained that she was asking if I wanted my coffee with cream and sugar. I didn't know—I'd only tasted coffee once in my life. When I sipped it now, it was unbelievably bitter. I poured in lots and lots of sugar.

I was curious to see New York's famous Chinatown, so, after parting with Tim and his friends, I made my way down to that part of town. I was so disappointed. The place looked dirty and sad compared to home, and the food in the restaurant where I ate dinner was truly awful, so sweet that it turned my stomach. When they brought me a funny little folded cookie along with my bill, I didn't know what it was. What a surprise to bite into it and find a little slip of paper inside that purported to tell my fortune. The proprietor tried to tell me that this was a Chinese tradition, but I'd never seen such a thing in China.

By now it was dark and I was tired. After such a full day, I decided to go back to Jon's place. I called him from the train station to tell him I was on the way. He was upset that I hadn't phoned sooner to let him know my plans; he had worried a lot about me. When we got home, I tried to lighten the tension making jokes in my newly acquired New York accent: "Would ya like a cuppa cawfee and a hot dawg?"

His anger dissolved into a big hearty laugh.

* * *

Soon I was on the train again, this time heading for Boston to meet Li Huang. Jon would meet me there in a couple of days. He was driving up in an antique van. He collected old cars, and this van was a favorite; he'd had it for twenty-five years. After Boston we were going to go touring.

I liked the Amtrak trains. The cars were clean and open, and the passengers and the conductor were friendly. In China a train ride was not such a pleasant experience. The air in the crowded cars was thick and rank. People smoked and spat on the floor, and little kids whined and screeched for the entire journey.

From the train station in Boston, I walked across the Charles River to Cambridge and the Harvard campus. There at last I had my rendezvous with Li Huang. I was thrilled to see her—we hadn't been together in more than six years. I was still struggling through medical school in 1990 when she moved to the United States to study physics, and I'd been a bit envious.

We were each surprised at the sight of the other. Li Huang was so skinny! In the big jacket she was wearing, she looked shorter and smaller than I remembered. She'd always been a tomboy with short-cropped hair, but now her hair had grown long and she looked sweet and girlish.

I was wearing a unique but not very traditional Chinese outfit in burgundy and had made up my face in the elegant manner I'd adopted when I moved to Shenzhen. I don't think she realized she was frowning as she said, "I've never seen you in makeup before."

A couple of days later she told me she thought my makeup was too heavy and my clothes too formal, but by then I'd figured that out for myself. Everyone in Cambridge was so much more casual than I had expected. Li Huang lived in a cluttered apartment with books lying everywhere and socks flung over the headboard of one of the beds. Her sweatshirted roommates seemed startled that I looked so starched and prim. When I went to Harvard for my interview I wore a business suit; however, the professor who spoke to me was in a T-shirt and jeans. It struck me as strange that he would dress like that when he was acting in his professional capacity. Still, the conversation we had was heartening. I would need to take the GMAT—the Graduate Management Admission Test that most American business schools required—but he encouraged me to proceed with my application. He was a friendly, straightforward man with a good sense of humor, quite unlike most Chinese professors, who tend to keep themselves aloof.

Aside from the difference in professorial styles, Cambridge and Harvard reminded me of Beijing and the university there. Both places are academic environments where intellectual discussions take place constantly. I was surprised, though, that unlike a Chinese university Harvard had no wall to isolate it from other parts of the city, no elaborate gate that one passed through to enter or leave the campus. City and university blended together almost seamlessly.

Li Huang took me to a Chinese restaurant where we sampled the famous New England lobster prepared Chinese style. I must say I didn't really care for this bicultural treat. I much preferred eating at the big Harvard cafeteria. I liked the variety of food that was offered, and I was impressed when Li introduced me to some American students who spoke to me in perfect Mandarin.

That evening Li's advisor invited us to a family dinner party, and I cooked chicken and fish. That was my first social party in the United States. Though our hosts were kind and welcoming, my feeling persisted that I didn't really fit into the Harvard milieu. My Chinese chic and flair seemed awkwardly out of style in this laid-back place.

* * *

I was happy to see Jon when he arrived the next afternoon. We spent a little more time with Li Huang, then took off for a beautiful drive into rural New Hampshire. This far north, the magnificent autumn colors were at their peak. It reminded me of Xiangshan Park, or Scent Mountain, near Beijing, which has maples that turn brilliant red in the fall. To the Chinese, red is an auspicious color, a harbinger of good luck.

After an overnight stay at the elegant White Mountain Hotel in North Conway, we left early in the morning, heading the opposite direction to make the all-day drive to Washington, D.C. My friend Ginger was there with her husband, and I was looking forward so much to seeing her again.

Washington was a beautiful city. In their parklike surroundings, the official buildings—the Capitol, the White House, all the monuments—gleamed white in the autumn sun, conveying a sense of strength and power.

We spent a lot of time exploring the museums of the Smithsonian Institute. One of the treasures we saw was the Hope Diamond. I marched straight up and snapped a picture of it. When I turned around I was embarrassed to see a long line of people waiting their turn to walk up to the showcase for a close look at the legendary blue gem. I made a face to show that I was sorry and hid myself behind Jon's big coat—I was tiny compared to his six-foot, three-inch frame, and he gave me good cover. We walked away quickly.

Downtown we witnessed a large protest demonstration. I was struck by the contrast between this gathering and the student uprisings I'd experienced while I was in medical school, the ones that were centered in Tiananmen Square. This was a gay rights rally, and it was the first time I saw people that I knew for sure were homosexual. Although they were serious about their cause, I liked the way they maintained a spirit of fun. The event was very theatrical. Many of the protestors were in costumes, and others wore nothing at all. Some of them had painted their faces to look like clowns. They struck me as being talented and creative people.

The second day in Washington, D.C., I finally got to see Ginger and Craig. We hugged each other in tears. Ginger was still the beautiful, kind woman I remembered, and seeing her again was like a miracle. I had thought when we said good-bye in Beijing three years earlier that we were parting forever.

She and Craig were now married, and they told me all about their wedding. Even though they didn't have much money, they were still able to get Ginger a wedding gown. They seemed happy together and very much in love.

Ginger was a little bit surprised to see that I was accom-

panied by a tall Caucasian man. At first she treated him with
some reserve. I think she was concerned that I might get hurt,
and, like a dear friend and sister, she worried about me. As always, she brought comfort and affection into my life.

We spent hours talking and walking around the city. Then
she was gone again, and just like the first time I felt empty and
lonely.

Before we left Washington, Jon and I went to a noted
restaurant in Chinatown, where once again I was disappointed. I couldn't understand how any chef could cook like
this and call it Chinese. It was not Chinese food at all. All of
the Chinese food I'd had in the United States so far was taste-
less, greasy, and much too sweet. The flavors, the subtleties,
the variety of true Chinese cuisine were totally lacking. Suddenly I realized how much I missed the food back home. I
wanted to taste chive dumplings with their garlicky sauce, or
Lanzhou beef noodle, pungent with vinegar and so peppery it
could bring tears to my eyes. Fresh vegetables and seafood,
tender chicken, succulent pork. Oh, how I longed for all of
these flavors and textures and scents.

Finally we drove back to Princeton, and I cooked my own
Chinese dumplings with Jon as sous-chef. He learned quickly
how to wrap a dumpling. We made about two hundred
dumplings and had a real feast. They were delicious. It seemed
as if I hadn't eaten for ages, and now I was in heaven. Sharing
this good Chinese meal was a significant experience for me. It
made me feel very close to Jon. He felt like family. He felt like
home.

* * *

A few days later I went to New York again, but this time with Jon. After a day in the city we were going to visit his sister Chris and her family.

Just like the tourist-bureau slogan said, I loved New York. It was such a fabulous city, and though I had enjoyed my adventure there alone, it was a real pleasure to explore it in Jon's company. This time I got to see all the famous sightseeing spots. We went to the top of the Empire State Building and stood on the observation deck with the wind tossing our hair as we looked out over the city. We took a boat to the Statue of Liberty and a helicopter tour over Manhattan Island. Strolling along a walkway on the bank of the Hudson River, we encountered a street artist who sketched a quick, comic portrait of the two of us, exaggerating all of our features. The picture made us laugh; Jon really loved it. At Penn Station, right before we left, I indulged myself by having my shoes polished—imagine, twenty dollars for a shoeshine! It was such an extravagance that we memorialized it by taking a photograph.

Then we journeyed north into the suburbs of Westchester County where Chris and her family lived. They had a large and comfortable house with a huge backyard surrounded by trees.

There I was introduced to the cutest children I had ever seen. Jenny and DJ just took my heart away. Jenny, at age five, was a sweet and sensitive girl, very curious about me and my Chinese-style clothes. She had tiny, soft hands and rose-colored lips. She was playful but very well behaved. I've always wished she had been my daughter. Three-year-old DJ was more willful and mischievous than his big sister, not very concerned with doing what someone else wanted him to do. I found him to be lots of fun and extremely clever, and I loved his red, plump chipmunk cheeks. They took me out into the backyard. As I stood there holding two little hands, one in my left and one in my right, observing the trees with their beautiful fall colors, I felt warm and satisfied inside.

Back at Jon's house, we settled into a happy routine. We spent our days together, strolling on the Princeton campus, going to the library, playing chess in the evenings in front of the fireplace. I would fall asleep in his arms. It was so peaceful, warm, and safe. I had never dreamed that such a feeling of contentment could happen this suddenly, and this wonderfully.

Toward the end of my visit, Jon asked me to go with him to his cousin's wedding. I was excited by the idea of seeing an American wedding—so much different from a Chinese wedding, according to what I had heard.

"What should I wear?" I asked. "What do people here wear to weddings? Do they wear something fancy or just put on jeans like they do for everything else?"

"Wear one of your pretty dresses. A wedding is a dress-up occasion, even for us super-casual Americans."

"Good," I said. Dressing up was more my style. "And I'll wear my fancy burgundy wig."

He stroked his hand on my shoulder-length black hair. "Don't do that. Your hair is beautiful. There's no need to cover it up."

"But I haven't had a chance to wear my wig since I got here."

"It's not appropriate, Diana. Your own hair is fine."

This simple, silly thing got us into an argument, and I became upset. Jon immediately tried to cheer me up by suggesting that we go out and shop for a wedding gift.

While we were in the jewelry store, he pointed out a big diamond ring and said, "That ring would look very good on you." I had no idea what he was implying, but I quickly found out.

That night, before we went to sleep, I was sitting in his lap and humming a little Chinese song while he watched the flames dance in the fireplace. He looked so handsome. All at once he looked at me with great tenderness and affection.

"Ah, Diana," he said. "I have never met a woman as wonderful and beautiful as you. Will you marry me?"

My breath caught in my throat. This was beyond anything I had imagined. I felt such a rush of affection as I put my arms around him.

"Oh, Jon! Yes! Yes, I will marry you!"

* * *

Arriving at the church for Jon's cousin's wedding, I couldn't help but think about my own. Would Jon and I be married in the American style or would we follow Chinese tradition? In China we would gather all our friends and family members in a big banquet room with a lot of handcrafted paper decorations in red, the good-luck color. As the bride I would wear a red gown or another bright color, but definitely not white. There is no white at a Chinese wedding since that is the color of mourning. Jon and I would bow three times—once to heaven and earth, once to our parents, and once to each other

—and then we would be pronounced husband and wife. There would be no kissing and no exchange of vows and rings, but there would be a lot of funny games to try to make the couple more intimate with each other.

This wedding was so very different. The flowers that filled the church, the sonorous organ music, the procession of the bridesmaids—how beautiful it was. Then all eyes turned to the bride. She looked a little nervous as she came down the aisle on her father's arm, the long train of her white gown sweeping behind her. As she reached the front of the church, her father stepped back and Jon's cousin extended his hand to her. As I watched the ceremony, I decided that this was what I wanted to have some day—my own fairy-tale wedding, pure, formal, and poetic.

The reception in the hotel ballroom was a real celebration. We ate, drank, danced to live music, and had a wonderful time, though I skipped the champagne toasts so that my alcohol allergy wouldn't embarrass me in front of Jon's relatives. It had been arranged for the whole family to sit together. The only ones I'd met were Chris, her husband, and her children, and Jon made sure to introduce me to everyone—his mother, his brother and sister-in-law, and various cousins, uncles, and aunts. At the end of the reception, someone began banging his knife against a wineglass, and soon almost everyone in the room was doing the same.

"What's going on?" I asked Jon.

"People want the bride and groom to kiss," he explained.

When the wedding couple had obliged their guests, Jon's uncle asked, "So, when are you two going to get married?"

A couple of people at the table chuckled, but Jon surprised them—and me—by saying, "Well, we haven't set the date yet, but I do have an announcement to make. I've asked Diana to marry me, and, to my great joy, she accepted. We're officially engaged."

After a second or two of silence, everyone began to congratulate us. Jon's mother gave me an affectionate kiss on the cheek. I sensed that some of them thought our decision was a little sudden, but they welcomed me warmly into the family.

* * *

Soon afterward Jon surprised me with that beautiful diamond ring we had seen in the store. I called my mother to tell her the big news, and she was very happy. I think she'd begun to worry that I never would be married.

Excitedly Jon and I began talking about our plans. He promised me that we would have a big wedding like his cousin's. I was just melting in his love and his affection.

My month in the United States was nearly over. It felt as though I'd been there such a short time. As I was packing up to return to China, Jon came into the room.

"Don't leave," he said. "There's no reason to go back. Why don't you just stay here?"

"We talked about this. I have things to finish up on my job, and I want to visit my family before I move here permanently." I kissed him lightly. "Don't worry, I'm coming back."

"But I *am* worried, Diana. What if the Chinese government

won't let you leave China again? Quit your job. They'll miss you, but they'll manage."

"I can't. I have an obligation to Draxler. I love my work; I can't just drop it."

Suddenly I realized what a big decision I was making. If I moved to the United States to be with Jon I'd be giving up a career that brought me great joy. I'd be giving up everything I had worked for in China, my culture, my way of life. I loved this man . . . but was I really ready to make such a monumental change?

"You could find a new job here," he assured me. "And we'll go into business together, like we've talked about. I'll take care of you. Please, Diana, stay here with me."

I couldn't bring myself to say yes. I promised to come back when I'd settled things back home, but that didn't assuage him. We got into a big fight. I could not deal with the huge pressure, so I called off the engagement and gave him back the diamond ring.

Suddenly we were saying good-bye. A few hours later I was on the plane.

* * *

I had arranged to stop over in Hawaii on my way home as a way to celebrate my twenty-ninth birthday. My breakup with Jon left me feeling lonely and sad—not at all the mood I wanted to be in while visiting a place billed as paradise—but I decided to stick to my plan. I was glad I did.

Hawaii proved to be a good salve for my misery. I loved the

tropical climate, the bright sunlight, and the atmosphere of fun. The local culture was full of color and music, reminding me of the open-hearted spirit I'd found when I taught at Northwest Minorities University.

Everywhere I went, I ran into couples on their honeymoons there, and I realized how much I missed my Jon.

Fortunately I met a lot of friendly people who helped keep my misery at bay. Some of them took me under their wings; they invited me to social events and showed me around the island. Such a beautiful place—I fell in love with Hawaii and almost didn't want to go back Shenzhen. If only Jon were here with me.

On the shuttle from the airport, I met a Hawaiian businessman who cordially invited me to a big Halloween party. Halloween was a new holiday to me; it sounded like a festival that belonged in China's Ghost City. My host told me that everyone would be in costume, so I dressed up as a hula dancer. It was a large, luxurious party and I really enjoyed myself. It was the first time I ever saw salsa dancing, and I couldn't keep my eyes off the dancers. I loved watching the way they moved. So passionate and sensual. They danced with all their heart. The music tingled through my body and made me want to join their dance, even though I had no clue how to do the steps.

While I was still in Hawaii, Jon called, sounding just as loving and affectionate as he was before. Hearing his voice on the phone gave me a thrill.

"I love you, Diana. I still want to marry you. Can't we work something out?"

Finally I told him I would try my best to work things out. "But I need time—at least three or four months to wrap up my work and arrange my life before I can think of leaving China."

He was overjoyed that I had changed my mind. "Honey, take your time. When you're ready I'll come to China and pick you up."

We talked for a long time about how we would create a business of our own and build a life together. I began to dream. Next summer I would have my fairy-tale wedding in America. I would walk down the aisle in my long bridal gown like other Western brides and take Jon's hand, and we'd be side by side forever.

When I arrived back in Shenzhen, my engagement ring was waiting for me. Jon had sent it, wrapped in old clothes to protect it. I was delighted to have it back. I hummed a little tune as I slid it onto my finger.

Yet at the same time a little voice was whispering in my mind. I loved Jon, I was sure of that. But to have him, I was about to give up my work, my culture, my country. Was I doing the right thing?

Diana's Stepping-Stones on the Journey to Success

Recognize that the only way to win in business is to satisfy your customers. The customer's interests always come first. They deserve and demand our best service and quality, and they will reward us with ongoing business relationships that are productive and profitable. Meeting a customer's needs may sometimes require us to give up a short-term advantage, but the compromise will pay dividends in the long run.

Create a positive personal brand based on trust and integrity. Our personal integrity represents our company's integrity; our personal image is the image of the company. The most effective branding is based on an unflinching dedication to the qualities of loyalty, honesty, credibility, fairness, decency, consistency, efficiency, and responsibility. These are the characteristics that earn us trust from those we depend on.

Learn to communicate effectively. Good communication is fundamental to any business relationship. This is all the more true in cross-cultural situations, where the people involved might not only speak different languages, but have different expectations about appropriate ways for business to be conducted. A word-for-word translation can sometimes create confusion rather than reduce it. A great translator can convey the meaning of the words, and also ideas and cultural nuances, helping the parties achieve mutual understanding and agreement.

Understand and respect each other's cultures. It is vitally important that we learn about and accept the differences in culture, customs, and modes of thinking between ourselves and those with whom we do business. International business rewards companies and individuals who are curious, flexible, open-minded, and receptive. These qualities promote a spirit of cooperation, leading to mutual benefit.

Bring together the best of both worlds. The people and companies who will have the greatest success doing business in China are those who can effectively combine and balance the logical, analytical, and strategic thinking of the West with China's intuitive, relationship-based business customs.

Don't be afraid of new people, places, and situations. They are gifts that enhance our lives in many ways—by helping us stretch our wings and discover our strengths, by teaching us valuable lessons, by expanding our knowledge and wisdom, by bringing us joy, by offering us love. Take the risk to embrace and enjoy these gifts.

With colleagues at an international telecom cable
and wire exhibition, Shanghai, November 1996.

希望和痛楚

Eight   Heartbreaks – and Hopes, 1996–1998

The minute I got back to China I jumped into my work, representing Draxler International at the big cable show in Shanghai. It felt good to be back in my own world—meaning not only China but also the fiber optics industry. Instead of being an outsider in a strange land, as I'd been for the past month, here at the show I was on familiar ground, among people who knew and respected me, talking about subjects in which I was an expert. And at last I was eating real Chinese food.

People admired my new ring, but not many of them guessed its significance. One of the few people with whom I shared my good news was my close friend Sally. She and I had first met at the Shangri-La, where she managed the computer department. After I left the hotel, she was my best support through the difficult job hunt that eventually led me to Draxler. She'd gotten married and had a sweet baby girl, and she'd given me the honor of being her child's godmother. I poured out my heart to Sally, all my fears and hopes, my doubts and dreams regarding the huge changes I was planning to make in my life. She was surprised by my sudden news, and while she was very happy for me, I could see she was worried, too, about the unknown future.

The industrial exhibitors and clients I met with at the show greeted me warmly. It was good to have them remind me that I was a capable, talented manager, and that I had their respect as one of the few strong female business executives in Chinese industry.

One reason they respected me was that I'd learned to put the customer first. I had always relied on the fact that Draxler International subscribed to the same philosophy. But with the fresh perspective I'd gained from being away for a month, I could see that things at Draxler were changing.

In late 1996, a challenging situation developed in our industry's marketplace—an extreme shortage of optical fiber. Clients were suffering big losses because of the short supply. To deal with the problem, I came up with a strategy for distributing the available fiber in an equitable way that balanced the needs of our various clients. I believed that even in a negative market cycle, loyalty and consistency would strengthen our long-term relationships with clients and ultimately benefit our business.

To my surprise, my plan was not appreciated. My boss insisted on taking a different approach. Whereas before we had agreed on business strategies, we now began to differ. I fought to keep the company focused on solving the clients' problems and satisfying our clients even in this seller's market.

The company's new approach led to complaints, confusion,

and distrust on the part of our clients. I will never forget what happened when my boss finished a meeting with one of our best clients. Mr. Ming Hua Zhu was the deputy general manager of Wuhan Research Institute, one of the top two optical cable makers in China. Though fairly young, he was intelligent, well educated, and experienced. Like most of his colleagues in the industry, I admired his integrity and his straightforward business style. He was furious with the company's new changes.

"The industry will not forget this," he said as he stood up, ready to storm out of the office. "You will pay the price for this one day, you will see."

I looked from Mr. Zhu to my boss. Did I dare translate this strong statement to him? Perhaps I should soften it a little. After a pause to think it over, I told my boss exactly what Mr. Zhu had said, but, as I did, I felt such shame. I absolutely agreed with Mr. Zhu and I could not believe this was happening.

Afterward we had a heated discussion, but my effort was futile; my boss had his own vision. He seemed determined to steer the company in a direction that was very different from the way I envisioned. I was disappointed that I could neither convince my boss nor satisfy every one of my clients, but my dedication to them and my battles on their behalf made a big impression on them, including some of China's largest cable companies.

Then another incident occurred that dramatically affected my interest in the company and emphasized my differences with my boss. To protect the company's reputation, I recom-

mended the dismissal of a salesman billing us for business trips
he hadn't taken. He was submitting his expense reports with
falsified receipts. When I realized what was happening, I
gathered the facts and called him into the office. Confronted
with the mismatch between the expenses his report claimed
and the ones that could be verified, he apologized. In accordance with company policy, I made him sign a written notice
of the infraction and gave him one more chance.

The next month it happened again. I called the clients and
the airlines to confirm that this man had not attended the
meetings or bought the travel tickets for which he was demanding reimbursement. Then I told him he was fired.

Then I reported immediately to my boss. I was shocked that
he seemed angrier with me than with the man I'd just fired.
"Why didn't you tell me when this happened the first time?"
he demanded to know.

"I wanted to take care of this burden for you. It's part of my
job."

"Send him in here to see me."

My boss met with the thief. When they emerged from the
office, his was red and the man I'd let go was smirking. My
boss had let him off the hook with the promise—which I
knew to be hollow—that he wouldn't cheat like that again.

I was so confused about what happened. I felt betrayed and
abandoned. How could I ever have the respect and cooperation of the employees if my boss didn't back me up? I didn't
understand it at all. Maybe he had other reasons that I did not
know about.

I was so disappointed, the idea of moving to the United

States to seek a better future with Jon became even more appealing.

In February 1997 I submitted my resignation, effective in three months. It wrenched my heart to take this step, because I had loved this company and this job. I learned so much from my boss and from the company—I'm grateful for my boss's trust and faith in me. I was devastated that my boss and I headed in different directions. But I was feeling more and more confident that I was moving in the right direction for myself.

* * *

Even though we were twelve time zones apart, Jon and I talked constantly—about our wedding, about the situation at Draxler, about the lives we would lead when I came to the United States. We were about to begin a new adventure together, and we both were eager to discuss all the details. Jon wanted us to get married as soon as possible. He was running up phone bills of a couple of thousand dollars a month.

While Jon was delighted with our plans, my boss was sorry to see me go. I didn't realize how important I was to the company until he asked me not to tell anyone in the office that I was leaving. He was afraid that the staff wouldn't work hard if they knew that soon I wouldn't be there to direct them. I was flattered by his request; it proved how valuable my management skills and power were to the company.

Draxler's vendors were also sad to learn about my departure. They had benefited from my work, and they enjoyed my cheerful company when they visited China. I had helped them resolve a lot of tough problems, and they'd come to depend on me.

I mentioned to some of them that I was thinking about enrolling in business school in the United States. Whatever work I chose to do there, I thought my career would benefit if I had an MBA, and I craved the intellectual challenge.

An Australian vendor tried to convince me to change my mind about leaving. He wanted me to stay and help build the market in China. He made a very significant comment: "You know, Diana, an MBA doesn't guarantee anything. You certainly don't need one to run a business. You're quite capable right now of running a business of your own."

A business of my own!

How I loved the sound of that. The vendor's words were a remarkable inspiration for me. I'd had idle, what-if notions about starting this business or that, but they were fantasies— I'd never really given serious thought to becoming an entrepreneur.

When I told Jon what the vendor had said, he was very supportive of the idea. "He's right, you could do it. We've always talked about being business partners. We should get serious about it."

We talked in depth about how we could make a business work. We concluded that I would run the enterprise while Jon kept his job, since start-up businesses rarely make money in the first couple of years. As a result of our discussions, Jon took the steps to set up a new venture called WJH Enterprises International. It was a loving gift from him to me.

We were now officially business partners, just as we were soon to become partners in life.

* * *

Late winter through early spring was a frantically busy time. I had to do many things in order to wrap up my life and prepare to leave China, perhaps for good. I closed up my apartment and got rid of my furniture, obtained the visa I needed to go to the United States, and arranged for plane tickets and a hotel for Jon's trip when he would come to Shenzhen to pick me up. Right up to the last minute, I was working hard at Draxler, doing my best to leave the company and my clients in good order.

At Spring Festival time I surprised my family by going to Lanzhou for a visit. It was wonderful to see them all and especially to meet my two-year-old nephew. It felt odd to realize that my sister Yan-Yan, who'd been a wild young girl, was now settled down with a husband and child. But I was very happy for her, and I enjoyed my role as Aunt Jing-Jing to this adorable little boy.

Lanzhou had changed a bit. New buildings had been constructed, and rows of new shops had narrowed the boulevard that led to the university campus where my parents lived. But some things were still the same, thank goodness. My first morning there, I indulged in two large bowls of spicy, delicious beef noodle—the wonderful taste of home.

I visited some of my high school and college friends, and I was surprised to see them looking so different. We were all aware of the contrast between them and me. While once we'd been a lot alike, now my clothes, my interests, and my lifestyle were vastly unlike theirs. Some of them had good jobs, but others did not. I was sharply aware of how far I'd come from Lanzhou, and how I was about to go even farther still, all the way to the opposite side of the world.

* * *

I was sad when my last day at Draxler International arrived. I had given two years of my life to this company, two years of my hardest work and best effort. And I had received so much in return.

Even though we had had our disagreements, Henry Smith had opened the door to international marketing for me. His trust and encouragement had made it possible for me to discover my strengths, cultivate my abilities, and establish my credibility in the business world. He gave me opportunities that were rare for a woman in the male-dominated fiber optics industry. He has played another monumental role in helping me to build a great foundation as a successful international entrepreneur. I'll be grateful for that for the rest of my life. I could now see clearly what my passions were, what would fulfill me, and what I had to offer. Now that Jon and I were starting to think about a business of our own, I was glad I'd had this chance to lay a solid foundation for becoming an entrepreneur.

My work with Draxler's customers, vendors, and staff had helped me crystallize my own business philosophy, the one I continue to operate by. I believe that several elements are fundamental to success in any business: integrity, self-respect, determination, persistence, loyalty, credibility, creativity, a spirit of adventure, and a long-range vision.

To ensure the longevity of a business enterprise, we must give 100 percent excellence to our clients under all circumstances. If we don't satisfy them, the business won't survive. The customer's benefit should always be the highest priority, even higher than an immediate profit. A profit is a momentary gain; it is only when we have the trust and respect of our clients that we can reap sustained financial rewards. If we focus only on profit itself, profit would turn into greed, which I believe would only drive the business to its grave. If we are providing something of true value to them and to society, then profit and success will follow. Some businesspeople may not find these ideas appealing, but this principle has worked in China, the United States, and every place in the Western world where I have conducted business.

A profit is a momentary gain; it is only when we have the trust and respect of our clients that we can reap sustained financial rewards.

I've often noticed that many Chinese companies are driven by profit as their only motive, without regard to the quality or value of the goods and services they offer. Business planning is based on market trends and a desire for quick earnings. If one firm appears successful, dozens of others will follow in its footsteps without considering their own financial or technical capabilities. If a new product becomes popular, other manufacturers jump in to produce copies, not considering whether the market can absorb them. As a result, China has gained a reputation for producing cheap products with poor quality. A common business model is to beat down competitors by charging lower prices and wringing out as much profit as possible. To me, this is a suicidal model, doomed to backfire. If we constantly compromise quality, in the end the customers will be dissatisfied, and they will go elsewhere.

> *When we explore new opportunities, we can expect a loss at first. We must be willing to pay the price of the learning process.*

When we explore new opportunities, we can expect a loss at first. We must be willing to pay the price of the learning process. Temporary sacrifices may be needed as we come to understand the market and the clients, create our business identity, and establish our credibility and integrity. If we take a farsighted view as we do these things, we will make wise, sustainable decisions.

As I shook Henry's hand and said good-bye, I was grateful for everything I'd gained from my time with his company. He wrote me a very good reference letter, appreciating my loyalty, ethics, and professionalism and emphasizing how much he had enjoyed working with me. I thanked him and wished him well. I was ending an extraordinary chapter in my life.

* * *

Jon arrived on a bright day in May, looking handsome in a pink shirt and nice tie. I was so happy to see him. He had a surprise for me—at the end of June we would be moving from New Jersey to California. His company was relocating him. Fine with me. I was glad that his employer was recognizing his merit by giving him an opportunity for advancement. What counted was that he and I would be together.

Since I'd given up my apartment, we stayed in a hotel for my last several nights in China. One evening Sally and her husband gave me a farewell dinner. I was beginning to get cold feet about leaving my own country. There were so many dear friends here, so many memories. But I had confidence in my love for Jon and in my own ability to create miracles for myself.

Before I knew it, my fiancé and I were on a plane heading across the Pacific. I could hardly believe it—I was about to marry an American. I was going to live and work in the United States. As a child in the coal-mining village, as an adolescent girl in Lanzhou, as a student in medical school, I never dreamed that my life would take this amazing turn. That such a thing could happen was completely beyond my imagination.

* * *

Fairy tales all end the same way: "And they lived happily ever after." Despite my dreams and expectations, that's not what happened to Jon and me. When we arrived in Princeton and he opened the door of his townhouse for me, I walked straight into chaos.

We were facing so many changes all at once. We had to pack up his home, plan our wedding, set up our new business, and move across the country. As two people accustomed to living solo, we had to make constant adjustments to get the jigsaw-puzzle pieces of our habits and preferences to fit together. He was preoccupied by the changes in his job situation, while all of the changes I was making at once—new marriage, new career, new business, new country, new culture—had my head spinning.

We began to argue a lot. In retrospect, that shouldn't have been surprising in such a hectic and stressful situation. But it was a huge jolt to me.

Jon was not the warm, thoughtful man I remembered. He seemed like a different person—distant and cool. To my surprise, he'd made no arrangements for our wedding despite all of the talking and planning we'd done. Adding to my disappointment, his enthusiasm for starting our business had waned in the face of his job relocation. He had to spend extra-long hours at the office, leaving me alone at home.

His family, who had embraced me last fall, gave me a far chillier reception now. Apparently they hadn't believed that Jon would really go through with marrying this foreign woman with such a huge cultural difference. Yet here I was, living in Jon's home, and, despite all the changes I saw in him, he was firm in his insistence that we hold our wedding soon.

One evening we had dinner with his brother and sister-in-law. What began as a dinner-table discussion about business ended up as a fight about the risks of starting our own.

"It's such a gamble, Diana," Jon said. "Look at all the businesses that fail." His brother nodded sagely in agreement.

"Look at the ones that succeed," I said. "Every business has risks. If you never take a risk, you never accomplish anything worthwhile. Think about the risk I've taken, giving up everything in my life to be here with you."

"That was your own choice," Jon snapped.

Before long we were yelling. Jon's brother took me aside to say, "Cut him some slack, Diana. You know Jon's not like this usually. He's stressed out right now, what with moving cross-country and your wedding coming up."

What wedding, I wondered. We still hadn't managed to make any specific plans.

Our battles escalated, until one night I ran out of the townhouse in tears. To my embarrassment I encountered one of the neighbors. He asked me what was wrong, and before I knew it I was spilling out my heart to him. He did his best to comfort me.

"If you love each other, you can work together to solve your problems," he reassured me. "Everything will turn out all right."

I nodded as I dried my wet cheeks. We did love each other, I was sure of it. I went back inside, and Jon and I had a long talk.

"Let's go ahead and get married, Diana," he suggested. "Right away. We'll just go to City Hall and do it. If we don't have a big wedding to worry about, everything will be a lot easier. It will cost less, too. That's important right now, with all the changes."

"Okay," I agreed. Perhaps he was right. The idea of a wedding was just creating tension. The wedding was just one day, but the marriage would be forever. It's the same as in business, I thought. Concentrate on the farsighted view, the long-range vision.

* * *

Two days later—on June 20, 1997—Jon and I stood before the mayor at the City Hall and exchanged our marriage vows. I wore a white dress I'd brought from China. Jon's best friend, Richard, and Richard's girlfriend, Lily, were our attendants and witnesses. None of his family attended the ceremony.

Afterward the four of us drove to Philadelphia where we had dinner at a restaurant noted for serving wild game. I had alligator—which was not the meal I had anticipated for my wedding feast.

No church, no bridesmaids, no gown with the long train. No reception with guests dancing and lifting their glasses in toasts to our happiness. No romantic honeymoon.

It was so disappointing to be deprived of the fairy-tale wedding I'd dreamed of. Jon assured me we'd still have a reception later, but in the rush to get ready for our move to California, that plan fell by the wayside. We did visit his mother, who gave us hearty congratulations.

Soon afterward we arrived in the Golden State and settled into our first shared home—a tiny suite in a Marriott hotel in Sunnyvale, a San Jose suburb in the heart of Silicon Valley. From the very first day I was miserable. I was not used to the food, the time zone—the entire environment was uncomfortable. Everything I was familiar with in China was so far away.

Jon put in long hours at work every day, stranding me at the hotel. I didn't know how to get around this strange place. I couldn't drive, and taxis were very expensive compared to those in China, so I had no way to go anywhere. I couldn't get out to meet people or look for a job, and the expense of using the hotel phone made it hard to begin working on our plans for WJH Enterprises International. I was trapped in those little rooms with nothing to do except to let my eyes glaze in front of the TV, a pastime I hated.

My loneliness was made unbearable by the fact that Jon was unavailable to me—financially, emotionally, physically, and mentally. He had become a stranger, cold and distant, even when he was lying next to me. We couldn't talk to each other without arguing incessantly over trivial things, so we said less and less. Sometimes we didn't speak for days.

I did not know what to do. I had no acquaintances in California to talk to, and I didn't dare tell my friends or family in China about my plight. The disgrace would be too great. I was still very Chinese, and in our culture saving face is extremely important. If anyone in China knew the truth, I was certain they would laugh at me or look down on me. That would bring shame to my parents as well as to me, and it would worry my mother and father tremendously since they were so far away.

Finally in my despair I thought of Jon's family. They were now my family too; surely they would help me resolve the problem. In China family members helped each other out when problems arose, and I assumed this would also be true in the United States. Having no one else to turn to, I phoned Jon's brother and mother. It turned out neither of them could help me out. They told Jon about my calls and he threw their opinions in my face. "They think it is inappropriate to tell our problems to them and you are overly sensitive. And you know what? I think they're right."

We stayed for a month in that hotel, and in that time my beautiful dream of marriage was destroyed.

* * *

In midsummer we moved to a house Jon had bought in Santa Cruz, a small city about seventy miles south of San Francisco. Santa Cruz is famous for its beach and its boardwalk filled with amusement park rides, but its summer weather tends to be cool and foggy. I longed for the tropical warmth of Shenzhen; I missed my homeland terribly.

Our new home was a plain, three-story, wood-frame structure in an older neighborhood. The main living areas were in the middle, with two bedrooms on the top floor and a third one on the first level, tucked behind the garage. This dark little room became my office.

Now that we had settled into a home of our own, I grew hopeful. We had made it through the months of stress and upheaval; surely our relationship would get better.

I did my best to be a good wife. I cooked for Jon every day, waited for him to come home, and tried to talk to him like we used to talk on the phone, those eager and affectionate conversations when we shared our ideas and feelings and the news about our day. Jon seemed not to want any of that. He rose at four each morning to go to work. When he returned home twelve hours later, he dragged himself in looking tired and showing no enthusiasm at all for seeing me. Sometimes he barely touched the food I'd prepared and avoided talking to me. By six o'clock he disappeared to take a shower and go to bed, leaving me to eat by myself and spend the evening with only the TV for company.

What kind of marriage was this? I'd given up everything that defined my existence in China—home, career, access to my friends and family—because I wanted to share my life with this man. Apparently this was his concept of sharing life together with me. It was painful and intolerable to have such a marriage.

I had also given up my financial security. Though I'd made a good salary in China, my savings were relatively small in U.S. terms, the funds that were available to me were very limited, and they were earmarked for investment in our new business. Now I was earning nothing, which meant I was totally dependent on Jon, and to my surprise the man who had thought nothing of a few thousand-dollar phone bills had turned out to be a real penny-pincher, at least when it came to spending money on our marriage. He gave me a small monthly allowance to cover my personal and household expenses, but it did not stretch far. If I decided to leave, I had no means to do so.

One day I tried to withdraw my allowance from the bank. Jon was supposed to have made the deposit into my account, but the money wasn't there. That night I confronted him about it, but he was unwilling to listen.

"I don't want to talk about this now, Diana. I need to get to sleep."

I stood my ground. "No. It's time we talked. You know this marriage isn't working. There are a lot of issues we need to discuss if we're going to make things better."

"I said not now." He turned his back and started to walk away.

I grabbed at his sleeve. "Yes, now! Is there ever a good time to have a discussion with you? How many times have you avoided talking to me? We have to talk now. It's important." At that point I was yelling.

He whirled around to face me again, his face red with fury. "You're out of control. Leave me alone or I'll call the police."

"You just go right ahead." I thought he was bluffing, and I was shocked when he picked up the phone and punched in the number.

Soon two policemen were knocking at the door. When they realized that we'd done nothing more to each other than raise our voices—no blows had been struck, no one was bruised or bleeding—they were angry with Jon for calling them.

"This is not a police matter, sir," one of them said.

"You should have called a therapist for your problem," the other said. "You're wasting police time and resources."

"Right," said the first. "You two don't need us. You need a marriage counselor."

Tears were pouring from my eyes. I was speechless with shock and humiliation. The policemen treated me with sympathy and gave me a card for a women's crisis center, where I could get help.

While the policemen talked to me, Jon walked straight up to the bedroom and disappeared. He didn't even wait until the police left our home.

I sat alone in the living room in the dark and cried for a long time after they departed.

* * *

Jon had torn my heart apart. Our marriage had turned into a nightmare. I realized I needed to do something to reclaim my life.

The business world was where I'd found my happiness in the past, but I knew by now that WJH Enterprises International wasn't going to work. Jon had lost interest, and it had become clear to me that we would never make effective partners. He was too frightened by the risk and too tightfisted to invest the necessary money.

I considered various options for my survival in this poor situation. One possibility was to study for a master's degree in business administration. Getting an MBA at an American university was almost standard procedure for Chinese immigrants. But I kept hearing the Australian vendor's voice in my head: "An MBA doesn't guarantee anything. You're capable right now of running a business of your own."

I decided to devote myself to creating a new company. For now I would borrow the WJH name, but this new enterprise would be all mine, not a partnership. I started to research what type of business would be right for me. I had established some contacts during my first trip to the United States, and through them I investigated some entrepreneurial opportunities, like a Hawaiian water company; however, those possibilities failed to spark my interest. I considered starting out by finding a local job to support myself, but, after a few interviews for positions I found in the newspaper, I was discouraged. None of the jobs appealed to me, and taking one would leave me no time for building my own business. I knew in my heart that I was not ready to give up that dream.

> *An MBA doesn't guarantee anything. You're capable right now of running a business of your own.*

Finally I decided my best bet for success could be stated in two words: optical fibers. The industry still sparked my passion and I knew it well. I had a solid reputation and excellent relationships with vendors and clients. After a mental pep talk to build up my confidence, I made a very bold move. I contacted the international headquarters of Corning in New York state.

It turned out to be one of my best-ever choices.

At that time, Corning was probably the top provider of optical fiber worldwide. Their marketing and distribution system had been well established in China for more than a decade. I knew that to squeeze into such a crowded circle and be accepted would be no easy task. But I was sure that I had something of unique value to offer Corning, based on my capability, my experience, and my reputation in the industry. I'm good at competition, and I love a challenge. It would never hurt for Corning to have someone like me to fight for them. My work with Draxler International had made me familiar with the company and its products, and it had provided me with a good reference to use as my introduction. Why not give it a try?

For the first time since arriving in the United States I felt hopeful, and I jumped to action. Checking the Corning organizational chart, I found out whom I should talk to: the international sales manager and manager of the Hong Kong office.

When I contacted them, I was asked to prepare a very specific market analysis as a way of demonstrating my knowledge and abilities.

Working from my office—the little dark bedroom behind the garage—I began phoning the cable companies that formed the market for optical fiber in China, asking them for information. My branch office was Kinko's. Jon had promised me a computer but had never made good on his word, so I rented one by the hour to handle my paperwork and draft the report. Jon complained about the phone bills and the Kinko's charges I was running up.

"Fine," I said. "If you don't like spending money this way, could you get me a computer—the gift you promised me?"

When I finished the ten-page report, I sent it in and held my breath waiting for a response. I knew it contained good, solid, valuable information, and I hoped it would substantiate to Corning that having me work with them could bring many benefits.

Sure enough, the report opened the door for me. I was invited to meet the two Corning executives in person. That was great news, made even better by the meeting's location—Shanghai.

Hooray—an excuse to visit China!

* * *

When I got off the plane in Shenzhen, I burst into tears. It was such a pleasure, such a relief, to see the familiar scenery and the faces of people who looked like me. I loved hearing the music of voices chattering in my own native language and smelling the delicious fragrance of the food. Even the noisy, dirty buses and the pushing and shoving of the crowds no longer bothered me. It was so good to be home. I hadn't expected to miss my country so much. I'd been away for only four months, but it felt like forever.

Sally had invited me to stay with her, and in the comfort of her apartment I told my dear friend everything—all of my dashed hopes for my marriage and all of my budding dreams for my new business. It was so good to be able to talk to someone, to be among people I knew and loved and who loved me in return. I felt as though I could breathe again.

I was grateful to her for putting me up, since I couldn't afford to stay at a hotel. I'd used most of my minimal pre-marriage savings on my plane ticket, and the rest would go to visits with prospective clients. My plan was to contact the cable companies and ask them if they would work with me if I were to represent Corning. That would strengthen my hand when I met with the Corning executives. The response I got was very encouraging.

I shared a bed with my goddaughter and food with the whole family. One weekend, I returned hungry from several days of visiting clients; I'd eaten very little on the trip. Sally's husband made chive pancakes. They were so delicious I ate seven of them, and everyone joked that I was Miss Piggy and had set the all-time consumption record.

During the meeting in Shanghai, I did my best to demonstrate to Corning that I was enthusiastic, ambitious, and capable. My strategy in selling myself to them was the same one I use for marketing products to clients: Be passionate about what you are doing and instill that enthusiasm and confidence in your customer. Be clear about your goal and vision. Emphasize the value you will add and the difference you will make. Once you get other people excited about your idea, then you have done your job.

I presented the operating plan I had conceived for increasing Corning's market in China. "I already have orders for you," I told them. "You have to supply me."

> *Be passionate about what you are doing and instill that enthusiasm and confidence in your customer.*

I knew in my gut that my passionate, determined attitude and my confident plan would convince them. They had heard positive reports about my reputation in the marketplace, which also persuaded them to work with me. They gave me a small segment of the market to work with so I could show them what I could do.

I was so glad I took the chance and tried. Otherwise I would have never gained such an opportunity. This very fruitful meeting officially opened another important era in my life.

* * *

By the fall of 1997, the shortage of optical fiber was well over and supplies were flooding the market. Competition was heated, and many people predicted that the days of having a successful business as an optical fiber representative were over. I'd be competing not only with the reps for other manufacturers but also with the rest of Corning's well-established team, including my former boss, who was still the agent for the Corning-BICC joint venture.

Jumping in as a newcomer would not be easy, especially because I was young and female, had very limited capital with which to finance my business, and couldn't afford to hire a capable staff. The marketplace would see these as negatives, but they never hindered my determination to succeed. I believed that I had a great deal to offer this crowded industry.

I convinced a good friend, whom I'd met through my social circle in Shenzhen, to work with me as a business partner. He was new to the fiber optics industry, but he was an expert at the complicated Chinese import-export regulations. He served as my trading house, handling letters of credit and customs clearing. Having him on my team gave me a real advantage.

All through the fall I remained in China, struggling to gain a toehold in the market. I was eager to establish credibility with Corning and keep the commitments I was making to clients. Operating internationally posed challenges, not the least of which was the irregular hours it required me to keep. One time when I called Corning headquarters it was three in the morning for me, though it was midafternoon in New York. I was trying to reach the international sales director for help resolving a problem. Instead, to my surprise, someone put me through to John Edward. At the time he was the director of international operations—one of Corning's most influential senior executives. I had heard his name mentioned many times at Draxler and in the fiber industry in China, but I'd never expected to be talking to him directly. Well, if anyone could help solve my problem, he could.

A clear, relaxed male voice came over the phone. "Young lady, what are you doing up in the middle of the night? It's three o'clock in the morning where you are!"

As calmly as I could, I said, "I'm begging you to ship the goods for my order. It's only three thousand kilometers of fiber. If I'm late in delivering, I have to pay a big penalty. It's extremely important for me to keep my credibility with my clients and protect Corning's reputation."

He said, "Don't worry, young lady. Let's talk at the IWCS show." He was referring to the International Wire and Cable Symposium. Held each year in a different U.S. city, it is one of the largest trade shows in the optical cable and fiber industry, drawing hundreds of attendees from around the world. This year it was to be in Philadelphia, Pennsylvania.

So in late November I attended the IWCS show for the first time. Though I knew some of the attendees would be casually attired, I dressed in a stylish black business suit that looked both professional and feminine. I didn't forget to put on my signature black hat. Getting ready in my hotel room, I looked at the mirror and gave myself a pep talk, repeating the words over and over: "I am an entrepreneur now. I'm ready for this new challenge."

Then I joined the throng in the exhibit hall. In the crowd were top executives of prominent wire and cable companies from all over the world, most of them male, most of them quite a bit older than I was. Strolling among them, I mustered my confidence and made my posture as tall and straight as I could.

I drew quite a few inquisitive glances. When I handed some-one my business card, the title under my name—vice presi-dent of WJH Enterprises International—helped them, and me, realize that I was truly part of the group.

While I was searching for the Corning exhibit, where I hoped to find John Edward, I browsed through the dozens of booths on the exhibition floor. The industry was even bigger than I had realized. Having had so few opportunities for real conversation in recent months, it was exciting to chat about business with the exhibitors, and I was pleased to find that I had no problem communicating with them. This show was different from ones I'd attended in China. People were more professional, and also more engaging, friendly, and sincere. Most of the people I talked to expressed interest in marketing their products in China—a confirmation that this industry held plenty of opportunity for me.

As I passed one of the booths, I saw that the exhibitor was putting on a magic show to draw the attention of the atten-dees, and I wandered over to watch. The magician was a young man named Kevin. Something about my stylish ap-pearance caught his eye, and he asked me to join the show. A small crowd was gathered around, and I blushed a little at be-ing made the center of attention. At first I was reluctant, but Kevin's lovely compliments made it difficult to refuse, so I got up on the stage.

While he bantered with the audience, I kept a close eye on him, curious about how he did his tricks. He displayed his empty hands to the crowd, then all of a sudden he pulled an object from my chest. Oh, my God, it was a sexy green bra!

"That's not mine!" I yelped. I was so embarrassed. I couldn't figure out how he'd pulled off the stunt, but I was anxious to have the spectators know that I was not flinging my lingerie around in public.

Everyone laughed, and I realized that it was a practical joke that Kevin and his employers had played to tease me and entertain the crowd. In the end I found it funny too, so I went along, pretending I was mad and joking back to him, "Kevin, you better watch out. Next time you'll beg me for mercy!"

"Oh, Diana, I can't wait for that moment. It will be my pleasure to entertain such an attractive lady as you." Kevin winked at me. What could I say to such a lovely joker? I admire the sense of humor that Americans have; they are so creative and relaxed. By now I felt at ease, and I enjoyed the little drama that put me in the spotlight.

When I finally reached Corning's booth, I didn't see John Edward. I introduced myself to the red-haired man who was staffing the booth. When I asked for John Edward, he said, "John isn't here. What can I do for you?"

"I was supposed to meet him here. We arranged to talk about Corning's supplying fiber to my clients. Could you tell me where to find him?"

The red-haired man's answer surprised me. "John is retiring. But if you insist, you can probably find him at the lobby coffee lounge."

I had no idea whether he was telling me the truth, but John Edward had invited me to speak to him about supporting my order, so I continued to search for him.

When I finally found him, I was very impressed. Here was a legend in the industry, striding across the lobby of the Philadelphia Marriott to greet a relative newcomer. He looked relaxed and confident, and much too young to be retiring; now I was even more puzzled by the redhead's comment. He recognized me before I could approach him and introduce myself.

"You must be the young lady who called me at three o'clock in the morning from China," John Edward said. His voice was warm, and his eyes sparkled with joy. His unruffled manner and humorous charm put me at ease right away. Over time I would come to know him quite well. He was the kind of strategic thinker and visionary entrepreneur I really respected, and he was a role model for the kind of entrepreneur I wanted to be one day.

At this first encounter I made my case for my place in the industry and the importance of meeting my old clients' needs, using every bit of my passion and persuasive skills. He laughed and said to me, "I've never seen anyone like you. It's only three thousand kilometers of fiber, yet you fight to get it for your clients as if it were a life-or-death matter."

"I know it's a very small amount," I told him. "But I always treat my clients' demands like a life-or-death matter. That way, I will have a long-lived and prosperous business."

"Well, young lady, keep it up. We need a lot more of that kind of attitude."

He agreed to help me out by shipping the goods right away. I'll always remember the way he endorsed my principles with his inspiring and encouraging words.

A man overheard our conversation. Although he was an American, he was the general manager—equivalent to the chief executive officer—of the largest government-supported Chinese joint venture, called Yangtze Optical Fiber and Ca-

ble Co. Ltd., or YOFC. As John Edward and I were wrapping things up, this CEO of YOFC joined us and introduced
himself. He told me that he was impressed by how persistently and passionately I pursued
my business on behalf of Corning
and my clients. Then to my surprise he said, "YOFC could use
someone like you to represent us."

*I always treat my
clients' demands like a
life-or-death matter.*

He extolled the virtues of his
product, a single-mode fiber, and John Edward backed up his
claims. YOFC's fiber was new to me, and I was astonished
that it was coming from a Chinese manufacturer. Optical fiber
in China had always been supplied by foreign vendors. I could
not imagine that a new domestic supplier with no brand
recognition and no reputation in the marketplace could be
good enough to get into the game when the competition was
so heated. Besides, I was already representing Corning. So I
said no to the CEO's proposal.

* * *

In early December I returned to Santa Cruz. I wanted to spend
the Christmas holiday season with Jon. I had been looking
forward to an American-style celebration—sleigh bells and
Santa Claus, decorating the tree and exchanging gifts. I was
hoping that the spirit of festivity, plus the fresh perspective
we'd both gained from three months apart, would bring us
closer again and let us recommit to our marriage.

Unfortunately, that was not to be. Jon insisted that doing

anything to celebrate Christmas was too much bother. We quickly fell back into a pattern of bitter arguments followed by long periods of deep silence. Obviously what I was looking for in our relationship was not what my husband wanted. We were far more different from each other than either of us had thought, and it was getting more and more difficult to be together.

Clearly our personal partnership wasn't working out, and neither was our business arrangement. I thought about divorce. If I were divorced, I would be much more vulnerable to sexual harassment, especially in China, where being a divorced female entrepreneur would not convey a very acceptable image. My status as a married woman gave me some protection in the commercial world. From the picture I presented to outsiders, they assumed my marriage was a happy and loving relationship.

Even more important, deep down I still could not believe this was the end of my marriage. Though the reality had turned out so different from my romantic dreams, I held a thread of hope that our relationship would grow better over time. I'd seen that pattern in many Chinese couples—they fought a lot but nevertheless stuck together for a long time. Eventually they would get used to each other and their affection would grow. That was how a harmonious marriage formed. How naive I was in my thinking about marriage.

But one thing was clear—it was definitely time to sever the final pretense of having a business partnership with Jon. In early 1998 I decided to establish a new company totally on my own in the United States.

I called my new business Allied Telecom International,

Inc., or ATI. Translated into Chinese, the word *allied* would make my little company sound very large.

Now I was truly an independent entrepreneur. My success was 100 percent up to me.

* * *

During the winter I entered into serious negotiations with Corning to finalize our business relationship. I felt I was dealing from a position of strength. I had established solid connections with clients, who liked working with me because they knew that I would deal with them honestly and fight to get them what they needed. As a result I was building a strong record in terms of sales numbers and client satisfaction.

But Corning wasn't my only option.

In March I attended the Optical Fiber Communication (OFC) conference in San Diego. Now that I was representing my own company, I could have printed my business card to say I was president of ATI, but I decided to continue listing my title as vice president of WJH Enterprises International. As was the case in Philadelphia, this was a much older, male-dominated crowd, and the lesser title would help ease my way, enabling me to avoid misunderstandings and gain acceptance.

While I was there I was approached by several companies—Sumitomo, Samsung, Alcatel, and some others—who wanted me to distribute their products in China. It was a crucial time for me. Should I continue to work with Corning or explore these other opportunities? To decide, I researched the companies and held discussions with key people. I began to see clearly how different they were from one another in the way they did business.

Corning had a very effective worldwide operation, and of all the companies I investigated they had the best plan for penetrating the market in China. They knew how to adjust to the local culture and use local experts to expand their market and influence. They also were very aware of how political power and influence worked in China, at the highest level of government as well as in the industry. Corning was creative and forward-thinking. Their products were always on the cutting edge of technology, and they invested heavily in marketing and branding. Working with Corning taught me many constructive business strategies and skills.

Samsung was one of the most aggressive and flexible new companies making optical fiber. Their determination was strong; their efficiency was high; and they were not averse to risk. They understood the concept of marketing and branding. But they already had one representative in China, which meant I would share the market. Moreover, I was not sure about the maturity and quality of their products at the time, since they were new in the industry.

In talking with a French company, I became frustrated with the process. Dealing with them became complicated because they were a little slow to make decisions. On top of that, they were negotiating to establish a large-scale joint venture; this meant that their marketing strategies and relationships would be likely to change in the near future. For my purposes, they did not seem like a good long-term bet.

Sumitomo, like other great Japanese brands, knew precisely what they wanted to achieve in their markets and what they wanted from a marketing agent. Yet they were flexible enough to accept constructive advice about marketing strategies. Their products were strong and reliable, and the company was efficient, well organized, and good with following through. A real advantage was that Sumitomo fully understood the Chinese business culture, and they treated their clients with courtesy and respect. They would be open-minded enough to satisfy my clients, even if some of the proposals presented were a little odd. Something else that appealed to me greatly was the high value they placed on integrity and credibility.

I was flattered that Sumitomo was courting me. I knew that they were extremely selective when it came to business partners. It was important for them to know whether the potential partner could ensure that they would reach the market they wanted. It would take time to earn their trust, but, once they trusted you, they would be loyal partners. Sumitomo was my favorite company, but there was one serious drawback to working with them: their market in China had already been developed by someone else for quite a while. I was concerned that they could provide me with only a limited market.

All this time, YOFC was urging me to work with them. I accepted their invitation to visit their headquarters in Wuhan, where I received a grand welcome. Though I'd been skeptical at first, I was becoming intrigued by the opportunity that YOFC presented. I liked the CEO and his team. The fact that the CEO was an American was a plus; I sensed that YOFC's management would incorporate the best of Western and Chinese business styles.

YOFC was a joint venture between the Chinese government's Ministry of Posts and Telecommunications and the Dutch corporation called Draka Holding N.V. It was the biggest cable company in China, and one of the biggest in the world. Thus it was one of the country's largest consumers of optical fiber. By manufacturing and distributing its own fiber line, YOFC would be altering many relationships in the Chinese market. It would reduce its need to buy products from outside vendors, and it would turn the competing cable companies into customers for the new product. At the moment, though, the fiber line had no sales, nor did YOFC have the marketing capacity to introduce it effectively. I was impressed with the company's determination and enthusiasm, and the challenge of opening the market to a product with zero presence had great appeal to me.

After analyzing the market and weighing the pros and cons, I narrowed the new choices down to two suppliers, Sumitomo and YOFC, though I didn't cut off my connection with the other companies, as I knew that somewhere down the road opportunities might arise for us to work together. I entered into serious discussions with Sumitomo, which went very well, while YOFC kept up a vigorous pursuit.

I was looking for a long-term business relationship with a solid company. If I could open the market for YOFC and help them to build and sustain a solid brand, they might have even greater potential for enduring success than either Sumitomo or Corning. Before making a final decision, though, I needed to see how the industry would respond to YOFC's new domestically produced optical fiber.

* * *

In May I went with a business associate to visit an ambitious young cable company called Cheng Du Huiyuan. It had been expanding aggressively, growing from a medium-size firm to take a place among the top ten cable companies in China. I learned that its new logistics manager—the key decision maker—would be at a conference in Nanjing that we were also attending. If I could see him there, it would be an ideal opportunity to present the case for the domestic fiber to an important prospective client. His response would be an excellent gauge of the market potential of YOFC's product.

When I approached the logistics manager at the conference to ask for an appointment, he brushed me off.

"I don't have time. I'm a very busy man."

"I understand," I said. "But if you could favor me with just ten minutes of your time."

"Not now. I have to go and rest. I'll tell you what, call me at my hotel room in three hours. Perhaps I will have time then."

I took a seat in the hotel lobby and settled in to wait.

My business associate wanted to leave. "We are wasting our time, Diana."

"We have to stay," I insisted. "This man and his company could be important to us. We need to introduce ourselves and get his opinion."

Three hours later, I called at the exact time specified, and our prospect told us we could come up to his room. He couldn't believe we had waited for such a long time and had followed his instructions precisely. He paid close attention as we briefed him about YOFC's fiber, which was a new product to him. He asked good questions and gave us a logical and practical assessment.

Obviously our ten-minute presentation worked. The customer invited me to visit his company for further discussions. I was encouraged by the sliver of hope he offered.

My test result on Cheng Du Huiyuan added to YOFC's promise to give me an open territory and their strong desire for ATI to help them break into the market, convinced me to sign on with YOFC rather than Sumitomo. It was a big gamble, but I was confident that I could accomplish this mission.

I began negotiating an agreement with YOFC to be its exclusive representative for this product in China. The major members of the executive team were involved in the discussions, including the CEO and Mr. Yan, the assistant sales manager. We went back and forth on both sides for several weeks as we hammered out the details.

On July 24, 1998, the CEO of YOFC signed the document. I now had been officially appointed by YOFC as its exclusive representative for its single-mode fiber in the People's Republic of China for the next three years. An appendix to the agreement specifically identified eleven major customers that I should target, but in fact the terms of the agreement placed every cable company within my exclusive territory.

As soon as I had the signed document in hand, I started promoting YOFC's single-mode fiber to the Chinese cable companies, and I assisted YOFC in creating a plan for penetrating the market.

Allied Telecom International—ATI, my very own firm— was up and running.

* * *

My colleagues in the industry were astounded to learn that I'd signed on with YOFC. Most of them gave YOFC's optical fiber venture little credence and little chance for success. It had several strikes against it. Strike one, YOFC's single-mode fiber was an unknown product. Strike two, YOFC's fiber was made in China, and people assumed that being domestically produced, it must be inferior to fiber from foreign sources. Strike three, as a major cable manufacturer YOFC would be in the awkward position of asking its own competitors to become its customers, a role that they were almost certain to resist. There was even a strike four: it was a buyer's market, flooded with foreign-produced fiber and crowded with rival suppliers who were fighting fiercely for market share. Most of them had the advantage of solid reputations and long histories with clients. Little room was left for YOFC. Industry experts predicted that it would take a miracle for YOFC to survive in the fiber business. My task—and it would not be an easy one—was to dispel the myths and establish a place in the market for YOFC. The situation should have been discouraging, but I had faith that with my capabilities and strategies, I could make it happen.

In August, at my suggestion, YOFC invited the top executives of Cheng Du Huiyuan to visit the YOFC headquarters. The chief executive officer, the chief financial officer, and the deputy general manager were among the warmly welcomed guests. The two companies engaged in long discussions to hammer out the terms and conditions for a major business deal.

When the negotiations had been concluded, we held a big dinner to celebrate the contract that would be signed the next day. I was one of only two women at the dinner. Everyone insisted that I share in the toasts to the success of the promising new business relationship. Poor me. I didn't want to drink any liquor at all because I feared the consequences of my allergy to alcohol. Yet to refuse to join in would be rude and offensive; it might even jeopardize the deal. So I raised my cup along with everyone else.

"To the success of Cheng Du Huiyuan! To the success of YOFC!"

I drank down the contents of my cup.

There was another toast, and another, and before long I had drunk fifteen more small cups of the Chinese hard liquor. I had requested to have a bowl of vinegar at my place, and every time I drained a cup of the liquor, I drank a few sips of the vinegar to help me throw up. Then I ran to the restroom and stuck my fingers down my throat. I hoped these techniques would keep the alcohol from poisoning my system. But the revelries finally proved to be more than my body could handle. Everyone watched as my face turned a deep purple color and then suddenly went white. My head was spinning, and I couldn't speak except in mumbles. I was too weak to move and in so much pain. The dinner guests finally realized that I really could not drink, so they stopped including me in their toasts.

The next day, I had the worst hangover of my life.

My suffering was well worthwhile, though, because the very next day the two companies signed a sales contract. YOFC would supply Cheng Du Huiyuan with one hundred thousand kilometers of fiber. I was wild with joy. In less than one month I had taken an unknown brand with no market share and no sales revenue and had established a foothold for it in a highly competitive market. I hadn't expected that success would come so soon, and with such a large order. Word of this fast, stealthy breakthrough spread quickly, and the whole industry in China was shocked. The theory that domestic fiber had no hope had completely been dispelled by the strong step I took into this market.

This victory was very sweet. After all the struggles and heartaches I'd endured in the past fifteen months, it gave me hope that I could have a bright life again.

Diana's Stepping-Stones
on the Journey to Success

When you are in despair, take action. When we feel down because life hasn't treated us well, taking action is the best antidote. Even in the worst circumstances, opportunities are present. Our best course is to find and seize those opportunities and turn them to our advantage.

Be farsighted. We make the wisest decisions when we have a long-range, forward-thinking vision and plan to guide us.

Keeping our plan in focus lets us achieve more in our business and personal lives. If we are entrepreneurs, the plan will help ensure greater longevity for our ventures.

Recognize your fears. Our fears can be powerful, and they try all sorts of tricks to derail our dreams. They present themselves in many disguises: ego, greed, jealousy, selfishness, and a need to control are just a few of them. Recognizing them for what they are is a first step toward diminishing their force and influence.

If you want to change your life, know that your best and only resource is yourself. We all sometimes wish that our fortunes would spontaneously change for the better. But the only way to guarantee a positive change is to take steps to make it happen. When we determine what we really want and dedicate ourselves to that goal, our passion and creativity will give us the power to achieve it.

With staff in the conference room of the Shenzhen representative
office of her firm, Allied Telecom International, Inc.

成功和背叛

Nine   Travels, Triumphs, and Treachery,
        1998–2002

I looked around the offices on the sixteenth floor of the New World Center in Shenzhen and felt a profound satisfaction. This thousand-square-foot space overlooking the ocean was the new Chinese representative office of ATI, ready for its grand opening in fall 1998. These premises were far more elegant than the company headquarters—the room behind the garage in Jon's house in Santa Cruz.

With the help of my newly hired assistant, whom I will call Annie, I had designed the office and coordinated the build-out of what had been an empty space with shear walls. Now its several rooms—a reception area, a conference room, an open-plan work area, and a nice office for me—had an ocean-blue carpet underfoot and modern, clean-lined furniture. I indulged in a little bit of smug pleasure that my new center of operations was even nicer than Draxler International's facility.

Annie was one of the staff I brought on board. It had been a challenge to find the right people, and I knew I'd experience some turnover, but some of my employees were proving to be excellent choices. Annie was one, and another person I will call Brenda. Even though she had zero experience in sales and marketing, Brenda was studying hard to make herself familiar with the technology and the industry. I sent her and my other hires to be trained at YOFC.

I had confidence that Brenda could do the job. She was intelligent and eager, one of hungriest and most ambitious candidates I interviewed. From the first moment, her strong desire to learn and her clear focus on achieving her goals impressed me. I saw the image of myself in her.

As the head of the company, I wanted to create an atmosphere of professionalism, cooperation, and respect based on the Western management model. In my experience, Western companies are more people-oriented than Chinese firms. The manager's role is to inspire, encourage, and trust the employees. Teamwork is valued, and the boss provides the resources the workers need to develop their capabilities and do outstanding work. As a result, the company operates with a high level of integrity, and everyone feels a sense of pride and ownership in its accomplishments.

The Chinese model, on the other hand, is one that gives great power to the executives and little esteem to the workers. The bosses believe that their positions of authority entitle them to exert control over their subordinates and micromanage the work. As a result, the employees become passive and resentful. Afraid to deviate from the rules, they stifle their intelligence and creativity. Not only is this approach inefficient, it promotes unethical behavior, and it robs the company of the valuable contributions the employees could make.

Yes, for me, the Western system was definitely the way to go.

At Christmastime Jon came over to visit me in China. He seemed pleased for me as I showed off the new representative office, introduced the staff, and described our accomplishments. When we went out together, we performed the charade of being a happily married couple. I still cared for Jon a lot, and I continued to harbor hopes that sometime we would trade the pretense of a loving relationship for the real thing.

* * *

The industry was paying close attention to YOFC's marketing and sales strategies. The new fiber was making a strong impact in the market as a result of my efforts. I was proud of the role I'd played in this accomplishment, because YOFC would have had no clue about how to penetrate the market on their own.

The first hints of trouble surfaced slowly.

In less than one month from signing the contract with YOFC, I started hearing from Chinese clients that YOFC was bringing in another agent and splitting up the clients in my exclusive territory. Such an action, if true, was totally contrary to our agreement. Worse, I heard the other agent was quoting lower prices to the customers than I was authorized to give, and in the process was undermining my reputation. I was horrified.

I raised a strong objection to YOFC and demanded a meeting to resolve the issue. After putting me off a few times,

YOFC executives finally invited me to their offices in Wuhan. But instead of discussing the issues at hand, they brought in a third party—the very agent who was working behind my back. They wanted to talk with me about the possibility of sharing clients with him under a redrafted agreement.

I could not believe it. It was an outrageous proposal, insulting to my integrity, my professionalism, and my intelligence. Naturally I refused.

Then I began having trouble collecting the fees ATI had earned. It appeared to me that YOFC would make any excuse to delay making the payments. Months would pass before we received what was owed us.

As 1998 turned into 1999, from my perspective the problems grew. I believed that YOFC, without ATI's knowledge or consent, had started using another representative to sell its fiber to one of the exclusive clients listed in our agreement. Under the terms of our agreement as I understood it, ATI was entitled to payment whenever this client made a purchase. So as soon as we found out about this, we put in a claim for our fees. We got no response.

Then it appeared the company began to arbitrarily reject the clients' orders despite having contractual commitments to fill them. Instead, I now believe, they diverted their supplies to customers in the United States and other Western countries where they'd earn a higher profit. This was a shock to me. The Chinese clients were the customers who had helped YOFC get into the market in the first place.

I thought this was suicidal conduct for YOFC. I'd always believed that if you plant a seed of hatred, you will be rewarded with hatred. When you do something wrong to your clients, they will remember that single problem far longer than they will one hundred great things you might do. Clients give you only one chance to hurt them; after that, they'll take their business elsewhere. So the best approach for all concerned is to treat customers right at all times. This is a fundamental principle that I've always applied in my business and fostered in my staff and my business associates. And I've benefited every time.

If you plant a seed of hatred, you will be rewarded with hatred.

It seemed to me that YOFC conducted business under a different set of rules. If their behavior was any indicator, I had to believe that the company's values were greed, arrogance, and shortsightedness. They seemed to exhibit a total lack of ethics in their dealings with the clients and me, and they were making life miserable for my employees, who chafed under YOFC's ill treatment of them. I had to keep encouraging them to rise above it and continue to work at their highest professional level.

Having signed an agreement with YOFC, I considered it vitally important to honor it. I had made a three-year commitment, and I intended to give YOFC no reason to claim I had broken it in any way. If I walked away, how could I protect my reputation in the industry? No one would hire me or do business with my company ever again.

So ATI continued to promote YOFC's products and ensure that clients' needs were met. We worked hard to give everyone exemplary service. We spent large amounts of time and money cleaning up the confusion and resentment instilled by YOFC's business behavior—a task made more difficult by the fact that YOFC's conduct was undermining my credibility.

I had never imagined that such a big company would operate in this fashion. I had turned down offers from Corning, Sumitomo, and other vendors because I believed YOFC's promises about its ethical standards and far-reaching vision. I was working hard to help the company achieve a bright future, and I'd expected that ATI would receive reciprocal support from it. Instead I was ensnared in a mess. At one point I overheard a YOFC executive make a comment that described the situation with great insight: "This company is like a big, red apple. It looks shiny and delicious, but inside it's full of worms."

ATI sent numerous letters to YOFC, requesting that the company fulfill its obligations and restore our credibility with the Chinese customers. It was a useless effort. The letters went unanswered and the Chinese clients' orders went unfilled. To complicate matters, the CEO of YOFC was leaving the company to return to the United States. YOFC was in a chaotic state of management transition. It gave me only small comfort to know that my firm was not the only YOFC representative with problems. Ganda, the firm's representative in the United States, complained of being treated as poorly and unprofessionally as we were.

At times it was very hard for me to maintain a calm front, suppressing the rage that constantly simmered just below the surface. Deep down, I felt lonely, hopeless, and helpless. Jon could not help me out, nor could my family resolve the problem for me. No one could.

* * *

In 1999 I had a busy year. My company was working hard to
develop YOFC's market, but it was clear to me that it was
time to expand my business into other new industries. I decided to broaden my focus beyond optical fiber and cable.
With a need for many kinds of components, subsystems,
and networking products, the telecommunications industry
offered many intriguing opportunities to explore. Since I was
stepping outside my immediate area of expertise, I invested in
independent market consulting so I'd have informed opinions
on which to base sound business decisions. But I wanted firsthand knowledge, too.

So I spent much of the year traveling around the world and
seeking out ways to expand ATI's presence in the industry. I
attended telecom conferences and executive marketing seminars, where I talked shop with high-level executives and entrepreneurs. I participated in exploratory talks with large
companies on the scale of America's Fortune 500 and with
small entrepreneurial startups in the United States, Canada,
Europe, Australia, Japan, and other Asian countries.

Every place I visited had its own charm and style.

Americans and Canadians were my favorite people to work
with. I liked the way they encouraged creativity and free discussion. They were straightforward, and no nonsense discussion was allowed; they were also open-minded and flexible,
approaching new clients, new projects, and new ideas with a
sense of adventure. They worked hard yet were relaxed and
easygoing, focusing on the final result and less concerned
about the process. They would not directly criticize you but

would give you enough hints that you could figure out how to improve. They tended to be a bit materialistic, and quick to take advantage of an opportunity to promote themselves. But I also found them to be generally warm-hearted people, non-judgmental, and accepting of cultural differences.

The Australians I dealt with, all of them men, were blunt and direct. They struck me as a bit superior about their country and their lives. But when it came to getting the deal done, they were efficient, hardworking, and down to earth.

Singapore and Hong Kong impressed me a great deal. Many of the businesspeople there were Chinese. Well-organized companies operated with a Westernized mindset tempered by a bit of the traditional Asian business mystique. I admired the female executives in Singapore and Hong Kong very much. They set high standards of professionalism and efficiency that women elsewhere would do well to emulate.

Japan was a productive place to do business. I went there several times, always intrigued by the mix of Japanese culture and Western philosophy. My trips followed a pattern. On the first day, we didn't talk business much. We would begin more socially with a visit to a nice restaurant. The Japanese businessmen I met had a habit of going out for drinks after work. Since I couldn't drink alcoholic beverages, including the sake they were fond of, it was hard for me to fit in, but they always were courteous enough to invite me. Sometimes, at my request, they would ask a lady friend to take me shopping.

The next day was also a social day. If I were a man, they would have taken me to a place featuring female entertainers, like a karaoke club or a geisha show. To avoid any awkwardness, I would come up with a request to go sightseeing or visit one of the famous Japanese baths.

On the third day we would finally get down to business. I was very impressed with the way the Japanese managed meetings. They always arrived on time and well prepared. Their discussions were efficient and to the point and always ended with a constructive result. They were cautious enough to test whether they could trust you; if you passed, you earned their business and respect.

I learned a great deal from doing business with Japanese companies and I came to respect them a lot. I was inspired by the pride they took in their productivity, quality, and knowledge of cutting-edge technology. More than people in almost any other country, the Japanese were perfectionists—focused, determined, goal-oriented, always eager to learn and to improve. They had grasped the essence of the Western business mentality, customizing it to their own culture and putting it to use in their own companies. They embraced self-value as well as corporate identity and national spirit. The Chinese could learn much from their example about having a sense of honor, a sense of ownership, and a spirit of teamwork.

Most of my business was conducted in Tokyo, a cosmopolitan city that seemed just like Hong Kong or large cities I'd been to in the West, except that the food was much better and fresher. I also visited Osaka, Sapporo, and Kyoto. I loved Kyoto the most. It was the capital of imperial Japan for more than one thousand years, and more than any other city it retains the look and feel of the traditional Japanese culture.

Though it's a thoroughly modern city, it still has an abundance of historic temples, palaces, shrines, and parks that give it a unique charm.

I had a touching experience at a cozy family restaurant in Kyoto. It was charmingly decorated and the fragrance of the food made me hungry, so I decided to have dinner there. The hour was early and I was the only guest. The owner and the waitress seemed surprised to see a pretty lady dining solo.

The waitress asked me for my order in Japanese, apparently not realizing that I wasn't from her country. Since my Japanese was poor, I tried responding in English, but the waitress didn't understand my English very well. We stumbled along in both languages and I managed to order my food: cold soba noodles with a lot of wasabi, miso soup, and two big rainbow rolls.

The owner, who was the chef, eyed me dubiously. "Miss, the rolls are quite big. Are you sure you want two of them?"

I hesitated, feeling slightly embarrassed. Did I look like a greedy little pig? But I was so hungry and the rolls looked so tempting. I knew I could eat two. I summoned a charming smile and said, "They look so delicious; my tummy cannot help wanting two."

He shook his head but smiled as he said, "I doubt it. You ordered a lot of food, miss, and you are tiny!"

That remark challenged me, and a tricky idea jumped to my head.

"How about this?" I suggested. "If I finish them both, the second one is free."

He laughed. "That's an interesting proposal. All right!"

I was almost intoxicated by my food, it was so good. As I

ate, a familiar melody started to play. I couldn't believe it—this was one of my favorite Japanese songs. I couldn't help myself. I leaped from my chair and sang along with the music. I was enjoying myself so much, and my excitement was quite infectious. The waitress and chef stopped working and listened attentively. They applauded when I was done.

"Wow, you have such a beautiful voice," the chef said. "How do you know this song? It is a very old song."

"I learned it from an educational TV show at home in China when I was a sophomore in college," I said proudly. "What little Japanese I speak, I learned from that Japanese-language program."

We continued to chat. I could tell they'd never met a Chinese businesswoman like me. They were fascinated that I was traveling alone from the United States. They had trouble putting my Chinese face and American attitudes together.

The food was delicious and I ate every bite, including both of the rainbow rolls.

The chef was impressed. "Wow, miss, you really finished both of them? I wonder where they could have gone to. You are too petite."

I teased him with a naughty wink. "Well, I'll tell you a secret. They definitely went to the right place."

The chef laughed, and to my surprise he didn't charge me at all for the rainbow rolls.

I really loved that little restaurant; it made me feel at home. I left my business card, and I promised that I would cook for them at my home in San Francisco one day when they visited the United States. I wanted to return their hospitality with a family-style meal of authentic Chinese food. Whenever I go to a Japanese restaurant, I remember that little restaurant. It was such a pity that when I went back to look for it on a later trip, it was no longer there.

In many ways, the Germans reminded me of the Japanese. They were similar in their perfectionism and in the pride they took in the quality and functionality of their products. The ones I worked with—as in Australia, they were mostly men —took their work very seriously. They liked to deal with people who knew their job and had a low tolerance for nonsense work and nonsense clients. They were persistent in their opinions, perhaps even a little bit inflexible, and they followed business rules and procedures precisely. When they took on a project, they delivered exactly what they promised, and they didn't appreciate sudden surprises in a business transaction. Although I couldn't share their passion for beer, my dedication and work ethic were very much on the same wavelength as theirs, which helped me work with them smoothly. It wasn't always easy to understand and meet their high requirements, but I found that once I did, working with German businesspeople was much simpler than working with Chinese businesspeople.

* * *

When it comes to business, China is like no place else.

As I worked more and more with Western companies, I came to the conclusion that the West is a better place to do business than China. The corporate structures and operational procedures are simpler and more efficient, and the laws provide a more stable and secure business environment, with legal remedies for breaches of contracts and unfair competition. However, I have to say that if I had not been trained in China, if I had not gone through hardships and learned to succeed in that tough, competitive business environment, then I would never have learned to appreciate the beauty of the Western system.

Conducting business in China is a marathon of negotiating and entertaining. Ninety percent of the time, what you're doing seems unrelated to the business at hand. Since everything is based on personal connections and relationships, you must build the relationships through rounds of socializing before you can even think of talking business, most of which is conducted in entertainment and recreational venues like golf courses, sauna centers, karaoke bars, or the many nightclubs that are filled with pretty young ladies whose job is to entertain businessmen.

Each company is different, with its own structure of political and financial power, and it can be difficult to discover what that structure is. Because nothing is standardized or systematic, you have to work case by case, making a specific operating plan for each client, factoring in the personalities, backgrounds, and levels of influence of the persons involved.

The lack of a strong regulatory environment makes it even more important to forge solid, harmonious relationships with the persons who have power and influence within a company. You depend on their goodwill to carry out a project and get paid. To a large extent, it appears to me that quite often a more traditionally managed Chinese company disregards the commitments and obligations of legal contracts.

Business relationships are complicated by the fact that

many transactions have three players—the manufacturer or vendor, the agent, and the customer. This creates a triangle of debt and obligation and makes it easy for the parties to shift blame if something goes wrong. One of ATI's areas of expertise was ensuring that clients paid our vendors in a timely way, without racking up overdue bills and debts. This service was a strong selling point that made us valuable to the Western companies we worked for.

The Chinese approach to business world may seem corrupt and disordered, and even lacking in good sense. Because of entrenched cultural attitudes and the legacy of China's history, many obstacles have to be overcome. However, I've noticed hopeful signs of change. In recent years the Chinese government, under determined and farsighted direction of leaders like President Deng Xiaoping and President Hu Jintao, has made investments and instituted reforms to encourage the development of the country and its economy. As a result the Chinese people are beginning to achieve better lives in an improved environment. The process has been painful and the price high, but, to the shock of the entire world, China has made extraordinary progress. I can see the day when China will be one of the strongest and most prosperous countries.

* * *

My travels taught me that when you do business cross-culturally, it's important to appreciate the culture and the people you're dealing with. In the best international partnerships, both sides reach out to understand each other's rules, systems, and mentality, and to adopt each other's best practices. When you make this effort, you will gain your partner's acceptance and trust and open the door to a productive and profitable relationship.

Many Chinese companies I encountered did not understand this. They seemed to think that learning to understand their international partners was too huge and too expensive a project.

Dazzled by the promise of short-term profits, they would relinquish their independence and identity and open themselves to exploitation by foreign firms. I found this attitude to be a national problem, limiting the growth and economic health of numerous businesses. Working with them through ATI, my goal was to encourage them to be open-minded enough to adopt the advantages of the Western business culture, cautious enough not to blindly embrace the aspects that are not beneficial, and proud enough to retain what is best about the Chinese ways.

In the best international partnerships, both sides reach out to understand each other's rules, systems, and mentality, and to adopt each other's best practices.

I found a niche for my company because I had a profound understanding of both cultures—their mentalities, their rules, and the sophistication of the business systems. Western and Chinese firms alike benefited from working with ATI because we could link their divergent business worlds, helping them find common ground and create common goals. They came to trust our ethics, our integrity, and our ability to promote success for everybody.

I loved dealing with all kinds of businesses around the world. Other people might find traveling on business difficult, but for me it was a joy. I always made time to take advantage of what the locality had to offer—the people, the culture, the language, and sightseeing. To me, the world and its people are endlessly fascinating.

* * *

In the summer of 1999 I took one of my favorite journeys, my first business trip to Paris and Italy.

I traveled to Milan to meet with high-ranking executives of Pirelli, which produces optical fiber and telecommunications cable in addition to its famous tires. They arranged for me to stay in a downtown hotel that, to my delight, provided a twenty-four-hour fashion show for its guests. After a rest, but still struggling to recover from my insane jet lag, I met with one of the senior vice presidents, who was a real gentleman and excellent company. Our productive discussions began at Pirelli headquarters and continued over dinner at one of the finest restaurants in Milan. Seafood, pasta, local olive oil— the food was so fresh and delicate, nothing like the Italian food I'd eaten in the United States. I cleaned my plate, impressing my Italian host with my healthy appetite.

That was only the beginning of the delights I found in Italy. I was overwhelmed by the great architecture and art to be found in Milan—visiting the home of the great Renaissance artist Leonardo da Vinci was an experience not to be missed. And I loved the fact that while Milan reveres its past, it has its eye on today and tomorrow; it's a cosmopolitan city that pulses with energy and excitement.

Milan is one of the world's fashion capitals, and the elegant taste of the Italian women I saw strolling in the central city just blew me away. I got dizzy trying to gaze in the windows of all of the beautiful shops. Let me tell you something—if I lived there, a fashion-loving lady like me, I would go shopping every day. There were so many exquisite clothes, shoes, hats, and bags, some of them handmade and all of them remarkably designed. Shopping in Italy was a sensational experience. It was interesting that most of the sales clerks took me for Japanese. Apparently they didn't see too many stylish Chinese women traveling alone.

A little distance from downtown, I discovered that even a glamorous city like this could have an ugly side when I wandered into a section of dirty streets and run-down buildings, just like bad neighborhoods in New York or Chinese towns. Something else that caught my attention was the mad traffic. The streets were filled with cars, all jockeying for the best position and weaving around other vehicles with as much speed and agility as possible. Horns blared, and the drivers yelled and gesticulated wildly to each other. This is the famous Latin emotion on display, I thought, yet I was astounded at how much the scene reminded me of China.

After Milan, I traveled to Venice. On the train several cute Italian men kept trying to flirt with me. I was flattered by their direct yet romantic gestures.

"Signorina, you are so beautiful!" they said in their charming Italian accents. "Why you are going alone to Venice? That's the city of love."

I winked at them and teased back. "Maybe I will find love there."

The young men were right. I lost my heart to Venice right away. It was such a romantic place—gondolas gliding along the canals, ornate palazzi that invited you to dream of being a guest at their banquets and masked balls, churches that were works of art with more art treasures inside.

I checked into the Hotel Danieli, located close to the Piazza San Marco, the city's pigeon-filled main square. A palace built for a duke in the fourteenth century, it had been beautifully restored with pink marble and gold leaf and many luxurious appointments. Walking through the public areas, I felt like royalty, so I was disappointed when the porter showed me to my room. It had almost no view and the bed was so small that it seemed intended for a little kid.

That evening I had a productive meeting with an old business associate from my work with Draxler, an experienced top executive who was working with an Italian chemical manufacturer. The company made chemical products for use in automobile manufacturing and large construction projects. He impressed me again with his technical knowledge and creative business strategy, as well as his adeptness at dealing with people from all over the world. He spoke perfect English, French, German, and Italian, and a little bit of Japanese.

As we wrapped up our discussion, I complained to him that I'd spent almost $600 and had to put up with a totally inadequate room. The hotel had apologized for the mistake and agreed to change the room the next day, but I was still unhappy about it.

He waited until I'd finished my griping, then smiled at me. "Diana, do you know how lucky you are?"

I was puzzled. Why would he ask me that? "Lucky? What do you mean?"

"Here you are, staying in the best hotel in Venice and one of the most prestigious hotels in Italy. You could even afford to stay in the most exclusive room. You have no idea how fortunate you are!"

That started me thinking. Yes, I realized I was very fortunate. My hard work was paying off, even if I had encountered enormous obstacles in my business dealings. As a result of my perseverance and diligence, I was able to live in comfort and style, travel to fascinating places, and enjoy the company of smart, creative, and sophisticated people. It was also true that my achievements hadn't come through happenstance. I had played a big role in creating my luck, through hard work, creativity, and a willingness to take risks and explore opportunities.

Venice held me in such thrall that I stayed for an additional day just so I could enjoy myself. I put on my white miniskirt, applied some light makeup, and went out to explore the many splendors of this magical, romantic city. I took my umbrella. I always avoid strong sunlight, as I don't want to get burned. I know that if I want to continue to be an attractive woman, I can never forget to take care of myself. Well, what can I say—vanity, thy name is woman.

As I wandered along the canals, I talked to strangers; I tried more of the delicious food; I listened to music. I indulged in the opera and the theater. I learned a few Italian words: *buon giorno*, good day; *grazie*, thank you; *arrivederci*, until we meet again. And I enjoyed a bit of attention from Italian men. I would give every one of them a PhD for mastering the art of flirting. They are tender and attentive, so delicate and sophisticated. They dress to impress you, and they treat a woman like a queen. They hold your arm as you walk along the bridges, hold doors open, and arrange your chair at the table. They will do just about anything to make you smile and giggle. They never miss a chance to whistle at a beautiful woman and express their appreciation with a romantic gesture. Some women find such behavior offensive, but I enjoyed the way they reminded me of how wonderful it is to be a woman, especially to be a beautiful woman.

When you pay personal attention to a client and make an effort to appreciate his culture and hospitality, you'll be rewarded with acceptance and trust.

My next destination was southern Italy, where I visited some earthy country villages. In one of them I watched as the proprietor of a restaurant came out into the piazza and yelled for olive oil. His wife appeared in a third-floor window. She put the olive oil bottle into a little basket, then lowered it on a rope from their window to the ground, where the man retrieved it and took it inside. That was funny.

Later that year I returned to Italy to continue the fruitful discussions with Pirelli and with the chemical manufacturer. This time I met my former Draxler associate and the company personnel in Bologna, where the company had its plant not far from where Ferrari manufactures its automobiles. I visited the facility and met the owner of the company. My former associate's assistance was invaluable as we talked business since the owner didn't speak English and my Italian vocabulary was so meager. I learned enough to become very interested in this company's products and goals.

Business is about people, nothing else.

They took me to a famous restaurant where the Spice Girls and other celebrities dined. As I'd done in Milan, I showed my genuine appreciation of Italian food by finishing every course. The chef was so impressed that he devised a special ice cream treat right in front of me. It was a splendid finale to an outstanding meal.

Thanks to that dinner, our business relationship progressed nicely. It proved again that when you pay personal attention to a client and make an effort to appreciate his culture and hospitality, you'll be rewarded with acceptance and trust. This is even more important in international situations. The bottom line is: "Business is about people, nothing else."

One thing I found interesting was that when it comes to families and food, the Italian culture is very much like the Chinese. We both take our time to prepare our food, and then to savor the meal and enjoy family interactions while we eat. Even though the Italians tend not to hold in their emotions in family or social situations, they are self-contained when doing business, which is another similarity to the Chinese. Both Italians and Chinese take an indirect approach to business deals, and it can take many rounds of negotiation to work out all the fine points of an agreement.

By now I had fallen in love with Italy—its passion, its history, its architecture, its arts, the opera, the food, the culture, the people, the myth of the Mafia. Everything is original, sophisticated, and passionate. And then, of course, there is its superlative sense of fashion.

I didn't need to define or limit myself by the circumstances I came from; what counted was where I was heading.

On the way back to Milan, I took a break at Lake Como, a blue jewel set among the mountains. I strolled along the lakefront, gazing at the tranquil waters and the alpine vistas, and reflected on my life. It was a therapeutic interlude.

My life was changing so fast and in so many ways. It really felt like a dream. I couldn't believe all the things that had happened in only two years. I'd moved from China to the unfamiliar Western environment of California, experienced a difficult marriage, and turned that poor situation into an opportunity to start my own business. Now I was running an international business venture, traveling all over the world and dealing with the top executives in my industry. I had taken many risks and had relied on myself to handle them well. I'd had to overcome many obstacles, but I loved what I was doing and I was happy with the choices I'd made.

It had become clear to me that I could control my destiny. Though I was proud to consider myself a daughter of the Yellow River, I didn't need to define or limit myself by the circumstances I came from; what counted was where I was heading. I deserved the best life I could achieve. Nothing could stop me from pursuing my joy, my love, my success, and my happiness. I had a great deal of value to offer, and I could make a difference in this world.

* * *

An unexpected accident at the Milan airport delayed my trip home. As I was riding an escalator down to the check-in terminal, I heard someone shouting at me. Thinking I'd lost something upstairs, I wanted to go back, but I couldn't see any escalator going up. So, my hands full of bags, I stepped back onto the down escalator and started to climb up. I'd almost reached the top when I tripped and fell.

As I pushed myself up, I didn't feel anything. All of a sudden I heard an Italian woman scream.

"*Mamma mia*, you are bleeding!"

When I looked down, I almost fainted. Oh, my god, I just saw my own bone! My knee was gashed and gushing blood.

The airport security officers rushed me to a nearby hospital for surgery. To my dismay, none of the doctors there spoke good English. One doctor suggested French, but my rusty French was of little use in such a complicated medical situation. We resorted to a mix of primitive French and clumsy English to communicate.

The doctor put ten stitches on my knee and wrapped it in a big cast. I could not bend my knee, and I had to use a cane to walk. I was worried that I would have an ugly scar, but the doctor promised me it wouldn't look that bad.

I missed my flight, of course, so I arranged to fly out the next day. On the way back to my hotel, I passed through the down-town shopping area, where I was distracted by the sight of one beautiful pink pump displayed in a shop window. While I was resting at the hotel, my injured leg propped on a pillow, the image of that striking shoe kept flashing into my head.

This was my last night here, my only chance. I had to get a pair of those shoes no matter what. The store was only a block from the hotel. So, maneuvering awkwardly with my cast and cane, I hobbled to the store and bought the beautiful pink shoes. The shop manager saw how much I liked the shoes, and he was impressed with the effort I'd made to limp there and get them, so he told me he'd give me a special deal. (God knows if it was true.)

Aha, I thought, look at what I did. I could not believe how determined, how tough and tenacious I was, just to get some-thing I loved.

* * *

In 2000 I bought my first house—a brand-new two-story home in an upscale neighborhood in Santa Cruz. Built in the French country style, the house had almost five thousand square feet of living space. It was surrounded by oaks on two acres of land and sat high on a hilltop.

California real estate was appreciating quickly, so I figured the house would be a good investment. Even more important, I wanted a real home; I was traveling constantly to China and elsewhere, and I longed for a haven where I could retreat and rest. I was thrilled to own a place like this, much larger and grander than anything I could have dreamed about when I lived in the hut in the coal-mining village or the tiny apartment on the grounds of Lanzhou University. Working with some talented interior designers, I selected all the colors and materials for the builder to use, adding artistic touches to make the house truly mine.

The foyer, with its cathedral ceiling and dazzling chandelier, made me think of the movie *Gone with the Wind*. For its floor I chose exquisite Italian marble in colors of coral and cream. Jade green carpet or pale hardwood surfaced the rest of the floors on the ground level. Fireplaces warmed the living room and family room. Large windows let in the sunshine and allowed me to look out at the backyard, which was edged by a little creek. Deer often wandered onto the property, and I loved watching them.

The house had five bedrooms, each with its own bathroom. The large master suite featured a third fireplace and a walk-in closet that was bigger than the bedroom of the first home I'd shared with Jon. In the master bath, I installed a Jacuzzi and had the floor and shower covered in more Italian marble.

The kitchen, with its homey breakfast nook, was one of my favorite places. Cooking is a creative activity for me; I get some of my best ideas when I'm preparing food, and I love to make meals for my friends. So I equipped the kitchen with high-end appliances, hoping they'd help me become a super chef.

I was a novelty among my neighbors. They were mostly in their forties and fifties, while I was in my thirties. They were married couples with children, but I was single—with great regret, I had recently filed for a divorce from Jon.

The neighbors gave me a warm welcome, which helped to

ease my solitude. They were surprised that someone like me, a young, single Asian woman, could afford to buy such a large, lovely home entirely on her own. I could scarcely believe it myself. Wow, from chicken coop to mansion—what a change!

* * *

While I was in Italy the previous summer I had received an urgent letter from my marketing director. YOFC had again rejected the Chinese clients' requests to ship fiber supplies they'd ordered. My deepest apologies to the clients had no effect in restoring their confidence in YOFC or in me. I realized I had to go back to YOFC to review our relationship and straighten out all our problems. Now that there was a new person in charge, perhaps we could make a fresh beginning.

Early in 2000, I flew to Wuhan to meet with the incoming general manager, the new CEO, and the assistant sales manager, Mr. Yan. We spent five days thrashing through all the problems, and we renegotiated and amended our agreement. When the meetings ended I felt very hopeful. The new CEO struck me as a professional and ethical manager, and in accordance with Chinese business custom he would be bringing in his own team.

He expressed his commitment to improving our relationship and working with ATI on a more effective level for our mutual benefit. He praised my dedication and diligence, saying, "Diana, I just wish everyone at YOFC was like you."

Unfortunately, nothing improved.

We still had to deal with our old problems. Customers were not satisfied with the products and service that YOFC provided. Our demands that YOFC respect its agreement and satisfy the clients' orders were ignored, even when we warned them of possible lawsuits if they failed to comply. My staff and I had to keep explaining and apologizing to our upset clients. We were extremely disappointed to be dealing with a supplier that worked with us in such an uncooperative and destructive way.

YOFC didn't realize how lucky they were to have us, a company that worked so hard on their behalf and was determined to get them market share and recognition. They didn't appreciate how many extra miles we went to provide outstanding service to their clients. Despite all the difficulties they inflicted on us, we had taken their unknown product line and established a strong brand identity, a reputation for quality, and a level of sales that had impressed the entire industry. We helped YOFC to get most of the major optical cable makers in China to accept YOFC's fiber products, and even more incredibly, all of the fiber sold to the clients had been paid for in full to YOFC, which was almost a miracle for the field in China. Imagine what we could have accomplished if YOFC had supported us instead of throwing up barriers.

To avoid the kind of shortages that YOFC had inflicted on the clients in the previous year, I spent the summer of 2000 obtaining pre-orders for 2001. That meant persuading clients to estimate their needs for the year and to commit in advance to making purchases in those amounts. In September I met with YOFC's top management to submit the new purchase agreements and discuss YOFC's willingness to honor these obligations.

Most companies would be thrilled to have advance orders for a year in the volume ATI had generated for YOFC. Based on what turned out to be the product's average price level in 2001, those orders would have been worth somewhere from $60 million to more than $100 million in sales for YOFC. So I was shocked on November 1, 2000, when a curt letter, just a note really, arrived by fax at ATI's Shenzhen office. It was signed by Mr. Yan, who had survived the change of leadership in the company to become the manager of optical cable sales for YOFC. Addressed to Brenda, my director, it said:

> For your information, as YOFC will concentrate on the production of G.655 and multimode optical fiber in the coming year of 2001, therefore YOFC will not be able to supply any single mode optical fiber to your customer [sic] in the year 2001.

In other words, YOFC was refusing to provide any fiber the customers had ordered in September for 2001, supposedly because the company would be focusing on a different business product line. Later on, I discovered that this was not true; ATI was the only representative to be cut off from the supply of single-mode fiber. YOFC refused to communicate with me and explain why they refused to supply the fiber.

This letter was a crushing blow. My last hope of improving this troubled business relationship was now completely destroyed. Regretfully, I forwarded YOFC's letter to the clients and told them that the fiber they had ordered would not be forthcoming. I deeply apologized for letting them down again because of YOFC's capriciousness. I explained that ATI was a victim, also, and I had no power to change this tragic situation. There was nothing we could do to make up for the clients' losses.

The clients were furious. Some of them threatened to sue me.

For years, through hard work, dedication, and loyalty, I had built strong, solid relationships with these clients. Now their trust in me was shattered. I felt ashamed to face them.

I could not understand what had gone wrong. Without ATI's diligent efforts, YOFC could never have created a market or a brand for its domestic fiber. In only two years, with just a handful of people, my tiny firm took a product line that had zero revenue and zero percent market share, and we developed a market for their products worth hundreds of millions of dollars, and we did this in the most competitive optical fiber market in the world. Moreover, we made sure that all of the customers paid in full; there was no outstanding debt for YOFC to collect.

Yet instead of treating us with honor and gratitude, YOFC sabotaged my business. Nothing in my dealings with this company happened the way it was promised when we signed the agreement. I was devastated. I cannot find the words to describe the anger, the pain, and the sense of betrayal I suffered. As I write this book now, my tears drop to my paper and blur the ink. I have to stop writing, settle myself down, and contain my rage so that I can reorganize my thoughts.

* * *

I tried hard not to be disheartened as the year 2000 closed and 2001 began. The two things that meant most to me—my marriage and my fiber business in China—had suffered brutal blows.

My relationship with Jon had been an ongoing source of anguish. Despite my best efforts, it had become clear to me that he and I would never find a way to make our marriage work. We differed too much in what we expected from marriage and what we believed a husband and wife should be to each other. Filing for divorce had been a painful and difficult step. But I still cared deeply for Jon, and I understood that he had genuine affection for me. If we couldn't succeed as partners, perhaps we could find a way to be friends. We spent the Christmas holidays together, taking tentative steps in this new direction.

YOFC's conduct had left ATI in a shambles in the Chinese optical fiber market. Somehow I would have to find a way to repair my small company. One thing was clear: I had been right two years ago when I decided not to limit ATI's focus to optical fiber and cable. That industry's misplaced emphasis on profit over quality and value was taking its toll. Unfair competition and suicidal low prices in a strong buyer's market had pushed almost every cable maker into large amounts of debt. Now, to branch out further, I began cultivating partners among Chinese and Asian original equipment manufacturers, known in the telecommunications field as OEM companies, to produce telecom components and other products to sell in the United States and other Western markets.

The professionalism and efficiency of the Western business system attracted me more and more. Making a deal was so much simpler; a few visits and some phone calls did the trick. We provided a sample, got qualified, submitted a competitive sales package, and obtained a purchase order. Then we shipped the goods, followed up on the sale, and received the payment. Because the systems for marketing and branding were regulated, precise, and easy to learn, a young company like mine could break into the market and create a positive identity of our own.

What a difference from the Chinese system. No drinking, no entertaining, no nightclubs, no exhausting nonsense negotiations, no ingratiating yourself to build personal relationships that only existed for business reasons, no endless chasing after payments.

One day I heard the general manager of Siemens Chengdu Cable comment in a meeting, "I don't understand how the Chinese can run their businesses like this. It is absolutely insane!" He was so right.

At first, OEM components proved to be a fast-growing, highly demanding, profitable direction in which to move. In the meantime I started engaging in other investment opportunities. But soon I could tell it was time for me to rethink my involvement in the telecom industry altogether. My risk-assessment, marketing, and branding skills were maturing, and my instincts, coupled with my marketing consultant's solid analysis, made me doubt the predictions of exploding growth being made by the industry's boosters.

I put my expansion plans for ATI on hold and began to contemplate my next steps.

* * *

After thinking about it long and hard, I decided to file a lawsuit against YOFC. It was an essential step if I was to recover the losses to my optical fiber business in China, regain my reputation, and protect my integrity. I could have no hope of reentering that marketplace or redeeming my fiber business in China unless I received justice by fighting in court. YOFC's managers probably assumed that because I was young, female, and Chinese, I would let them push me around. I might complain, but I would be too timid, too acquiescent, or too naive to stand up for my rights.

They were in for a serious surprise.

I started searching out legal representation. I needed attorneys who understood both American and Chinese business law. I searched and interviewed quite a few prominent international firms, and I finally selected a United States–based firm with offices in eighteen countries. It had been the first American law firm to open an office in China, so it knew that country well. On May 4, 2001, my attorneys filed a lawsuit against YOFC in the California Superior Court on behalf of Allied Telecom International. Now we would begin the long, slow crawl toward justice.

* * *

Late in 2001, with pain in my heart, I bade farewell to my ATI staff and closed the representative office in Shenzhen that I had opened with such happiness and hope. Since YOFC had betrayed my trust, my fiber business in China was destroyed.

My new business interests were concentrated in the United States and Europe. It made no sense to keep a Chinese office going.

More and more, I was beginning to think of the United States as home—something I would have found hard to believe just a few years ago, when I was a homesick bride feeling trapped and miserable in a lonely hotel room.

My Santa Cruz home had appreciated greatly in value, and I decided to purchase more residential property in California as an investment. I started to search for other investment opportunities in the United States, too. My interest in China was waning.

* * *

All of the struggles and heartbreaks I'd suffered in recent years had exacted a huge toll. I was worn out emotionally, physically, and mentally. With comfortable financial rewards from my hard work in business ventures and investments, I decided to step away from the telecommunications industry and give myself a rest. I would look for pursuits that would bring me more joy and comfort my heart.

So at the age of thirty-four I opted out of the telecom business world that had given me so much.

"Wow, Diana, you're retiring so young," a friend commented in amazement.

I was astonished myself. I had loved all of the excitement and challenges of being in business, and I was proud of what I had accomplished. In an industry dominated by men, I never backed down in the face of intimidation and prejudice. I demonstrated my strength, my capability, and my value. Instead of dressing and behaving like a man in order to compete with them, I used my own brand of femininity—a combination of professionalism, high principles, style, and attractiveness—to provide freshness and balance in a stifling male atmosphere. Through my spirit, my skills, and my integrity, I had achieved a miraculous success.

But I had no regrets about the change I was making.

I looked forward to enjoying a more relaxed and balanced life in the United States. I'd arrived here five years ago with limited funds, a lot of hope, and an unknown future. I had journeyed a long way on a sometimes rocky road. I was confident that many more paths lay ahead for me to explore.

Diana's Stepping-Stones on the Journey to Success

Understand that business is about people, not products or profits. When we put our clients, our staff, and our associates at the center of our business, we gain the means for the company to achieve longevity and success. The secret: listening to them and meeting their needs. "People first" is a fundamental principle for sustaining our business, no matter how competitive an environment we're working in.

Encourage your employees. Excellent employees are among the chief assets of any business. We help our employees achieve excellence by giving them opportunities to be creative, develop new skills, make real contributions, and meet their own goals as part of their long-range vision for themselves. If we resist the temptation to micromanage them, productivity will improve. But we should never condone negative or unethical conduct, which will only ruin the team and jeopardize the company's reputation.

Become a marketing expert. Marketing is everything we do that gives someone an impression of our business or ourselves. To be an expert in marketing is simply to be aware of and act on that truth. Successful marketing means sharing our beliefs and enthusiasm for what we are doing in a systematic way. The goal is to create a recognizable brand with a solid reputation. How do we accomplish this? By making sure that our services and products are of top quality, by establishing a single, consistent image and message to convey who we are and what we are doing, and by clearly and continuously delivering that message to our audience.

Maintain a sense of urgency. Setting a deadline increases the chances that we will accomplish our goals. It requires us to put forth our best effort—to make a real commitment and to perform the work efficiently. This puts us steps ahead of other people and enterprises, enabling us to be winners, not only in a competitive business world but also in our personal lives.

Open yourself to what the world has to offer. The world has an immense and endlessly fascinating variety of places, people, languages, and cultures. When we reach out to embrace them, whether through studying, traveling, or befriending a stranger, we have an opportunity to make our lives richer and more joyful.

Always fight for your principles and your integrity. These are the qualities that earn us respect, trust, and support, and, in business, lead us to prosperity. We must guard and protect them as if doing so were a matter of life or death.

Performing a Latin dance with a professional dancer in the Metronome
showcase at the Cowell Theater, San Francisco, August 2003.

Photograph by Marty Sohl, former official photographer of the San Francisco Ballet and the San Francisco Opera.

心灵之乐

———

Ten　A Song Within My Spirit, 2002–2003

———

As I toasted the arrival of the New Year, 2002, I was set-
tling into a life that many people might envy. I had achieved
what some see as a dream—retirement at a youthful age, no
demands on my time, and the freedom and means to choose
where I wanted to live and what I wanted to do.

Santa Cruz, where I had bought my first house, was a
charming seaside city in an area with many scenic splendors
—white beaches, rugged hills, and redwood forests. But just
sixty miles away was one of the world's most beautiful, cosmopolitan cities—San Francisco. I couldn't resist its siren call.

For my home in the city, I picked a spacious condominium
in a building at the foot of the legendary Telegraph Hill. The
condo was so large that my family's first Lanzhou apartment
could have fit within the living room. The dining room was
nearly as big, and the condo also had a gourmet kitchen, a master suite, a second bedroom that I used as my reading room,
and two marble-lined bathrooms. The days of heating wash
water on the stove or hauling it in thermoses from the *kaishui
fang* seemed so long ago. From my new windows I could

watch the sailboats and ferries crisscrossing San Francisco Bay. When I stepped outside my door, I was in the midst of the nightlife, the symphony, the jazz bars, the theaters, the restaurants—all of the energy and stimulation of a place where many cultures met and mingled.

I was still sorting out the last phase of closing down my telecom business, and I kept a close eye on my investments. I was also paying attention to my lawsuit, though little seemed to be happening on that front. To keep up with the fascinating world of business, real estate, and the stock market, I made a habit of reading *The Wall Street Journal*, *New York Times*, *Fortune*, and *Financial Times* and watching CNBC and CNN on television. But more and more of my time was devoted to exploring and enjoying urban life in all its luxurious sophistication.

Wow, I thought. How fortunate I am to live in such a splendid place!

* * *

My days fell into a pleasant routine. Every morning when I woke up I lay in bed watching the sun coming up over the bay or the famous San Francisco fog drifting outside the window. Then I got up to do my yoga or take a long walk along the marina, listening to the birds, smelling the fresh flowers and the tang of the saltwater, and listening to the sounds of the city and the ocean. San Francisco has gorgeous weather all year long, never too hot or too cold. On sunny days it sparkles like a gemstone, and the fog has its own magic and mystery. I love the sight of the Golden Gate Bridge when one of its red towers is hidden in the fog, while the other tower steadfastly awaits the smile of sun.

Sometimes I walked to Ghirardelli Square to have breakfast at one of my favorite restaurants, McCormick & Kuleto's, where I'd watch the boats on the bay while I drank my chamomile tea and ate my omelet without cheese. Or I might stop at a crab house on Fisherman's Wharf and eat a whole crab by myself for lunch.

In the evening I sometimes simply relaxed at home, reading and listening to my favorite music. Often, though, I went out with friends for dinner or a movie, or got lost in a music store or a bookstore, or donned a sexy dress and shoes and danced nonstop to the salsa beat at the lively Club Cocomo.

San Francisco had so many restaurants to try. My taste in food was expanding to include what to me were new and exotic cuisines—French, Italian, Spanish, Greek, Mexican, Thai. I enjoyed going to small neighborhood cafes as well as restaurants with international reputations and a four-month wait for reservations. Sometimes I went to the Cliff House, perched on a bluff at the edge of the ocean, to watch the sunset. A couple of times when I was there, I had the privilege of watching a young couple become engaged to marry. Both times, the young man got down on his knees to propose to his intended bride in front of all the restaurant patrons. These were really touching moments, and I wondered if I would find love like that again.

Despite all the excellent restaurants, I hadn't found even one with really good Chinese food. Nothing could compete with the food in China. So I cooked a lot for myself, and I entertained my friends with big dinner parties, serving eighteen or twenty dishes. The parties were especially fun on the Fourth of July, the U.S. Independence Day, when we had the added attraction of watching from my windows as the fireworks exploded above the bay. My friends told me that the best Chinese food in the Bay Area was found in my kitchen. Their appreciation of my cooking was such a comfort. To me, cooking was not only a special art but also an amazingly therapeutic activity.

An enjoyable part of my routine was a regular visit to my favorite salon for a hairstyling, a facial, a manicure, and a pedicure. I indulged myself by choosing a high-end establishment. The people who worked there were highly skilled professionals who provided impeccable service. But the service came at a price. In China, people worked much harder than these Americans, yet the cost of my afternoon in the salon was just about equal to a typical Chinese worker's salary for three months.

I joined a health club and went there frequently. I knew the Bay Club was an excellent facility, catering to individuals with money and style, but I didn't realize the reputation it had until a cab driver said to me, "Oh, that's the club where all the women with attitude go."

After my workout, I liked to relax in the sauna or the Jacuzzi and then indulge in an irresistible treat—a great massage. But my favorite program at the club was a class for ballet-style stretching and exercising, specially taught by Evelyn Cisneros, the former principal ballerina of the San Francisco Ballet. I loved to watch her dance and to imitate her exquisite movements. The elegant sweep of her arms, the precision of her steps, the grace with which she balanced on her toes, even her smile—with every motion she made me appreciate the beauty and profundity of the ballet. Her artistry went beyond what I could describe in words, but it spoke very clearly to my heart.

* * *

I soon became addicted to musical and dramatic events. The opera, the symphony, and the theater are now such an important part of my life that I don't think I could live without them. I spoil myself by buying the best seats in the auditorium.

I became a big fan of Joshua Bell, the young genius of the violin, and was thrilled by the artistry of the multitalented cellist Yo-Yo Ma and the young Chinese piano sensation Lang Lang. I will never forget Marina Domashenko, the Russian dramatic mezzo-soprano who sang the lead role so beautifully in *Carmen*, and I adored hearing performances by the extraordinary sopranos Renée Fleming and Kiri Te Kanawa. Through their instruments and their voices, these stars could transport me to realms of joy and sadness, laughter and tears.

American musicals were a new kind of entertainment for me. I'd never heard of them in China. They were so much fun, all the music and dancing entwined with a dramatic story. I tried to see everything that played in the big theaters in San Francisco, and sometimes I jetted to New York for the weekend to catch a new Broadway show. *Mamma Mia*, *The Phantom of the Opera*, and *Les Misérables* were among my favorites.

I loved to go to open-air concerts where I could wear jeans and eat American barbecue with my friends. One of my favorite venues was the Saratoga Winery—a little ironic since I can't drink wine, but the concert series there, featuring performers like jazz vocalist Diana Krall and rock singer Linda Ronstadt, was a true delight. What could be more intoxicating than sitting under the stars, listening to beautiful songs sung by such fabulous voices?

It wasn't just the music that attracted me to the opera and symphony; I relished all the pomp and circumstance of the gala opening nights and the fundraising balls. I had so much fun on these festive occasions, dressing up like a movie star in a designer dress, putting on my most alluring makeup and jewelry, and stepping out into high society accompanied by a handsome, tuxedo-clad gentleman. As a schoolgirl in Lanzhou, watching the glamorous actresses in Hollywood films, I never dreamed that one day I'd be the one in the elegant gown, drawing attention and compliments with my unique sense of style.

Over dinner in a five-star restaurant or a meal catered on-site at the performing arts center, I hobnobbed with many sophisticated people—bankers, entrepreneurs, politicians, lawyers, financiers, professors, journalists, and of course actors and musicians. Like me, they devoted their hearts to the arts as well as to their professions. Many of them soon became my valued personal friends as well as good business contacts. Talking to them, I came to appreciate Western music, culture, and people even more.

They accepted me easily, and I never felt like a new immigrant among them. To my surprise, no one guessed that I'd lived in this country for only five years. Most of these new acquaintances assumed I'd been here much longer, perhaps fifteen or twenty years. Apparently I was adapting into the society smoothly and quickly.

My one disappointment was that there were so few Asians among them. I have yet to meet anyone else in these circles who was originally from mainland China, though I hope to one day.

* * *

Like a real Californian, I was beginning to love outdoor activities—skiing at Lake Tahoe, hiking in Yosemite National Park, biking along the back roads in the Bay Area, or rollerblading along the Embarcadero, the roadway that curves along San Francisco's waterfront. Backpacking never tempted me because I couldn't tolerate the idea of not being able to shower every day, but I tried many fun and adventurous things, like parachuting, bungee jumping, and piloting a private jet with a friend who let me take the controls for just a few seconds. That was a thrilling experience.

Sometimes I received the greatest pleasure from a simple activity that reminded me of my childhood in China. One Saturday morning I was walking in Golden Gate Park with a friend when we came upon a group of people playing volleyball. All of a sudden I felt the same surge of excitement that I experienced as the team captain in junior high school. My hands were itching to hold the ball.

I asked if I could join the game. The players looked at me with doubt in their eyes. I knew why—I was wearing a narrow red skirt and a pair of red Charles David high-heeled shoes, and my recently manicured fingers had long red nails.

"How can you play in that fancy dress?" one of them asked, but with a smile. The others began to tease me.

"And those heels. You'll sprain your ankle."

"We don't want you to cry if the ball breaks one of those delicate red fingernails."

I teased them back. "Hey, I will play barefoot. Don't worry about my nails; I can get a new manicure. If I cry, will you lend me your shoulder?"

They all laughed, and one of them said, "Okay, hop in."

I kicked my shoes onto the lawn, and soon I forgot what I was wearing. All I thought about was hitting the ball and playing well. I was pleased that I hadn't lost my powerful serve. They were impressed that I kept up with their game despite my attire, but they continued their teasing.

"Watch out, John! She's a scarlet woman. Red shoes, red lipstick, red dress, red nails, red everything!"

"Hey, Tom, keep your eye on the ball, not on her. You don't want to get hit in the head again."

We played for an hour until my arms were burning and I had to say good-bye. I had such a wonderful time. The players had been warm and generous, welcoming a stranger into their midst. They were easygoing and so much fun, and their dry sense of humor was infectious. These were the kinds of qualities I have always loved about Americans.

* * *

I became a travel fanatic, and now I was able to travel wherever and whenever I wanted—as long as the trip didn't require me to drive a car.

My friends couldn't understand how I managed to get around without knowing how to drive. You can see by now that I'm a strong, brave person, so how could I be such a chicken when it came to driving? I will tell you honestly: driving is scary, and learning how to drive is a pain in the ass. Believe me, I have tried.

My first attempt to learn came while I was still married. Several times Jon took me to a parking lot and tried to teach me. The experience was not pleasant. I found it boring and stressful; he found it frustrating. Each lesson ended up in an argument. All the pedals and buttons and dashboard controls made me feel dizzy and confused, and I was going crazy just driving around in circles in the parking lot.

"Let's go on a real road," I insisted. "I can handle it."

"You're not ready yet," Jon argued. "Don't be impatient."

But I kept insisting and finally Jon gave up. He let me take his big car out on Highway One in Santa Cruz. Instantly I knew he was right; I didn't belong on the freeway. All the cars zooming past us like rockets made me so nervous that I thought I would have a heart attack. What if one of them hit me? To compound the problem, Jon kept nagging me.

"Stay straight!" "Go faster!" "Slow down!" "Keep in your lane!"

It made me feel like an idiot. Finally, though, I seemed to be handling the car well. I was excited to be at the wheel as we rolled down the highway.

That's when Jon said, "Stop the car."

"Stop it? Why?"

"There are two cop cars after you. Pull over," Jon said with obvious frustration.

"What? Cops! Why, what did I do?"

I finally managed to pull to the side of the highway. In the rearview mirror I saw a highway patrol officer approaching the car. I waited nervously, clutching the learner's permit I'd gotten from the Department of Motor Vehicles.

"Lady, please step out of the car," one of the officers commanded.

I did. "Why did you stop me? I couldn't have been speeding."

"You're zigzagging all over the highway. Two motorists reported you as a drunk driver. Let me see your license."

"Drunk! I never drink. Alcohol makes me sick." I handed over my learner's permit and gave him a sheepish look.

He studied the permit, then handed it back, along with a bit of advice. "Young lady, next time you should practice in a parking lot."

"I did practice there," I explained to him.

"Well, obviously, you need to practice there some more." He gave me a small smile, then headed back to his patrol car.

No way, I said to myself. I don't want to go back to the parking lot. This driving business is no fun. It's too much trouble, too scary. I could kill someone, or someone could kill me in an accident. Well, forget it, I am not going to try to drive anymore. I'll manage some other way.

Once I made that decision, I felt relieved. I'd rather spend my money to have someone else drive me. Cabs and chauffeur services were safer and more convenient for business meetings, and stretch limos for nights on the town were much more fun. So why bother to drive? A car was nothing but a burden to someone living in the city; fighting through traffic was a hassle and parking was a headache.

Besides, I clearly had no talent for driving. One day on a golf course with some gentlemen friends, I couldn't even manage to control the golf cart. Reaching for the brake, my foot failed to find it. With me frantically turning the wheel, the cart slipped all the way from the top of the hill into the bushes at the bottom, startling the landscaper who was working there. Fortunately nothing was damaged, but I was so embarrassed. All I could do was join in as my companions laughed themselves to tears. Here I was, a basically smart and capable person, yet so inept that I couldn't even handle a golf cart. Well, that's me. What can I say!

* * *

Even if he didn't succeed in teaching me to drive, Jon and I were forging a more comfortable relationship. I encouraged him to accept an offer for a different job, one that would permit him to have more time for himself. Even better, his new position was on the East Coast; he had wanted to move back there since the day he arrived in California. Each year we exchanged birthday gifts, and on his birthday I would sing him a special song over the phone. Sometimes we called each other to chat like old friends, and we would get together whenever our travels brought one of us to the other's city. I was really happy that we were able to put our miserable past behind us and create a friendship we could value.

Meanwhile, I was enjoying one of the benefits of my new life: the long line of interesting men who were chasing after me.

Dating in the Western world was fascinating, very different from my experiences of dating in China. Of course my taste in men and my requirements for a romantic partner had changed too. I had become more selective. The men I found attractive were over six feet tall and preferably blond. More important, they had to be able to challenge me intellectually and stimulate me artistically. I'm sure my rigid qualifications drove some perfectly fine men crazy.

The men had their own expectations, of course, and I was surprised to learn that the qualities I considered most positive —my lifestyle and achievements, my talents and capabilities, my independence, my intelligence, my worldly experience, my zest for life, and my physical beauty—were detriments on the dating scene. Although the gentlemen I dated were successful and sophisticated, they were often intimidated or threatened by the whole package that was Diana. I wouldn't have been surprised if this had happened in Asia, but I never expected it in the modern society of the West.

A few men were strong and assured enough to embrace who I was and what I had achieved. I enjoyed their romantic gestures and enthusiastic attentions, and it was a pleasure to engage in various activities with them. Their lovely company gave me many pleasant memories. Some of them were wonderful, almost flawless. Yet even when I grew really fond of someone, I pulled away. I didn't understand that at all.

* * *

Yes, I was leading a dream life, with everything I wanted. Yet sometimes I found myself feeling restless, bored, and confused. Even with all of my success and freedom and access to luxuries, I felt unfulfilled. Something was missing, but I didn't know how to find it.

Winter is the season of storms in California. One day I watched through my windows as clouds darkened the sky and the wind whipped up whitecaps on the bay. Then rain began to pelt the glass. The weather suited my mood perfectly.

I was a strong person, but the deep pain inflicted by my marriage and by YOFC's betrayal had not fully healed. I felt weak and fragile. For years I had kept up an incessant pace of work and travel.

Now that I'd cut way back on my business activities, I had a powerful realization—I had often used business as a shield, a way to avoid confronting the emotional and spiritual issues that now made me restless. That strategy was no longer working. I craved inner peace, and I needed to take time to reflect on my life and learn about myself.

I didn't know it yet, but I was about to embark on an amazing journey of healing and exploration.

* * *

Late in the winter I received a phone call from a friend.

"Diana, I've just been through an amazing experience. A self-awareness training program. You should take it. I can really recommend it highly."

I decided to sign up. I needed a chance to assess my life up to this point, examine the potentials I might want to pursue, and chart a course for the future. I had so many questions about my life. Perhaps this program that excited my friend so much would give me some answers.

So in February I traveled to Southern California for the three-day seminar, which I followed up a couple of weeks later by attending the seven-day advanced program. They were long, grueling days, beginning at eight o'clock in the morning and sometimes not finishing until midnight. We had little opportunity to eat. The forceful techniques of the seminar leaders reminded me of brainwashing. The idea was to break people down in order to push them through their personal emotional barriers, and then rebuild them with new insights and new behaviors.

Some participants found this process beneficial, but for others it proved destructive—not so much a matter of self-discovery as a way to shift blame for the failures they perceived in their lives from themselves to their parents or other outsiders. There was an exercise in which all the participants pounded on their chair, condemning their parents for all the wrongs that were done to them. I refused to participate. I'd had plenty of difficulties with my own parents, especially my mother. But I could recognize that they loved me and did the best they could for me given the limitations of their own personalities and circumstances. Perhaps it was helpful to recognize the ways in which my own negative patterns and emotional barriers stemmed from things that happened to me when I was younger, but what would I gain from blaming my parents for my problems? The only payoff was the chance to say, "It's not my fault"—and that was not really helpful. I believe that you are the only one who's the victim when you play the victim game; you set your own trap. Better to forgive your parents and forgive yourself. That's when you can move forward in a positive direction.

Out of two hundred participants, only five of us challenged the attitudes, assumptions, and techniques of the seminar leaders.

One of the unruly five was a slender woman with large dark eyes and an intense voice. She asked a question that showed her to be both intelligent and wise. Later I approached her in the restroom. "I liked your question," I said.

"Thank you," she replied, and we fell into a conversation. From that point on we sought each other out so we could participate together in the games and teamwork exercises. Over time I learned that she had graduated from optometry school and now worked as a legal secretary for her lawyer husband. She had five kids, now grown, and a phenomenal ability to reach out and touch people's souls.

> *You are the only one who's the victim when you play the victim game; you set your own trap. Better to forgive your parents and forgive yourself. That's when you can move forward in a positive direction.*

My enduring friendship with Patty was born at the seminar—one of many benefits of being there, despite the program's flaws. The seminar gave me a chance to break through barriers and let myself be vulnerable. It helped me confirm my intention to be a vulnerable, tolerant, nonjudgmental woman and my commitment to pursuing achievements based on the passions and desires within my heart.

I got another big gift at the seminar: I discovered my talent for acting. On one of the last days we had an exercise in which we took turns miming other participants. We would imitate their posture, their movements, and their body language, without speaking a word. As we began the audience would be standing, and as people recognized who we were miming, they would sit down.

My first subject was a fellow I will call Ron. I became totally absorbed in copying his heavy-footed walk, his habit of thrusting his arms out, and the way he twisted his mouth and knotted his brow. A couple of the spectators identified my subject right away and quickly took their seats. Another person giggled at my performance and then sat down, followed by two more. By the time I was finished, the whole audience was seated. Next I mimed Patty as she fought back against an insult tossed at her by the seminar leader. Again, everyone instantly recognized who I was pretending to be.

Afterward I received admiring compliments from the participants and a hug from Patty. I had never realized that I could be good at portraying a character. I decided that when I got back home I'd look into acting lessons.

At the end of the seminar I said to Patty, "I'd like to bring a seminar to China. People there need something that can show them how to tap into their potentials and passions. But not this program—a better one."

"Go for it," Patty said. "I'll help."

Right then a seed was planted. We had no idea if it would ever grow.

* * *

The seminar left me hungry to understand myself better. I began spending time at bookstores looking for nurturing and inspiring books that would guide me on my journey of self-discovery—so much time, in fact, that the staff had to kick me out at closing time. On the recommendation of the seminar leaders, I bought Deepak Chopra's *The Seven Spiritual Laws of Success*, which really opened my eyes. Reading it became my daily ritual for guidance and reflection. Its ideas were so simple, yet profound and powerful. Before long I had read all of Chopra's books, and I was thrilled when I had a chance to attend a program he presented. I regard him as a mentor who guided me to new levels of joy and peacefulness.

Other authors also helped me answer my thousands of questions: Wayne Dyer, Don Miguel Ruiz, Dr. Phil McGraw, Anthony Robbins, Joe Caruso, John Maxwell, Zig Ziglar, Dale Carnegie, and many more. As soon as I finished one book, I grabbed up another. As the months passed, I read more than one hundred books—enlightening works about spiritual guidance, self-awareness, and psychology; insightful memoirs and autobiographies; instructive volumes about business management and leadership. The profound spiritual philosophies and business wisdom I encountered helped me grow to another new level. Soon I was feeling greater contentment and peace.

I took up meditation and made it part of my daily routine. At first the process of becoming quiet and focusing deep within myself felt odd. It was a real departure for someone like me who is accustomed to being busy all the time. But soon I recognized the difference this spiritually nurturing practice was making in my life, as I began to build my inner peace.

Gradually I was learning where my fears are, and how to bring greater peace, strength, and harmony into my life. A new Diana was beginning to emerge.

* * *

Despite all the time I was putting into my new pursuits, business was never far from my mind. My lawsuit against YOFC was always in my awareness, even though its progress was painfully slow. Also, I had my real estate investments and other interests to manage. I still maintained some sidelines in the telecom industry, and now I received an offer from a Canadian firm to merge my business with theirs. They were seeking to expand into the Chinese market, and, aware that doing business in China is vastly different from doing business in Canada or the United States, they hoped to have the benefit of my expertise and my network of resources.

So in April I took an extended trip. I flew to New York, where I visited friends, and from there to Ottawa, where I met with the Canadian firm to talk about the proposed merger. My next stop was Paris; I wanted to check on some business interests there. Boarding the plane in Toronto, I noticed a fellow passenger—a Canadian man who was tall, thin, blond, and insanely handsome. Though we didn't speak, he naturally caught my attention. When we disembarked, we went our separate ways, and the memory of him faded as I turned my attention to Paris.

My visit there was brief but enjoyable, especially because of one middle-of-the-night encounter. At one o'clock in the morning I was struggling with bad jet lag. Unable to sleep, I decided to go to a dance club. As I left the hotel it was drizzling. I was standing on the sidewalk trying to hail a taxi when all of a sudden a Jaguar sports car pulled over right in front of me. A gentleman opened the door and asked if he could give me a ride. I looked at this man with salt-and-pepper hair, well dressed, well mannered, looking very sophisticated and kind, and I decided to trust him. I got into his car.

He introduced himself as Laurent and commented, "You are a very brave girl."

"I have my cell phone with me. If anything happens, I will call *les gendarmes*."

We both laughed. "You are very lucky that I am a real gentleman," he said.

He delivered me to my destination, the Latina Café on the Boulevard de Champs-Elysées. Before he let me go he kindly invited me to dinner the next day. I was delighted and accepted his wonderful invitation.

I stayed in the crowded nightclub until four in the morning. By then I was hungry, so I went to a pizza restaurant on the Champs-Elysées. French guys are not used to seeing a beautiful woman eating alone at that late hour, and I was subjected to a lot of unpleasant and unwanted attention. Fortunately the manager stopped the male patrons from harassing me.

My supper the next evening with Laurent was far more enjoyable, but it was nothing compared to my flight back to Toronto. I had just boarded the plane and was searching for my seat when I spotted the insanely handsome man; he just appeared right in front of me. We'd taken the same plane to Paris and here he was again. How odd—and how wonderful.

We sat next to each other and chatted all the way across the Atlantic Ocean. I learned that his name was David. I found myself powerfully drawn to this man, which was very unusual—normally I didn't feel such a quick attraction to a man I just happened to meet. Maybe I really was changing, becoming more open to my feelings. David had a natural calm and a gentle charm. I felt comfortable in his presence, and by the end of the flight I had a huge desire to be in his presence again.

After landing in Toronto I returned to Ottawa for another meeting with my potential Canadian partner. The discussions went well, and I was excited about the possibilities of the merger—until the CEO made a pass at me.

I was furious. Our business arrangement would mean working in close cooperation with one another, and how could I do that if I'd constantly have to be fighting him off? So many times, I'd had to give up a great business opportunity in order to maintain my principles and integrity.

To make matters worse, the CEO invited me to join him for a private dinner. I had no interest in mixing my business with my personal life, even less so since I knew the man was married. I had to set clear boundaries, and I had to do it diplomatically so I wouldn't jeopardize the business negotiations.

As I was pondering this dilemma, providence intervened. David, who had just moved to Ottawa, called to ask me to go out on a date that very same night. I quickly accepted his dinner invitation, which meant I could politely decline the CEO's. I couldn't get out of that office fast enough.

David and I enjoyed a great meal. Afterward he took me dancing at a salsa club. Despite the big crowd we hardly noticed the other people. The two of us moved very well together, our bodies in perfect synchrony. I felt a magnetic attraction between us; it was exhilarating. At one point, as he held me in his warm arms, he whispered, "Honey, you don't have to struggle anymore. You can relax and rest."

These words were so comforting, so profound. David hardly knew me, yet he understood so well all that I had been going through. I melted in his arms and let my tears run quietly down my face.

Right at that moment I knew I was falling in love with my whole heart. I could not believe it. It was an unexpected joy.

I was overwhelmed by the sudden change in my heart. And I was scared to death.

* * *

The trip to Canada marked the end of my involvement in the telecommunications industry. Although I was still excited by the technology, I encountered too many people in the telecom business who lied to me, cheated me, or wanted to harass me sexually. Yes, I had met many wonderful people also, but this latest experience was discouraging. It was part of a pattern I wanted to break.

I decided it was time once again to follow my heart. Always my most reliable guide, my heart told me that a new arena was out there waiting for me, a place where I would find stimulation, challenge, and joy—the theatrical stage. Singing, dancing, and acting became my new passions.

Well, perhaps not so new. The fact is, I was born with music and the theater in my blood. When my mother was young, she was a popular and gifted entertainer. My own talents and enthusiasm were gifts from her. As a child in the bleak coal-mining village, as an awkward adolescent in Lanzhou, as a resentful and frustrated medical student—all through my childhood and youth, my happiest times came when I was singing and dancing on the stage. I loved the creativity and vitality of people in the performing arts. I loved the rehearsals, the process of bringing a show to life and making it better and better over time. I loved the costumes and makeup that transformed me into someone new and magical. I loved the performances and the chance they gave me to share my wonder and joy with my audience. I loved the validation of their applause.

But since leaving school, I had done little to acknowledge this important part of my soul. It was important not to deny it any longer.

I began a search for an excellent singing instructor and found one of the best—Dr. Lee Strawn. An experienced teacher with a PhD from the renowned Eastman School of Music, he sang in the San Francisco Opera Chorus and had performed for several years in *The Phantom of the Opera*. Under Dr. Strawn's expert tutelage, I began to sing again, with my voice and my heart.

* * *

I was excited by the changes in my life. The one hard part was not being with David. We talked on the phone for hours and hours; we missed each other very much.

Finally, in early May, came the chance I'd been waiting for. David was going to be in Victoria, British Columbia, for the weekend, and he suggested that I join him there.

When I arrived at the Vancouver airport, David was there to meet me. I was very nervous at first. In the limo from the airport, I spoke only to the driver. But soon David and I fell into easy conversation, and from that point it seemed that we could never stop talking. I was impressed by his intelligence and knowledge and energy.

We took the ferry across the Georgia Strait to the charming city of Victoria, which was abloom with flowers. We had dinner, went dancing, and then strolled along the harbor, watching the lights sparkling on the water. After walking for a long time, my feet were sore. David carried me piggyback all the way back to the hotel. I was in heaven all weekend, comforted and protected and loved by this man whose soft strength broke through all my walls.

We arranged to meet again in New York for a weekend later in the month. The magic continued as we took in a performance of *The Graduate* on Broadway and rambled in Central Park, talking about life. We visited galleries and the Metropolitan Museum, and we discovered we shared an interest in the arts.

We also did a lot of shopping. In one store the manager was touched by the sight of us. "I'm always happy to see people in love," she said. "I've been married for twenty years and in love for every minute. I hope that will also be true for you."

I looked at David, and he nodded to me. I was pleased to know we wanted the same thing. I was surprised that I was able to open my heart so completely even though I barely knew him. But there was something special about him, and I could not hold back my heart anymore. My feelings for him were so intense. I felt bound to him, and at the same time I felt free in a way I'd never felt before, my soul soaring like a bird.

After that trip we were inseparable even though three-quarters of a continent lay between us. We talked on the phone for two hours every day. David touched parts of my heart and soul that I had never noticed before and soothed the pain that had lodged there.

I invited him to come to my home in San Francisco for the Fourth of July weekend. We celebrated the holiday by hosting a big dinner party to introduce him to my friends. I cooked eighteen dishes, and we finished the meal by watching from the windows as fireworks lit up the sky above the San Francisco Bay. Over the next two days, I showed off my adopted hometown. We dressed up to see *Madame Butterfly* at the opera —David had packed his tux—and we rode a boat to Alcatraz where we explored the famous prison on a rocky island in the middle of the bay. One evening we went to the Cliff House restaurant and watched the sun descend into the Pacific Ocean as we dined. And, as always, we spent a lot of time simply walking and talking and learning from each other.

On July 6 we phoned his mother to wish her a happy birthday. I learned that she and I had something in common—we were both born in China. Her parents were missionaries. At the time their daughter was born they were in Beijing, although most of the time they worked in Henan province. Knowing this made me feel even more closely connected to David and his family.

"Oh, Diana, I really don't want to leave," he said sadly as he departed for his flight home. That sentimental moment is still inscribed on my heart today.

I never thought that weekend would be the last time we'd spend in each other's company.

All summer we continued phoning and emailing. The communication between us was getting better and better. A letter he sent me, dated July 16, 2002, is something I will

TOP: Diana at her home in San Francisco.
BOTTOM: With Peggy at Diana's business suite.

ABOVE LEFT: In Rome.
ABOVE RIGHT: In Trianon Park, France.
RIGHT: At the Vatican.
BELOW: A business visit to Hong Kong.

Diana with her family in China, winter 2004.

CLOCKWISE FROM ABOVE:
Diana singing at her birthday party, 2004;
with Mike and Woody; Diana walking out of
her backyard; with Jim and Diana P.; with Patty
and Lindsay. (*Birthday party photos by Lonnie Dean.*)

ABOVE: Diana's Chinese girlfriends from all over the country, gathered for her birthday.
BELOW LEFT: Waiting in the lobby of Diana's condo for a special art gala, 2003.
BELOW RIGHT: At the loge seating area for a concert in Davies Symphony Hall.

ABOVE LEFT: With a friend at a business networking function, the Fortune Innovation Forum, in New York, 2005.

ABOVE RIGHT: At a luau party at the San Francisco Bay Club.

LEFT: Socializing and networking.

BELOW: In Las Vegas for a CES conference, January 2005.

TOP LEFT: With Deepak Chopra, fall 2005.

TOP RIGHT: In Shanghai with Jim and a Chinese government official at the World Management Forum.

MIDDLE LEFT: With Bill Keller, executive editor of the *New York Times*, 2005.

MIDDLE RIGHT: With San Francisco Mayor Gavin Newsom in the VIP lounge at a Commonwealth Club special event.

BOTTOM: Diana with IGI executives and business associates in San Francisco.

TOP LEFT: Playing games during a seminar testing in Beijing.

TOP RIGHT: After an eight-year separation, a reunion with Sally and Zhang Li in Beijing at the Beijing China World Hotel, summer 2005.

MIDDLE: At a business dinner in Beijing with Diana's brother and other business associates.

BOTTOM: At an ice-skating rink inside a modern shopping mall in Shenzhen, fall 2004.

Diana at the opera.

A dance performance with a Metronome professional dancer
at the Cowell Theater in San Francisco, August 2003.

Diana with her vocal coach, other singers, and some audience members after a recital in San Francisco.

ABOVE LEFT: Dressed up at the Black and White Ball, San Francisco.

ABOVE RIGHT: Disguised as Cat Woman with opera fans at a Merola Opera Masked Event at the Four Seasons Hotel, April 2005.

BELOW LEFT: Watching a musical at the Gershwin Theater in New York.

BELOW RIGHT: A gala event at Davies Symphony Hall in San Francisco.

ABOVE AND BELOW:

Celebrating with a close friend at the San Francisco Symphony's New Year's Eve gala, December 31, 2005. Diana joyfully welcomes the new year of 2006.

forever treasure for the wisdom it offered me. David pointed out that my success was rooted in my spirit, not in any material accomplishments I might have. He told me that I don't need to look to external sources to affirm my identity; it is my virtue, my heart, and my soul that define who I am. Today, whenever I feel the old urge to seek approval from others, or to let them dictate my course of action, I look at his letter to remind me. Thank you, David, for that gift. Thank you for challenging and stimulating me in all the right ways. It was such a rare experience for me.

Sadly, fissures began to appear in our relationship. Ottawa is a very long way from San Francisco. With so much geographic distance between us, it became difficult to maintain our emotional closeness. Frustration led to stress, and the stress led to heated arguments.

At the end of August, all the tension boiled over into a huge breakup.

To my deep regret, David vanished from my life as suddenly as he had appeared.

* * *

Hoping to escape the pain of losing him, I traveled to Hawaii and then to China, making stops in Beijing, Shanghai, and Shenzhen. I knew I would find comfort in the familiarity of my home country, my native culture. The cities were experiencing astounding changes. New buildings were everywhere; the old ones were gone, simply swept away. The telecommunications industry there was in the toilet, and while I knew that it would prosper again—I'd experienced the highs and lows of the industry's business cycle often enough—I was glad I was no longer part of it.

In Beijing I had a chance to spend time with my brother and his wife, a former ballerina. Hui-Hui was doing well; he had a good job in information technology. Then I visited my parents in Shenzhen. When they had retired from Lanzhou University in 1999, I'd helped them move, buying them a pleasant house by a park. Shenzhen was a livelier city than Lanzhou, with a much milder climate, and the change suited them. My sister came to see me while I was there. Yan-Yan was raising her son and running a restaurant in Lanzhou. One day she came into a room and found me crying.

"What's the matter, Jing-Jing?" she asked.

I started to pretend that it was nothing, but then the whole story about David spilled out.

"Oh, Jing-Jing, I'm so sorry," she said, "He must have been really special. I've never seen you cry over a relationship before." She comforted me as best she could.

When I returned home, I did what I could to put my life back in order. My lawsuit wasn't going well; I'd lost the man I loved; and these setbacks had tossed my feelings into upheaval. What sustained me was the joy I found in music, the tingle it put in my heart. It was even clearer to me now that my musical studies had to be a central part of my life.

With the help of my talented and inspiring instructor, Dr. Strawn, I was making progress with my singing—or so I thought. During the summer I had achieved a personal milestone—my first audition for a musical. I tried out for a part in a production of *Miss Saigon*, and, while I didn't get the role, I was proud of the effort I'd made. I was learning that there are many ways we can assess our accomplishments, and taking the risk to try something new can be an accomplishment in itself.

However, my emotional ups and downs and my frequent travels were disrupting my training. I was missing too many lessons and I'd come unprepared to too many of those I did attend. Dr. Strawn was patient and understanding at first, but, naturally enough, my on-again, off-again approach soon began to make him question my dedication. When I got back from China he told me he had to drop me as a student.

Fired by my own teacher! I was so upset with myself—I'd had an incredible opportunity and I had blown it. I begged him to take me back but he refused to reconsider.

The winter was a miserable time. I don't know if it was really colder, wetter, and drearier than other years, but it felt that way to me. Once again, I packed my bags for a trip, this time to Europe. This was an old pattern—traveling to a distant place was one way to avoid situations I needed to confront. It was as if when I left home, I could leave my pain behind. But no matter how much I pretended otherwise, I always carried it with me.

This trip, I vowed, would be different from all my travels before. It would not be a business trip, not a family visit. It would be a time to sort through the turmoil in my life, not to run away from it. I was determined to make this a journey of healing and recovery.

* * *

Paris, Barcelona, Cannes, Marseille, Monaco, the French Riviera. For twenty days in March I roamed from place to place, basking in the bright city lights and the warm Mediterranean sun.

In Paris, my first stop, I visited the Musée d'Orsay, a former train station that has been transformed into an inspiring art museum. It houses a collection mostly of nineteenth-century masters, including some of the world's most magnificent impressionist paintings. As I stood surrounded by all this beauty I suddenly burst into tears. I missed David so much. He was gone. I felt incredibly lonely.

This time, I didn't fight the pain; I didn't ask myself to hold back the tears. I let them run all down my face. Other museum-goers were staring, I knew—some sympathetic, others distressed, most of them merely curious. It didn't matter. I cried until there were no more tears left to wring out of my heart.

At first I traveled in a daze, but as I moved from one city to the next, the trip began to seem like a meditation—a chance to keep company with myself and with all my hopes and dreams and fears, and to come to understand them better. Gradually I felt myself waking up. The people, the scenery, the cultures around me, all were beautiful. Life was beautiful. There was no reason to me to feel disappointed or discouraged.

It was time for me to focus again on the positive. My own life was a rich one, not so much because of my comfortable lifestyle, but because of the accomplishments in which I took pride and the many wonderful people I counted as friends. Yes, I had been disappointed to lose David, but I could wish him well and move on.

I realized that our lives will be what we choose to make

them. It's not the job of other people to define us; we can't rely on them to make us complete and whole. We must do that for ourselves. If we want to live in a way that's true to our passions, that honors our authentic self, the power to do that lies within us. We need to be clear and focused about what we want, and invest the time and energy necessary to achieve it. That can be a daunting challenge, but the rewards are immeasurable.

Our lives will be what we choose to make them. We need to be clear and focused about what we want, and invest the time and energy necessary to achieve it.

I decided to begin by picking up the broken pieces of my music work. When I returned to San Francisco, I brought with me renewed energy and resolve. I also carried a written plan I'd created for searching out the best teachers and the best facilities for training in singing, dancing, and theater.

* * *

As soon as I got home, I put my plan into action.

My first step was to enroll in acting classes through the American Conservatory Theater in San Francisco. My training curriculum at ACT would include classes in subjects like basic breath work, singing for musical theater, improvisation, and comedy craft, taught by working professional actors.

I continued going every week to Evelyn Cisneros's ballet practice at the Bay Club. Each time I was in that dance studio I felt pure, graceful, and harmonious. I recall a moment that occurred as we danced to Tchaikovsky's *Swan Lake*. A picture crystallized in my head of that peaceful, clear lake with a beautiful view and a ballerina dancing and singing there. In that instant a wonderful feeling enraptured my heart, tingled my soul, breathed with my body. My arms, my legs, my whole being felt intensely alive. Laughter, tears, sadness, joy—everything that lifts me up was captured in that moment. I wished that the music would never stop—just go on and on forever.

To expand my dancing skills, I signed up for lessons at the Metronome Dance Center, which offered intensive classes and workshops in many varieties of dance. I especially loved the Latin dancing—so sensuous, and so full of passion and energy. The spirited Brazilian samba, with its complex rhythms and intricate steps—not to mention the fabulous costumes—was the greatest challenge and biggest delight.

Now that I was throwing myself into my plan, my stress was diminishing. I felt free and light. The biggest disappointment was that I hadn't found another vocal coach. I asked friends for recommendations and checked out possibilities through the San Francisco Conservatory of Music. I tried out several instructors, interviewing them and taking sample lessons to try them out, but none of them made me feel as though I'd found the right one.

Eventually someone suggested that I go the National Association of Teachers of Singing. I found a number of San Franciscans listed on their website and started calling randomly. Dr. Jay Pierson was one of the first to call back.

When I stepped into his home studio on July 5, 2003, I was instantly at ease. Dr. Jay was tall and thin with a rakish smile, a strong yet warm man with an engaging sense of humor. He

had performed with a number of opera companies and symphony orchestras, and he was on the music faculty at Santa
Clara University down in Silicon Valley. That first class
passed quickly—a warm, relaxed, joyful hour. I knew I'd
found the right instructor—a great teacher and a true artist.
When he sang, his creamy, emotional baritone voice touched
every single nerve I had and penetrated into my blood. I listened quietly and attentively, thinking, What a miraculous
voice he has.

After hearing me sing for him, he pointed out that I might
be a soprano rather than mezzo. That was a huge surprise—
everyone had always told me I was a mezzo.

"You can reach all the mezzo notes," he agreed. "Your voice
has a great range. But soprano works most easily and naturally
for you, and sounds the best."

I told him I wanted to audition on July 11—less than a
week away—for a production of *The Sound of Music* in San Jose.
He kindly didn't laugh but helped me practice the song I
planned to sing: "Losing My Mind" from *Follies.*

At the end of the lesson, Dr. Jay said to me, "In September
I'm producing a recital. All my students will be singing arias
from various operas. I'd like you to be part of it if you're willing to do the preparation."

I couldn't believe what I'd heard. "An opera recital? Me?"

He said, "That's right."

Just the thought of it made me nervous. "Do you really think
I'll be able to do it?"

He looked me in the eyes and calmly and confidently said,
"Why not? I think you can. Let's give it a try."

When I stepped out of his studio, I danced all the way to

Union Square, humming the new songs I'd learned. From then on I was on fire about my singing; I couldn't wait to go to Dr. Jay's class every week.

* * *

Being on track again felt wonderful. I had a goal and a plan for reaching it, and every day I took another step forward.

The progress I was making in my musical studies was having a huge impact in my life, opening another path of adventure and joy. Dr. Jay's faith in my ability gave me the power and courage to take a chance on myself, and it affirmed for me that we all have the power to create miracles in our lives. He reminded me how important it is to encourage people whenever we can. You never know when your words of support might change someone's life.

We all have the power to create miracles in our lives.

I continued to seek out inspirational books, and I kept to my meditation routine. I took up yoga, too, a beneficial addition to the mix.

Ever since my retirement I'd been exploring the ideas and insights of wise authors, examining my accomplishments, and reevaluating my life. Through my efforts to assess my life's real meaning and purpose, I was building a solid base of self-awareness and understanding. As a result, I felt stronger and calmer, more in harmony with myself and the world. I was learning to face some truths about myself, to recognize my fears and push past them, to be kinder to myself and less judgmental. I was more accepting of other people too, and better able to support and encourage my friends and help them when trouble struck their lives.

My definition of success began to change. Money, status, fame, and admiration are not true measures of success, I realized; they are side products. Success isn't a destination, a pinnacle to strive for. It is an ongoing journey, the steps you take to discover and become your authentic self, and to honor and encourage that process in others. When you move forward to new accomplishments that are based on your courage, your creativity, and your own strong spirit, that's when you are achieving success.

It important is to encourage people whenever we can.

I felt challenged and uplifted by the ideas I encountered in my reading. At first it was hard to reconcile the Western philosophies and wisdom I was studying with the traditional Chinese beliefs I'd grown up with. But the effort to understand them proved very fulfilling.

Most Chinese people, including me, are taught to be someone else—not our true selves, but a person who meets the approval of our parents, our teachers, the government, and the society. The authority figures in our lives don't use encouragement to mold us into what they want us to be; instead, their tools are criticism and pressure. We are forced to behave according to strict standards, and our individuality and creativity are suppressed in our families, in our schools and universities, and in our workplaces.

As a result, few Chinese people have a real belief in their own abilities and worth and power. Most lack the self-confidence even to figure out their own dreams, let alone find ways to achieve them. So they seek validation from external sources, competing with each other for status, money, material goods, and approval from outsiders.

Success isn't a destination, a pinnacle to strive for. It is an ongoing journey, the steps you take to discover and become your authentic self, and to honor and encourage that process in others.

Most Chinese people are conservative and cautious, fearing change, fearing loss, fearing the future, fearing anything that seems uncertain. This, as they see it, is the way to survive. Taking risks or acting boldly is considered strange and unacceptable behavior. That's one of the root reasons why China today is not an innovator in business, and why so many people there lead restless, stress-filled lives.

This prevailing mentality has had a profoundly negative impact, destroying the spirits of the children and ensuring that adults will fail to fulfill their potential. As I'd learned from bitter personal experience, an individual who wants to blaze his or her own path to happiness and satisfying personal achievements will find that many barricades have been placed in the way.

So it was a joy for me to find so many books and authors that offered maps and guidance for this kind of journey. Even better, I discovered that these Western principles had much in common with the wise teachings of Taoism and Buddhism. I was glad to be able to keep within me the great values of

Chinese culture, and at the same time absorb the spirit of Western thought—so healthy, earthy, open, and free.

Miraculously, the insights I was gaining and the changes I was making within myself led to a huge breakthrough in my relationship with my mom. Her opinion had always had a big impact on me. I craved her approval, and I was devastated whenever she was critical or harsh. I finally realized that I'd wanted her to be someone that it was impossible for her to be.

When she was disapproving or judgmental, it wasn't because she didn't love me. Our clashes occurred in part because of our personalities. In some ways we are much alike—both of us are strong-willed and stubborn. In other ways we are poles apart—she is always cautious, while I believe we must take risks at times. Both the similarities and the differences provided fertile ground for conflict.

Her personal experiences also had contributed to our problems. She had suffered many hardships and disappointments, and she wanted to spare her children from the kind of negative experiences she had endured. That noble wish led her to be demanding and overprotective of her children.

The traditions of Chinese culture were another factor. In China, the reverence for parents goes beyond respect to entitlement. Parents believe it is their prerogative to make decisions for their children, even when the children have become adults. The attitude is, "I raised you, so I have a right to run your life." Most families constitute a small culture that is a rehearsal for the big culture, and ours was no exception.

Chinese parents are supposed to live for their children and through their children. They see everything they do as being for their kids' benefit, often at the sacrifice of the parents' individual lives and happiness. Having successful children with prestigious careers or high positions in society elevates the parents' status and adds to their honor.

As a result, the purpose of child rearing in China is not to give kids the skills and self-confidence to achieve their dreams; rather, it's to pressure them to fulfill the dreams of the parents, who use blame and criticism as tools in their effort to exert control. In the process, they too often destroy the children's creativity and hope. This system has a negative effect on the health, growth, and happiness of both the children and the adults.

> *The purpose of child rearing in China is not to give kids the skills and self-confidence to achieve their dreams; rather, it's to pressure them to fulfill the dreams of the parents.*

Once their kids leave home and become independent adults, the parents often feel their own lives have little value, especially after they retire. That's when Chinese parents start to push their children to have babies. Having grandchildren lets them feel they still have some importance and use.

While I value the Chinese tradition of children taking care of their own parents, I certainly don't appreciate the sense of ownership that makes their parents feel entitled to control their lives. Parents have to know their own lives have equal value to their children's. They are entitled to live full and rewarding lives on their own but not to depend on their kids for happiness.

Western society takes a different approach. The culture respects each person's individuality, creativity, independence, and choice. Parents live their own lives, and they allow and encourage their kids to find fulfilling paths for themselves.

This mentality is much more free, relaxed, and natural, and it creates an environment that supports creativity and originality. I like it very much.

Western society respects each person's individuality, creativity, independence, and choice. Parents live their own lives, and they allow and encourage their kids to find fulfilling paths for themselves.

So many times in my life I had defiantly insisted on treading my own path instead of following the course my mother had prescribed for me. I saw her as controlling and critical; she saw me as disobedient and disrespectful. Each of us was convinced we were doing what was best, and each of us in our own way was right.

As I came to understand myself better, I also learned to understand my mom. I began to listen to her more, and to my surprise she responded by listening to me. Instead of talking at each other, we began to have real conversations. Soon we all began to see each other as adults. By breaking the pattern and responding to my parents differently, I forced them to respond differently to me.

My mom is slowly releasing her tight grip, becoming less overprotective of my brother, my sister, and me. It's hard for her not to worry about us, to not involve herself too much in her children's lives. But she has become more understanding of the choices we have made.

It is vitally important for every person to claim his or her own life. I had known that through instinct all along. Now my parents were beginning to grasp the notion of finding their own dreams and paying attention to their own needs and desires.

"Look to the future and focus on making positive things happen," I keep telling them. "Go for the hope and the strength and the love."

* * *

I loved my singing and dancing classes, but my work at the ACT training studio was proving to be a challenge. Acting demands creativity and spontaneity—the opposite of the logic, analysis, and controlled thinking that had become customary for me as I ran my business. I felt stiff and awkward onstage, especially in situations that involved intimate interactions among the characters. With my Chinese upbringing, I found it hard even to watch the other students perform in those scenes.

> *Look to the future and focus on making positive things happen. Go for the hope and the strength and the love.*

I cared tremendously what others thought about me in the performing arts, and the more I focused on that, the less I could let go of my fear. I envied the talents of the Western kids, including the American-born Chinese and Asian students. They were all so brave and natural about discovering and expressing their feelings and passions in a theatrical way. Feeling like a failure, I began to avoid my classes. Maybe studying acting in the Western theater was not for me after all.

"Why don't you try taking an improvisation class?" one of my classmates suggested.

"Yeah," another student agreed. "It's a good way to loosen up and become more comfortable onstage."

"It builds your stage confidence, too," someone else said.

So, pushed by curiosity and desperation, I signed up for the next improv class on ACT's schedule. It turned out to be an amazing experience. The class opened my eyes and removed some of my fear as I realized how creative and talented human beings can be when they get encouragement and great instruction.

The students in the class came from all over the world, and every one of them was like a magician. One minute someone was a grandmother, the next minute an infant crawling on the floor. Another person was deaf and couldn't speak, and then transformed to a soprano with a melodious voice. We could be anyone or anything our wild imaginations could dream of. We learned to use our movements, voices, expressions, and postures to bring our creations out of our heads and into the world. Even silence could deliver a dramatic meaning.

We all supported each other as we became more adept at our craft through games, skits, exercises, and lots of surprises and laughter. For me the class was a real breakthrough—I started paying less attention to what others thought about me and concentrating more on my own creativity and sense of fun. Everyone was sorry when the class ended.

Dynamic Comedy Craft was another class I loved. The students were divided into teams to prepare and present comedy scenes. My two male partners and I did a humorous sketch in which I played a sex maniac called Nurse Ratchett. What a huge challenge that was for me. In the beginning I couldn't get into the role at all; it was too hard to let go of my fear of being judged. In one scene, I was seducing a pair of young boys and I had to grab their butts. At first I couldn't bring myself to do it. It was much too difficult and embarrassing. The Chinese are not direct and aggressive like that, not even in private, let alone in public.

We rehearsed the scene over and over. With the help of my fellow actors, I gradually found the fun in playing the silly part.

Even so, when the time for our performance arrived, I was nervous. I dressed for the part in a white nurse's jacket and, beneath it, a provocative, tight-fitting miniskirt. My makeup —red-hot lipstick and a lot of black, purple, and blue eye shadow—was deliberately applied to look as dramatic, colorful, and messy as possible. I couldn't bear to look at myself in the mirror, for fear I would gross myself out. One good thing—in this ridiculous getup, no one would blame me if I looked like I had the jitters.

Finally my big moment came. I picked up my prop—a bicycle pump that was intended to symbolize the action of seduction. As I waved it around at the boys, pushing the handle in and out, I heard a big laugh. How gratifying it was to crack up my audience!

Comedy, I discovered, is very rewarding, but it's not as easy as it looks. In fact, I was learning that being a real artist of any kind is just like doing business—creativity is important, but the secrets of success are practice, dedication, and hard work.

Though I loved singing and dancing, I wasn't certain that acting was for me. The acting I was doing also required a deeper understanding of American culture, people, and history than I'd achieved at this point. If I couldn't really get into the part, my performance felt detached and fake, which made me uncomfortable. This was especially true if the part required me to behave in a way that was contrary to my own culture and values—I wasn't sure I could completely let them go, and that contributed to the awkwardness and fear I sometimes felt onstage.

> *Being a real artist of any kind is just like doing business— creativity is important, but the secrets of success are practice, dedication, and hard work.*

But one thing I did know—if I were interested in a part, I would devote myself to getting it and put every bit of my passion and skill into the performance. I hoped that with more training and practice, I would improve my techniques and enjoy acting more.

* * *

Practicing in the studio is one thing. Performing onstage in front of an audience is quite another.

I didn't have high hopes when I tried out for *The Sound of Music*—in fact, no hopes at all. It would have taken a miracle to get me cast in the show. I was far from ready to pursue a real role. I hadn't even prepared head shots or a resume. Still, when it was my turn to get up on the stage and sing, I gave the best rendition that I could. I knew auditioning would be a great experience, and I was right. I learned how the auditions were conducted and what to expect, and I boosted my confidence by giving it a sincere try. Taking advantage of this opportunity would help me be ready when an audition really counted.

A month later I was on a different stage, the one at the Cowell Theater at Fort Mason, a former military base on San Francisco Bay that has been transformed into a center for arts and environmental groups. Metronome was presenting its dance showcase, and I would be in two numbers. I was happy and excited. Dancing had turned out to be good for me. Thanks to all the exercise I had lost eleven pounds; Western dancing was a more athletic activity than the stylized Chinese dancing I'd done as a child. Not only was I slimmer, but my strength and physical energy had increased. And there was no better remedy for tension and stress. Now I was about to receive the payoff from my three months of hard work and intense practice.

My first number was a samba. With six other women I pranced onto the stage to perform the intricate choreography. We wore glittering bikini costumes in a rainbow of colors—mine was green—and huge Brazilian hats. I was so nervous that my smile muscles froze in place, but I could tell we were dancing beautifully. We were also getting drenched in sweat under the hot lights. I loved it.

When I went onstage for the second time that evening, I felt more relaxed. I was becoming more at home with the lights, the music, the high energy of the dancers waiting backstage, the hush of the audience that would suddenly erupt into applause. This dance was a duet based on the cha-cha, and my partner, Eldon, was a fine dancer. Our steps and motions were in complete synchrony. I twirled in my pretty fuchsia dress and flirted with the audience. Then I launched into a series of solo steps that brought me my loudest applause yet. After the showcase was over, my friends rushed up with flowers to celebrate the joyful moment with me. I was so happy.

* * *

My dancing feet had hardly stopped moving when it was time to get ready for the singing recital. This annual event was produced to give Dr. Jay's students valuable performance experience and the chance to show off what they'd learned over the past year.

The piece he picked for me was from *Don Giovanni*, Mozart's opera about the womanizing nobleman from Seville and how he receives his final comeuppance. Cad that he is, Don Giovanni tries to seduce a peasant girl named Zerlina on her wedding day. I would sing one of Zerlina's arias, the one beginning "Vedrai, carino." It was perfectly suited to my voice.

Dr. Jay taught me the aria word by word—how the vowels were pronounced, which syllable was stressed, where the pauses fell, what the meaning was of the word and phrase. We also worked on the character, so I would understand who Zerlina was and how the aria fits within the context of the story. His coaching was an excellent complement to my training at ACT. There the instructors focused on singing technique. Dr. Jay not only improved my basic vocal technique but also went beyond that to teach about music theory and help students express what was in their hearts. As he worked with me he was never discouraging, but always kept me on balance in a diplomatic way.

Between July and September I learned more about music than I ever thought possible. How lucky I was to have such an encouraging coach. Dr. Jay empowered me to conquer my fears, to challenge my limits, to help me learn about the real music in my heart.

Before I knew it, the evening of the recital had arrived. My mouth was dry and my heart was pounding as I took my place at the front of the Old First Presbyterian Church, which was lending its splendid facility for the occasion, and looked out at rows and rows of expectant faces. All of their eyes were fixed on me. I was wearing a long gown, but the sides of the skirt were slit to the knee and I just knew everyone could see how my legs were shaking.

The pianist gave me my cue. I put my heart in my voice and began to sing.

I'd like to report that I did brilliantly, that I presented a perfect performance and received a standing ovation. That isn't quite what happened. At the start my breaths were too short, thanks to my nerves, which threw my phrasing off. In the middle I forgot a few words, so I had to mumble quickly through that part.

But I did it—and that is what counts. With only two months of training I had performed a difficult opera aria before an audience, which rewarded me with their attention and applause. Next time I would do even better. And there would

definitely be a next time, because this had been such a profound experience.

Look at me, I thought, taking my bow as the clapping re-
sounded. Here I am—Jing-Jing, daughter of the Yellow River.
Now I'm Diana, singing and dancing on Western theater
stages in the fabled city of San Francisco. Now I'm living like
a star. Who could ever have imagined that I'd be where I am,
doing what I'm doing, and loving my life so much?

Diana's Stepping-Stones
on the Journey to Success

Let yourself enjoy life. It is never too late to learn new things,
try new adventures, explore new places and ideas, and develop new interests. Life is a huge banquet; we should taste
and enjoy all of the good things it has to offer.

Reexamine your definition of success. Success is not a destination,
a spot on a map where we might someday arrive. We achieve
it through the way we make our journey, living lives of integrity and passion that honor our true selves and our heartfelt goals. Riches, accolades, and other tangible symbols of
success are nice to have, but they come from external sources.
They are neither as satisfying nor as lasting as the success that
comes from within us.

Don't get attached to material things. Material abundance is a side
product that comes from using our spirit and our strength.
Accumulating goods is neither the purpose of life nor a valid

measurement of success. Possessions can enrich our lives, but they can make our lives more difficult if we allow them to be our master.

Seek out the best teachers you can find. When we stop learning, we derail our journey to success. Good teachers can be found in books, in classes, in mentorships, and in informal relationships with stimulating people who, through their accomplishments, knowledge, and example, can guide us toward our goals.

Open your heart to others. The love that we give to others and receive from them is what makes life worthwhile. Sometimes we avoid love because we fear that it will cause us pain, but when that's the case we create for ourselves a hurt that's far greater. Remember, allowing ourselves to be vulnerable takes more courage and strength than pretending to be tough.

Open your heart to yourself. The more we know about ourselves, the more power we unleash within us to achieve a better future. When we are able to accept ourselves and embrace who we are, then we have less fear. We are able to conquer any challenge and to attain any goal.

With attorneys Steve Hemminger and Ellen King of White & Case LLP
at their Palo Alto office, working on ATI's case.

蚂蚁斗象

Eleven Diana Versus Goliath, 2003–2004

The sweet musical notes of the recital had barely faded away when I began to prepare for my lawsuit against YOFC. It was almost time for the long-delayed hearing. In this drama I would have the starring role.

At last I would get the chance to let the world to know about this company. The lawsuit itemized the long list of its wrongdoings.

First of all, YOFC allegedly had breached its contract with my firm, ATI, in several ways, one of which was using other agents to sell to customers that had been exclusively assigned to ATI.

YOFC also allegedly had failed to pay substantial sums of money that it owed to ATI: commissions on sales made to YOFC's single-mode fiber customers in China, lost commissions for sales contracts that YOFC failed to honor, and late-payment penalties provided for in the contract.

Furthermore, YOFC allegedly had committed fraud by falsely representing that they could not provide their Chinese customers with products ordered for 2001 because the company would have no single-mode fiber available. It was bad enough that this assertion was untrue. Worse, I believe it was a knowing and deliberate lie.

The lawsuit also claimed that ATI's optical fiber business had suffered irreparable harm from YOFC's actions. Because we could not meet the commitments we had made to the valuable clients, we lost them as customers. We lost the good will and reputation that we had built with considerable time, effort, and expense. Although my firm had not relied on YOFC for all of its business—from the beginning, we had worked to develop other business lines and penetrate into Western markets—YOFC's unethical business conduct, at least as it appeared to me, had forced my firm out of the fiber market in China.

It had been a long, frustrating journey to reach the point where we had a hearing scheduled. My attorneys had filed the suit in the Civil Division of the California Superior Court nearly two and a half years earlier. Ever since then, I believe that YOFC had been throwing its weight around, trying to obstruct the proceedings.

The company created endless impediments and postponements. Maybe that was their strategy for victory: to drag the case out as long as they could until they destroyed my courage and confidence. They were sure I'd lose heart, and the pesky little problem of my lawsuit would simply go away.

I was determined never to give them that satisfaction.

As the case dragged on, I began to wish I could amend the lawsuit to demand compensation for the impact on my mental health.

* * *

YOFC's first action had been to petition to have the case thrown out, claiming that the U.S. court had no jurisdiction. Their top executives asserted that they had never communicated with me or solicited me to be their representative while I was in the United States. When I read their sworn testimony, I could not believe that they could make this statement for what they did.

"On or about July 24, 1998, in the afternoon, the CEO asked me to go to his office. At his office, I met Diana for the first time in my life."

This statement was from Mr. Yan, YOFC's manager of optical fiber sales. He simply denied that we had met three months earlier, in April 1998, when, at the warm invitation of the former CEO of YOFC, I had traveled from Santa Cruz to visit YOFC's headquarters in Wuhan. For several months, ever since I met him at the IWCS show in Philadelphia the previous November, the former CEO had actively solicited me to become YOFC's representative. Mr. Yan failed to mention that during that April visit he had given me a grand introduction, providing me with rich information on the company's great history, its honorable reputation, its production capacity, and its spectacular plans for expansion. Other YOFC managers backed up Mr. Yan's statement with equally strong declarations. I believe they were determined to wipe out any record of what they had done to enlist ATI. Apparently they could conveniently change their memories whenever they needed to defend their position.

What they didn't consider was that I would have kept our initial written communications dating back to early 1998. My records proved to be convincing evidence that the court had jurisdiction over YOFC in California.

At a hearing early in 2002, eight months after the suit was filed, the court denied their request for dismissal and ruled that the case could move forward. One point on the scoreboard for my team.

Then YOFC offered to submit our quarrel to the China International Economic and Trade Arbitration Commission, or CIETAC. This organization, which is headquartered in Beijing, was established to provide resolution of commercial disputes in which at least one of the parties is a Chinese individual or economic entity.

To me, this was just another game that YOFC was trying to play. Their motive seemed obvious: by dragging the case to China, they expected to gain some measure of favor or protection from the government. After all, YOFC was a joint venture partially owned by the government.

In May 2002 my team scored an additional point: the court agreed that the lawsuit should be handled in California and appointed Judicial Arbitration and Mediation Services, Inc., to conduct an arbitration. This organization, familiarly known as JAMS, complements the court system by providing alternative modes for resolving disputes so that the combatants can avoid litigation.

The hearing was set for October 2003 in San Francisco. The proceeding would resemble a civil trial in that both parties could present evidence, have witnesses testify, and cross-examine the witnesses for the other side. Instead of a judge

and jury, we would be arguing our case before an arbitrator—
a "neutral" in the language of JAMS.

I was determined to win. I wanted every cent of the money
I was owed, just on principle. Even more I wanted justice. I
knew I was right. I wanted the legal record to redeem me
and expose YOFC's business conduct—a chicanery, as it appeared to me—to every one of the customers and my former
colleagues.

* * *

With only a month to go before the arbitration hearing, and
even less time before I was scheduled to give a deposition
to YOFC's lawyers, I dived into preparing for the case. As
I tried to discuss plans and strategies with my attorneys, it
quickly became apparent that they and I were not the best fit.
Our styles and objectives were very different. Why had I not
realized that until now? To my great disappointment and regret, I realized I should have placed less trust in the lawyers
to handle matters and paid more attention to the lawsuit.
Instead I had allowed myself to be distracted by other things
going on in my life. Now time was tight, and with such
a complicated case, I didn't see how we could possibly be
ready.

What a nightmare. I felt furious and helpless. If I asked for
a postponement, the hearing might not be rescheduled for another year or two. But if I moved forward, given the way the
case had been handled, I could only imagine that the worst
might happen.

The fear of losing the case almost buried me. Every day, I

tortured myself with blame for this awful mess. If only I'd been alert, if I'd been competent, if I'd been on top of things, I could have, and should have, prevented the problem.

The world felt hopeless and dark as I became mired in an unbearable depression. I did not want to eat, and I could not sleep. Even a quick nap brought me nightmares. My regular activities ground to a halt as I lay around all day in my bed or on my sofa. I had no strength, no energy. My head would not stop spinning. What could I do? Was I going to let these people get away with it, let all these years of effort go to waste? I could not bear the thought, but I could not figure out any solution. I was losing all faith in myself.

One morning, after a week of self-pity, I looked closely in the mirror. I could not even recognize myself. My hair was tangled, my face had lost its usual glow, and a few wrinkles had appeared. Glancing around I saw that my home was in shambles, with papers scattered everywhere. Oh, my God, what had I done? How could I have let myself sink like this? This was not me. Enough was enough. I had to pull myself together.

While I was taking a long, hot shower, my tears flowed, but the crying felt good. I stayed in the shower stall for a long time, letting the water pelt me as I reflected on my life. So many dramatic changes had happened to me; so many miracles had occurred. I had been in sad situations before, and I'd always managed to make them better. I could, and would, do it this time too.

When I made that resolve, I felt myself pulled out of my depression. I began to think deeply about what really made my miracles happen. The answers were clear in my head: it was my unstoppable desire for a joyful life; it was my infinite passion to explore the world; it was my unbreakable insistence on living life with integrity and principles; it was my persistence and dedication and years of hard work. The spirit and the power to make miracles lay within me. And they were still there, stronger than ever. The obstacles I was facing now would not stop me. I would overcome this mess. I deserved better and I wouldn't give up.

My unstoppable desire for a joyful life; my infinite passion to explore the world; my insistence on living life with integrity and principles; my persistence and dedication: the spirit and the power to make miracles lay within me.

I made up my mind to find the solution. If I gave 100 percent of my effort to fighting to achieve what I wanted, then even if I didn't get it in the end, I would have nothing to regret.

The first step was to find better legal representation. After interviewing more than twenty attorneys in the top ten international law firms, I found two extraordinary litigators, James Burns and Christopher Vejnoska, and hired them to help me prepare for my deposition.

I was gratified to realize I'd chosen well. James and Chris believed in me; they were encouraging and sympathetic. Even better, they had a great deal of knowledge and experience and high standards of professionalism. With the help of these two lawyers, I felt hopeful and strong. They pulled me back from the brink of my depression.

The deposition was an unpleasant experience, even a little

scary. It took place at the San Francisco offices of the law firm that YOFC had hired to represent them. The lead attorney on the case—let me just call him Mr. A—hammered me with questions. He was a tall man with dark hair, olive skin, a voice that was deep and intense, and a manner that was impatient and pushy. He smiled at me, but I felt it was a courtesy smile; there was nothing genuine about it. As he badgered me, I focused on the place on his suit jacket where one of the buttons was missing. Thanks to James and Chris, I handled the situation well.

I was still unsure, though, about the wisdom of completely changing my legal representation. Was it too late, with the arbitration hearing almost upon me? Perhaps I should go back to the original team.

When I had almost made up my mind to transfer my case to James and Chris, events took a sudden twist. YOFC's key witness—its manager of optical fiber sales, Mr. Yan—was unable to get a visa to come to the United States, so the firm's counsel requested another continuance. YOFC refused to accept videoconferencing as an alternative, which would have been perfectly workable. Once again I believe the company was using delaying tactics in an attempt to derail the case.

But JAMS would have none of it. The arbitrator assigned to our dispute ordered the hearing to take place as scheduled. I was so happy—something had finally turned out in my favor.

* * *

My mood was light on the October morning when I arrived at the JAMS arbitration center on the eleventh floor of San

Francisco's Embarcadero Center. I was accompanied by one of the attorneys who'd been with me from the start. The Honorable Daniel "Mike" Hanlon, a distinguished-looking white-haired gentleman, was our neutral. He had impressive judicial experience, having been a presiding justice on the California Court of Appeal and a presiding judge on the San Francisco Superior Court.

No one from YOFC showed up. Just the three of us were present, and the hearing lasted less than one hour. We assumed Judge Hanlon would issue a default ruling in my favor since YOFC didn't appear. I was astonished that after thirty months of buildup, it could be over so simply and quickly.

More than that, I was relieved and grateful. At last I could put the whole wretched episode behind me and move forward with my life. A fresh beginning—what a wonderful gift for my thirty-sixth birthday, which came near the end of the month.

It turned out that I celebrated too soon.

As we anxiously awaited word of the award, YOFC notified Judge Hanlon that Mr. Yan's visa had come through. To my shock, the judge granted another continuance. We would have to have the hearing over again, at some new date that hadn't been decided.

All of my hurt and anger pushed to the surface. How could this happen? Why had no one told me there might be such a consequence? I felt as though my case were being fumbled. So much time had been wasted in the last three years. Well, I decided no one would waste any more of it.

I was discouraged with my original attorneys, and James and Chris were unavailable to take my case further. So I began all over again to research the issues and seek out the first-class legal representation I needed. It was a painful and tedious job. Selecting the top twenty global law firms, I spent several weeks in November interviewing senior litigators and managing partners.

At last the long effort paid off. I found two excellent lawyers—Steven Hemminger and Ellen McGinty King of White & Case LLP, a prestigious and powerful law firm with considerable experience working in China and dealing with Chinese companies. Steven, who had warm eyes and a distinguished beard lightly touched with gray, headed the firm's Palo Alto office and was a leading expert on intellectual property disputes. Ellen, an energetic brunette with a wide smile, specialized in litigation involving trade secrets, unfair competition, and patent and trademark infringement. Working in the heart of the fabled Silicon Valley, they had both dealt with numerous clients in high-technology fields.

As soon as White & Case took over the case, I knew I'd made a wise move. When you are uncomfortable with your lawyer, listen to your gut and find a different one. Generally, as you may know, bad attorneys can make your life miserable, while good ones, like the ones I had now, can work wonders. Very quickly I knew that Ellen and Steve were ethical, caring, and highly professional. Their strategic minds, their rapid grasp of the core issues of the case, and their attitude of strength and self-assurance convinced me that I'd placed my case in the right hands.

* * *

My stomach tied itself into knots as I walked into the conference room to face the enemy. It was February 24, 2004, and I had come to White & Case's Palo Alto office, where Ellen King would take Mr. Yan's deposition. For the first time in more than three years, I would be face to face with someone from YOFC.

When Mr. Yan arrived I greeted him courteously. He didn't say a word to me, not even hello, and I could tell he didn't want to look at me. He'd always struck me as arrogant and insulting; now, as he ignored my presence in the room, I was reminded of a meeting we'd had at which he spent the entire time speaking to someone else on his cell phone. From the beginning of my association with YOFC he had doubted my ability, and he didn't change his mind even as I built an outstanding record of promoting YOFC's products.

Mr. Yan was accompanied by two lawyers, whom I'll call Mr. B and Ms. C, as well as Mr. Yu, the chief operating officer of YOFC. Ellen and I were outnumbered two to one—a ploy of YOFC's to intimidate us. Also present were an interpreter fluent in English and Mandarin and a certified shorthand reporter to transcribe an official record of the questions and answers.

The deposition took two full days. At first Mr. Yan avoided answering most of the questions. His responses were a litany of forgetfulness: "I can't really remember. . . . I can't really be sure. . . . I can't clearly recall. . . ."

Despite his high position within the company and his supposed expertise, he was very vague on what one would think would be basic information—how much production capacity YOFC had, how much optical fiber was actually produced and sold, or what the sales quotas were. He could not hazard a guess as to how much of the fiber that YOFC produced—zero percent, 100 percent, or something in between—was reserved for YOFC's own use.

If the issues weren't so serious, it would have been funny to watch his testimony. In my mind I nicknamed him Mr. I Don't Remember.

He denied having seen the representation agreement between YOFC and ATI prior to July 24, 1998, the day it was signed, even though his handwritten amendments appeared on an earlier draft.

According to his version of events, my contract did not make ATI YOFC's exclusive representative in China; it covered only the eleven customers named in the agreement's Appendix A.

Ellen asked him to look at Exhibit 9, a copy of the agreement, and directed his attention to the first paragraph. "It says that ATI is appointed by YOFC as exclusive selling representative in the territory of the People's Republic of China for a period of three years."

"Yes, I have seen it," Mr. Yan acknowledged.

"Was ATI YOFC's exclusive selling representative in the territory of the People's Republic of China for that three-year period?"

"It should not be within the territory of China," Mr. Yan insisted. "It should be the exclusive representative for the listed customers."

"That's not what the agreement says, though, is it?"

"Yes. According to the agreement, it was written that they were the exclusive representative in China."

Hooray, I thought, Mr. Yan just slapped his own face. Ellen had caught him. A day and a half into the deposition, and he has finally conceded this crucial point.

Then Ellen asked about the sales representative YOFC had used in violation of its contract with ATI, whom I will call Mr. J. Mr. J had had an earlier agreement to represent YOFC in selling to certain customers, but that agreement was superseded by mine. "Did you tell Mr. J that he should not attempt to make any sales to the eleven customers after July 24, 1998?"

"Yes," Mr. Yan agreed.

Ellen pointed out the paragraph in the ATI agreement that said YOFC would pay ATI commissions on all sales within the People's Republic of China. Then she asked about a company I will call Client Q, which was one of the eleven customers listed in Appendix A. Even though Client Q was supposed to deal with YOFC only through my company, Mr. J had continued to make sales there.

"Did YOFC pay ATI commissions on all sales made to Client Q?"

"No."

"Why not?"

"Because Client Q, this client, is somehow special." Mr. Yan explained that the general manager of Client Q wanted to work with Mr. J because they had studied at the same science research institute.

If you asked me, that should have made no difference. In the United States, the connection between the two men would be considered part of the old boys' network. In China, it

would come under the heading of *guanxi*, a back-door relationship. In either country, Mr. J's continuing to represent
YOFC in making sales to Client Q would violate the representation agreement.

Mr. Yan confirmed that indeed this had occurred. His testimony demonstrated that, to many Chinese businesspeople,
political relationships are far more important than contractual
obligations. This mentality is one of the biggest problems of
doing business in China.

Ellen asked, "Did YOFC sell single-mode fiber to Client Q
after July 24, 1998?"

"Yes," Mr. Yan said.

"And these sales were made through Mr. J, correct?"

"Yes."

"And ATI never agreed in writing that Client Q would not
be on its exclusive list of customers, did it?"

"The CEO told me that after a meeting they had decided
that the two representatives would share the commission."

"Mr. Yan, I'll repeat the question. ATI never agreed in
writing that Client Q would come off its customer list,
did it?"

"Yes."

"Yes, there was no written agreement?"

"No."

"There was a written agreement?" Ellen's head must have
been spinning by now. I know mine was.

"I said there's no agreement."

Finally he had admitted it—ATI had never given up any
of the Chinese customers or commissions to Mr. J or anyone
else.

Ellen proceeded to another issue involving Client Q. This one concerned representations about products. As she asked Mr. Yan about it, I recalled how shocked and upset the incident had made me.

Every fiber manufacturer shipped its fiber on spools labeled with its own brand name. At the time, Corning's marketing strength influenced the entire industry, and most large cable projects specified that Corning fiber must be used. Even YOFC, in its role as a cable company, was required to use Corning fiber rather than its own for certain projects.

During one of my visits to this special client, their logistics manager asked me to arrange to have orders of YOFC fiber delivered on Corning spools. I was appalled, though I understood his motivation. He wanted to take advantage of the competitive price offered by YOFC, yet be able to claim that he was using Corning fiber. Of course I denied this absurd request. It was totally contrary to my principles. I would never exchange my reputation and integrity for anything, let alone this kind of greed.

In the world of Chinese business there are no secrets. I heard rumors that this client was indeed passing off YOFC fiber as Corning's. I couldn't believe that they'd gone ahead and done it. So I visited their factory again and asked to see the Corning spools. Someone on the staff obliged me.

Sure enough, there were the Corning spools wrapped with what I believe was YOFC fiber, just as the logistics manager had requested. I tried to take photographs, but the factory staff stopped me. This incident demonstrated just how far greed could drive people to go. Not only had YOFC violated my exclusive representation arrangement, but it also appeared that they were complicit in an underhanded and unethical practice.

I wrote to YOFC to protest the situation, but they never responded. My letter was just another piece of paper they buried in their file drawers. But now, in the deposition room, they couldn't ignore the questions that their conduct raised.

"Do you recall that Client Q wanted to have YOFC fiber wound on Corning's spools?" Ellen asked Mr. Yan.

"No." Mr. Yan seemed confident as he answered.

Ellen handed Mr. Yan a copy of the letter I had sent, then repeated her question: "Do you remember YOFC selling Client Q its fiber on Corning spools?"

"That's impossible. We never do such a thing. YOFC never does such a thing." Mr. Yan raised his voice.

"Does YOFC purchase product from Corning?"

"Yes."

"So there are Corning spools located at YOFC, is that right?"

"Yes."

"And that would have been true in 1998 and 1999, correct?"

"Yes."

A few hours later, after testimony on other topics, Ellen suddenly returned to the issue. "Earlier today, Mr. Yan, you testified that YOFC would never have used Corning spools for YOFC fiber."

"That applies to most of the time," he replied. "There was once when Corning asked us to supply fiber to them, and they asked to use their own spool."

"So YOFC fiber was wound on Corning spools and supplied to Corning. Is that your testimony?"

"Yes."

"Is it your understanding that if YOFC put its fiber on Corning spools and sold it to another company, it would not be legal?"

"Yes," he conceded.

Wow, that was refreshing news. But I couldn't believe Corning had made any such request. I wondered how Corning would react if they heard this testimony, since infringement of trademarks and intellectual property was and still is a very sensitive problem in China.

* * *

In the fateful fax Mr. Yan sent to ATI on November 1, 2000, he told us that in the coming year YOFC would be concentrating on making other products instead of single-mode fiber. For that reason, YOFC would not be able to supply the Chinese customers with the fiber they'd requested. However, when Ellen asked Mr. Yan about sales to foreign customers, he made a very interesting admission. YOFC had sold substantial amounts of single-mode fiber to non-Chinese companies in 2001—far more than would have been expected for a company that was redirecting the focus of its production and marketing. Moreover, most of these sales were not made through a representative but by YOFC directly, which spared the company from paying commissions and gained it a higher profit.

In other words, YOFC had shut ATI out of the market because it thought there was more money to be made elsewhere. At least, that's how I heard what Mr. Yan was saying.

No one but ATI was sent a notification about the decrease in supply. Mr. Yan said that he himself had made the decision to send the fax to my company. Earlier in his testimony he had remarked that he had not wanted YOFC to continue doing business with ATI, especially with me, in 2000 because I had complained about him in a memo to the CEO of YOFC.

ATI was the only company he had treated so poorly and with such disrespect. Perhaps dealing with a capable and independent Chinese woman was too intimidating for him. If I were a Westerner or a Chinese man, maybe my situation would have been different.

I was frustrated and angry to think that a personal vendetta might have played an important role in YOFC's destruction of ATI.

* * *

Mr. Yu, the chief operating officer of YOFC, broke out in harsh criticism of Mr. Yan in Chinese in the middle of the deposition, in which he was not allowed to speak; that was really unbelievable. I had been shocked by the insulting words that came from the mouth of YOFC's COO. Angry with one of Mr. Yan's answers, he had interrupted the testimony to say: "You are simply bullshit." It was the most shameful moment I'd seen in the whole deposition. What was it that made so many Chinese executives feel entitled to insult their subordinates that way, with no regard for their self-respect? Poor Mr. Yan, I almost felt sorry for him.

* * *

I will never forget the moment when Mr. Yan proudly announced, "I conducted business according to the agreement." He was referring to YOFC's agreement with ATI.

It was hard for me not to laugh. How could he make such a claim? In his own testimony he had been admitting that he didn't always comply with the agreement. I guess that this was his true style of business conduct—promising one thing and doing another, and saying whatever was convenient.

While Mr. Yan continued to defend his statement, Ellen caught him again.

"Mr. Yan, do you remember telling ATI that you would not make contacts with customers in China?"

"I don't remember."

"Mr. Yan, do you remember signing rules and regulations about how to deal with YOFC's customers who were also ATI's responsibility?"

"There is no such rule in the agreement," he answered, twisting the question.

"Mr. Yan, my question is whether you remember signing the rules and regulations about the dealings with ATI's customers."

"I didn't sign it."

Ellen showed him a pair of documents stapled together, one in English and one in Chinese. They spelled out rules and regulations for dealing with YOFC's clients. She had them marked for the record as Exhibit 4.

I knew these documents well. I had drafted them myself. I believed YOFC's disorganized way of doing business caused

ATI and the customers so many problems and so much confusion that it became difficult to continue promoting the product. So I negotiated with YOFC's CEO to create a set of rules and regulations to organize and coordinate the sales and marketing process. This was one of the ways I tried to guide YOFC toward conducting business with greater efficiency and clarity.

"Mr. Yan, have you seen Exhibit 4 before?" she asked.

"Yes, I have seen it," he said.

"Do you recognize the handwriting on the first page of Exhibit 4?"

"Yes."

"Could you read what you wrote out loud so that the translator can translate it into English?"

He complied, and the translator reported his words: "Quote, when it comes to the optical cable clients which were exclusively represented by ATI, we will execute according to these rules and regulations." Then he pointed to the page. "And this is the signature."

"Signed by you, Mr. Yan, is that correct?"

"Yes, I did sign it."

Bingo! Ellen was amazing; she didn't let Mr. Yan get away with his denials. It was an honor to observe a first-class lawyer at work—just like watching a mystery movie, where you have to stay really focused to catch everything that's going on. Calm and graceful, sharp-witted and strong—she was a consummate professional, and her power shone throughout the room. You have no idea how proud I was that she was representing ATI and me.

The deposition testimony and documents gave us quite a lot of evidence we hadn't known about. Our case seemed stronger than ever, and I came away with greater confidence that I would win. About time, too. I deserved to get back the reputation for integrity that YOFC had stolen from me.

* * *

When we gathered at the JAMS arbitration center the following week, my head was still spinning with all of the false statements, distortions, and evasions I had heard during Mr. Yan's deposition. I was glad I had two capable lawyers beside me. My attorneys and I took our seats on one side of the large hearing room, and YOFC's battery of attorneys and witnesses arranged themselves on the other side. Judge Hanlon presided from the end of the long conference table. I was nervous but also excited. Soon, I thought, this whole unpleasant business will be over.

On the first day I was questioned by Mr. A—YOFC's lead attorney. It was a long and exhausting day, and only the beginning of what I would have to endure in the witness chair.

On the second morning YOFC brought out its expert in Chinese law. The witness was glib and confident as YOFC's lawyers questioned him, but when Steve Hemminger began to cross-examine him, his assuredness crumbled. Many times when Steve asked him to be specific about the law he was citing, he couldn't. Instead he kept insisting, "It is simply common sense." It became apparent that Mr. Common Sense—this quickly became his nickname—didn't understand the case. He was misreading the laws or attempting to apply laws that were inappropriate. He treated ATI as if it were a foreign investment company, an obvious mistake. I couldn't believe how poorly YOFC had prepared its so-called expert. So that day of the hearing began on a high note for me.

Things quickly grew more difficult. Early in the afternoon I was put back in the hot seat for more cross-examination from the opposing counsel. Mr. A flashed his courtesy smile and then did everything he could to destroy my credibility and con me into lying—at least, that's how it felt to me. His questions were accusatory; his tone was insulting. When I answered one question, he implied in the way he asked the next one that my response had been dishonest and deceitful. His bag of tricks contained questions designed to pressure me, confuse me, or scare me. But he didn't succeed. I knew I had no reason to lie and nothing to fear if I spoke the truth.

I returned to the witness chair several times during the proceedings, testifying for a total of more than two days. Only once did I seriously lose my composure. In the middle of the hearing, my tears suddenly began to fall. I couldn't help it. For almost six years I'd felt betrayed and tortured because of YOFC. Now that I finally had the chance to tell what YOFC had done, I couldn't control my tears.

My lawyers asked for a brief recess, and I went off for a few minutes to regain my calm. Ellen and Steve stayed by my side to comfort me. To lift my spirits I sang the Rodgers and Hammerstein song "I Have Dreamed" from *The King and I*. As always, the act of creating music soothed my spirit. I wiped my tears away, took a deep breath, and returned to the hot seat. *I shall not fail*, I chanted to myself. *I shall not fail*.

On the third day of the hearing, Mr. J replaced me in the

witness chair for a while. I had never been so happy to give up a seat. Through his questions Mr. A established that Mr. J's firm did in fact work as a sales representative representing YOFC to clients in China. The lawyer asked Mr. J about the occasion when he and I first met.

"That was in '98," Mr. J said. "In '98 she signed a representation agreement with YOFC. And we all went to YOFC for a meeting, and I met her at the meeting."

"What was the purpose of the meeting?"

Mr. J called it a marketing meeting. We did talk about marketplace trends that day, but YOFC had a more specific agenda: to bring together their representatives in the hope of working out conflicts over customers. For motives I'd never understood, YOFC had assigned the rights to certain Chinese customers to both Mr. J's firm and ATI.

Mr. A asked, "Was it a surprise to you, sir, that the CEO was getting you and Ms. Lu together to try to come to some resolution about the customers?"

"I just didn't feel that good within me," Mr. J replied. "Within my heart I didn't feel that good because since you already signed a contract with me, why did you sign a contract with ATI? I did not find that too reasonable."

On that point, I couldn't have agreed more. I did not find it reasonable either. In fact, it didn't feel good at all within my heart.

Mr. J was supposed to be YOFC's most solid and persuasive witness. Instead his testimony helped make my case. He even brought with him an unexpected but welcome bit of evidence—a copy of his own agreement with YOFC, which demonstrated irrefutably that even though YOFC signed exclusive agreements with ATI, they secretly had a separate agreement with Mr. J. What a sneaky, shameful company.

The next witness in line was Mr. Yan. I was eager for the long, exhausting ordeal to be over. Unfortunately, I would have to wait. What was supposed to be a three-day hearing had already extended to four, and we were still far from finished. But scheduling conflicts prevented us from pushing on. Judge Hanlon declared a continuance, setting a date to resume in mid-May.

Two more months. I was disappointed but hardly surprised. This battle had lasted so long that I was beginning to think it would be part of my life forever.

* * *

At the end of May the hearing dragged on for five more days, and for three of them I was back in the witness chair, enduring another cross-examination. Mr. A used all of his brainpower and energy to accuse me, insult me, and try making me angry enough to lose control—at least, that was what I believed. It was the toughest test I had ever been through in my life. I don't know why he thought his tactics would work this time when they hadn't before. I knew I was right. I knew what the truth was. Over and over my head and heart repeated: *I shall not fail*.

At last it was time for Mr. Yan to testify. Just like his deposition, his testimony in front of the arbitrator was full of deceit and evasion. Frequently he contradicted what he had said in earlier testimony. My two brilliant lawyers did a fantastic job of catching him in the act.

Mr. Yan confirmed his personal feelings against me when Ellen asked about a memorandum of understanding, or MOU, that ATI and YOFC signed in January 2000 to amend and clarify the original contract. "Now, you personally were opposed to YOFC even entering an agreement for 2000 with ATI, isn't that right?"

"Yes," he said.

"But your CEO made the decision to supply at least some single-mode fiber to ATI, right?"

"Yes."

"Now, the reason you were opposed to entering the agreement with ATI to provide them with any single-mode fiber in 2000 was that you didn't like working with Diana, isn't that right?"

"Yes."

I'd known that all along, so I felt vindicated when I heard him admit it.

"Okay, and you didn't like working with her because you felt she made criticisms of you to your boss, right?"

"Yes." Oh, poor Mr. Yan, how fragile he was. He sounded like a sulking kid.

I believe his testimony completely contradicted what he'd said in his first letter to me, back in 1998: "Your effort and success will determine the level of our fiber inventory."

Not only that, he denied YOFC's entire motivation in hiring ATI, which the former CEO of YOFC stated in a letter he wrote to me at an early stage in our cooperation: "I expressly hired Allied for two reasons. First of all because I believe that Allied could help YOFC open the Chinese market for YOFC products. Diana, your past accomplishments in China speak for themselves. Your reputation was impeccable, professional and competent."

That was the reputation I was fighting to have restored.

* * *

Much of Mr. Yan's testimony had to do with YOFC's behavior in 2000. That was a frustrating year. ATI had generated a large volume of sales orders from Chinese customers, amounting to 550,000 kilometers of single-mode optical fiber. But YOFC had been persistently unable to fulfill those orders. At the time, YOFC told me that this was because the customers' demand for the fiber had outstripped the supply.

Hoping to avoid similar problems the next year, I spent the summer of 2000 working with the Chinese customers to estimate what their needs would be and obtain advance purchase orders. I had assumed this information would help YOFC in making its production plans. Instead, in November ATI received that abrupt and painful fax of dismissal.

Here in this arbitration center in San Francisco, a different picture of the supply problem was emerging.

Mr. Yan had admitted in his deposition that the contract with ATI, signed in 1998, was YOFC's first long-term agreement for single-mode fiber sales. Two years later, in 2001, YOFC made sales agreements with two Western firms—the British company BICC and Draka Holding N.V., the large

Dutch firm that was one of the partners in the joint venture known as YOFC.

Now, as Ellen asked him how YOFC handled its obligations for supplying fiber, Mr. Yan insisted, "It depends on the contract and agreement. In a shortage period if we have the long-term contract, then we have to follow the contract."

Since ours was the earliest long-term agreement and it was still in effect, our customers should have been first in line for any fiber YOFC produced. So Ellen asked about YOFC's production and sales in 1999, 2000, and 2001. Mr. I Don't Remember answered with his usual refrain: "I can't recall; I don't know the exact quantity. . . ."

But while he might have forgotten the figures, our side had a pretty good idea of what they were. During our investigation, we had found an interesting document—the official minutes of a meeting of YOFC's board of directors, held in Brazil in April 2000. Because Mr. Yan claimed not to know of the document, Judge Hanlon didn't allow it on the record, but it gave us greater confidence in ATI's case.

At that meeting, the board confirmed a resolution to expand, not reduce, the production of optical fiber. The CEO presented an ambitious production plan for 2000. It called for YOFC to produce and sell 1.5 million kilometers of single-mode fiber, as well as a much smaller amount of multimode fiber.

The board requested the CEO of YOFC to submit a cost-saving plan and a report on YOFC's representation agreements to sell optical fiber in China (ATI's contract) and North America (the company's contract with a firm called Ganda).

The board also consented to a proposal made by the vice chairman regarding the division of the international market. Interestingly, YOFC's vice chairman was S. J. van Kesteren—who was also the chairman of the board of Draka.

With the numbers from the production plan at her fingertips, Ellen said to Mr. Yan, "All right, now, in the year 2000, YOFC had the capacity to provide the entire 550,000 kilometers of single-mode fiber to the customers on ATI's list, didn't they?"

"Capacity, yes."

There it was—he admitted that YOFC had made enough single-mode fiber in 2000 to supply its Chinese customers, whose orders they had a contractual obligation to fill. But they hadn't made enough for both China and the potentially lucrative Western clients served by BICC and Draka. YOFC decided that it would be more profitable, as well as politically expedient, to ignore the Chinese customers who were first in line and serve these foreign latecomers. Based on my experience, I believe that YOFC's policies and principles were subject to change whenever they thought they might benefit, regardless of any contract or legal commitment.

Ellen brought this point to light. "Isn't it true that YOFC decided it would sell the single-mode fiber to other customers instead of selling to the customers on ATI's list?"

"No."

"In fact, you sold at least 200,000 kilometers to Draka, right?"

"I don't know; where is the figure from?"

It came straight from Mr. Yan's deposition. Ellen read aloud the testimony in which he had confirmed that in 2000

YOFC had provided Draka with 200,000 to 300,000 kilometers of fiber—the entire quantity that Draka had requested.

For a moment Mr. Yan seemed confused, though he quickly recovered. "Draka is one of YOFC's shareholders, so they asked for fiber in the shortage, and they signed a long-term contract with YOFC, five years. So that's why the YOFC general management tried to sign this agreement."

Aha, now it was on the record—Draka had been pushing YOFC to supply them with fiber.

Suddenly Ellen stopped short. Turning to the judge, she said, "Excuse me, Your Honor, the witness has just been handed a note. I don't know whether is has to do with his testimony or with some emergency or what, but Mr. Yu at the end of the table just passed him a note."

All eyes fixed on Mr. Yu. I couldn't believe it. The chief operating officer of YOFC had given a note to his company's key witness in front of everyone, including the honorable judge. That was absolutely forbidden. How could he think he was entitled to coach his colleague on his testimony while Mr. Yan was in the witness chair? He must have assumed that he was still in China.

"Counsel," said Judge Hanlon with a look at Mr. A.

Mr. A retrieved the note from Mr. Yan.

Ellen wasn't about to let the matter slide. She asked, "It's in Chinese?"

"Well . . ." Mr. A seemed reluctant to say more.

Steve Hemminger cut in. "Can we have it read into the record?"

"Okay, hand it to the interpreter," Judge Hanlon ordered.

The interpreter translated the note aloud: " 'If ATI believes that YOFC did not supply sufficient optical fiber, they have the right to find optical fiber elsewhere. This is fair.' "

"Your honor," Ellen said, "could we ask either that Mr. Yu be excluded or that he at least be asked to refrain from coaching the witness?"

"Yes, why don't you talk to him," Judge Hanlon said to Mr. A.

Mr. A tried to explain the awkward situation. "Obviously, this is the first time any of these folks have been involved in any kind of . . ."

Ellen stressed that a similar situation had occurred during the deposition, so Judge Hanlon ordered Mr. A to take care of it. This theatrical and embarrassing incident ended there, but none of us will forget how one of YOFC's senior executives made such a negative impression on the Western court system. What a shame.

The fact is, I met a lot of good, hard-working people in YOFC, who were not at all like Mr. Yu or Mr. Yan. However, it was leaders like these who represented the company in the eyes of the industry and the outside world. An unavoidable reality of business is that one bad impression can destroy one hundred good ones. Bad news always travels faster and farther than good news, and it prints itself more indelibly on people's memories. Whether you work for someone else or for yourself, your personal image is the company's image. Never underestimate the impact, whether positive or negative, your personal image can have on the business's reputation.

* * *

Watching Ellen at work was impressive. She seemed to remember every statement Mr. Yan had made in his deposition, and she never missed a chance to catch him contradicting his own words. As she asked her sharp questions, he finally surrendered to the truth.

"Now, isn't it true that ATI entered the MOU in January of 2000, prior to your having an agreement with Draka for fiber sales in the year 2000?"

"Yes."

"Well, did Draka insist that you send them 200,000 to 300,000 kilometers in 2000?"

"Yes, they have a, they also were very eager to commit to buy YOFC fiber in three years from 2000, 2001, 2002." Mr. Yan was anxious to explain Draka's strong will.

"What were the political reasons that you were referring to about there being a concern about providing Draka with fiber in 2000?"

"Because Draka is YOFC's shareholder. In a time of shortage, they had the right to get the fiber because they own 37.5 percent share of YOFC."

Wow, I never would have thought that a giant public telecom company like Draka would have played a role in the unfortunate dealings that so adversely affected ATI's fiber business in China. I wondered why the Chinese government would allow Draka, as a Western investor, to involve YOFC in such a situation—one that placed YOFC in danger of damaging its reputation and credibility and could put the government's huge investment in YOFC at risk. The decision to cut ATI off and cut the supply to the clients was more complicated than I'd thought, not only involving YOFC but apparently influenced by other players.

* * *

After Mr. Yan, there was one final witness, who appeared on an additional day of testimony that had to be scheduled in June. He was our own expert in Chinese law, Dr. Pitman B. Potter of the University of British Columbia. Dr. Potter is a renowned authority on Chinese history and law, especially in the areas of trade, investment, and business. He is also an authorized arbitrator for CIETAC, the Chinese international arbitration committee.

Dr. Potter speaks and writes perfect Mandarin, and he has mastered the essence and nuances of the Chinese language. At one point, when we discussed a certain translation error, he was able to make the subtle but critical distinction in the meanings of two similar words. Applying the correct word had a very different legal impact in the hearing.

With a rich fund of knowledge and experience to draw on, he had no trouble distinguishing the earlier statements of YOFC's Mr. Common Sense and defusing any power they might have had. When he cross-examined Dr. Potter, the opposing counsel played every trick he could, trying to discover something damaging that would help YOFC's case at the last moment, but to no avail.

* * *

As a partnership between China and the West, and as a major player in a cutting-edge industry, a joint venture like YOFC should have been a role model for other Chinese enterprises in the global market. Unfortunately, from my experience and that of other Western businesses that have dealt with them, YOFC is not a worthy example to emulate. In my opinion it damages the credibility of reputable Chinese corporations in the eyes of the West. I'd like to appeal to the Chinese government, as one of the joint-venture partners, to give a high priority to correcting YOFC's business conduct. I believe YOFC's international image has cast a dark shadow over China's telecom industry.

ATI has not been the only company to suffer at YOFC's hands. In mid-2005, I learned that YOFC was facing at least two more lawsuits. Ganda, its representative for fiber sales in North America, filed a suit for breach of contract and conspiracy, and a huge global telecom company called OFS (formerly part of Lucent Technologies and now owned by Furukawa Electric North America) commenced federal litigation proceedings, alleging that YOFC has infringed at least four U.S. patents. OFS is seeking a permanent injunction barring the importation and sale of many YOFC products.

In China there is a saying: "Whatever you plant, that's what you will get as a result." It is similar to: "What goes around comes around" or "You will reap what you sow." In the case of YOFC, I believe the repercussions of its bad behavior would come back to haunt its own business.

* * *

When we walked out of the JAMS center after the last day of the hearing, I breathed a long sigh of relief. I thought we were finally done with this long, dragged-out, and frustrating arbitration process.

But it turned out we had more steps to take. Both sides had to prepare case summaries—essentially, their closing arguments—and present them in writing in September. My attorneys insisted that serious damage had been done to my company and me because YOFC broke a valid contract. YOFC's counsel argued the contrary point of view and continued to contend that Chinese law should prevail.

All through the autumn we anxiously awaited the verdict. The hearings had greatly weakened YOFC's case, but that did not make the delay less nerve-racking.

In December 2004, Judge Hanlon issued his decision: the contract was not governed by Chinese law. All of YOFC's claims that the contract was invalid were disregarded. He ruled that Singapore law should govern the case, citing language in the agreement specifying that any dispute would be resolved under the laws of a third country.

Yes! This was the result we had been hoping for.

We now could begin the process of assessing damages. Judge Hanlon would handle that also. He asked to be briefed on the relevant Singapore laws. In January 2005 an additional briefing was held under Singapore law to determine if any financial compensation was due and settle a few other leftover issues.

I filed my lawsuit in May 2001. In March 2005—three years and ten months later; I could probably cite the hours and minutes too—I received the final decision from the arbitration proceeding: ATI was indeed entitled to financial compensation. Since this was nonbinding arbitration, we will proceed with litigation in Superior Court to determine the amount of damages. I look forward to obtaining a deposition from Draka's chairman, Mr. van Kesteren, to see if

> Only truth can beat lies. No one can take away our right to keep our honor and integrity intact, with passion, and happiness, and love.

we get better answers about Draka's involvement with YOFC. I don't care who people are, how powerful they are, or how high a title they have, I will confront them without hesitation when my rights and honor are at stake. I've always believed in an ancient Chinese maxim: "When the emperor breaks the law, he shall be penalized the same as the average citizen would be." In my opinion, this should also apply to YOFC.

ATI's lawsuit has taken more time than earning a college degree usually does, and it has given me just as intense an education. As I sat in lawyers' conference rooms and in the arbitration center, I had a chance to review my life and reflect on how much I'd accomplished. From a rugged start in a rough and remote coal-mining village, I had moved to the other side of the world—and not just in a geographic sense. I'd learned so much about cultures, languages, and the infinite possibilities of the human spirit.

The traumatic ordeal of the lawsuit taught me how strong we can be, how much potential we have, and how we can create miracles in our lives as long as we believe in ourselves. Passion and strength can conquer anything and take us anywhere.

Naturally I'm glad I prevailed, and I look forward, of course, to receiving the final financial compensation. Once I do, my hope is to donate some of it to help Chinese children who cannot afford an education, to encourage their creativity, integrity, and professionalism, and help them avoid the mistakes of YOFC. But the real achievement of this four-year combat was that I never gave up. The real reward was the opportunity to tell my story, to have the truth be heard and acknowledged. Only truth can beat lies. And no one can take away our right to keep our honor and integrity intact, with passion, and happiness, and love.

As I recovered from the hearings and awaited word about their outcome, I began to think about ways to help people benefit from my experiences. How could I use my knowledge and wisdom to help companies build better businesses that profit by operating with the highest integrity? How might I inspire people to pursue their dreams and fight courageously for the truth and for their rights?

I began to burst with ideas. The next step—putting them into action.

Diana's Stepping-Stones
on the Journey to Success

Remember that the truth is the best weapon for beating a lie. Lies can be disguised in many forms, but they will always collapse before the power of truth. When we stand on the shoulders of truth, we are wiser and stronger.

Look forward; never look back. What happened in the past belongs to the past. If we cling to it, it will only weigh us down. The past is too heavy a burden to carry if we are going to move ahead.

Put it in writing. Whenever we make a business decision or arrangement, with ourselves or with others, we should document it in writing. Good notes and records of plans, discussions, schedules, and agreements serve several valuable purposes. They make a vague vision more concrete; they enable us to track our progress; and, in the case of a disagreement or dispute, they provide evidence of what really transpired and what both sides really promised.

Enlist the help of strong, capable allies. We cannot fight all of our battles alone, nor can we carry out our action plans for success without assistance. Professionals who have the expertise we lack are invaluable members of our team. But expertise is not enough. Good rapport and a commitment to the task at hand are crucial. It pays off when we trust our instincts and take action when someone turns out not to be right for our team.

Allow yourself to make mistakes. If we experiment and take risks, a few mistakes are inevitable. Accept them as opportunities to learn and grow. Perfectionism can get in the way of our creative mind and be an excuse that stops us from making progress toward our dreams. It takes strength to admit a mistake, and it can be even harder to make the change that is needed. But being willing to do so is the only shortcut to success. Once we take those steps, we are that much closer to our destination.

Stand up for your rights. We should never let a person or company mistreat us. When someone takes advantage of us or fails to honor a commitment, we should take action to correct the situation. Sometimes we may not prevail, even when we are in the right. But we always gain in terms of strength, wisdom, pride, and confidence. In that, we win no matter what the outcome.

Take ownership of your life. Victimization is another form of fear. Sometimes we create an illusion of victimhood and allow ourselves to indulge in it to escape our own responsibility for our success and happiness. The truth is, we control what happens to us. If a situation is not what we would like it to be, we have the power to change it. When we acknowledge this truth and act on it, then we have truly learned the secret of success.

With vocal coach Dr. Jay Pierson and his partner Paul.

创举无畏

Twelve My Soul Is Not Afraid, 2004–Present

Istrolled along the terrace with my good friend Patty, gazing out across the bay. On this July evening, the last sailboats were skimming the waves, their sails catching the wind as they headed to their home marinas. The sun was disappearing into a bank of fog that half hid the gleaming towers of San Francisco on the far side of the water. The breeze tugged at my hair. I hugged myself as I breathed in the fresh air scented by the flowers growing nearby.

Turning to Patty, I said, "I'm beginning to feel hopeful again."

Since the beginning of the summer, I'd felt flattened. The nonbinding arbitration proceedings had bled away my positive energy and filled me with negativity and confusion. Now that the hearings were over and the lawyers were preparing their closing-argument summaries, I had nothing to do but wait and worry.

I continued my lessons in acting and dance, and I went every week for my singing training. But the joy I usually found there was eluding me. I had no strength. I was exhausted and I had put on weight.

My life felt out of sorts. I knew I had much to be grateful for, but it was hard to focus on those good things. The battles and heartbreaks I'd been through had formed a dark cloud over me, and all of a sudden I felt that, try as I might, I couldn't break through and find the sun. It seemed that there was nothing around me now but obstacles and the deceitful, dishonest, and destructive people who had put them there.

Now and then I thought about a tiny, frightened, pigtailed girl, locked in a tight dark space full of noisy, flapping chickens, spending her days sweeping up their endless shit. Often I believed I'd put that child behind me, but lately she didn't seem so far away.

So when I heard that Deepak Chopra would be offering a Renewal Weekend in nearby Berkeley, I signed up to attend, and I invited Patty to join me. The program included times to practice yoga and meditation and sessions designed to enhance the well-being of body, mind, and spirit. I had met Dr. Chopra the previous year at an evening lecture, and I'd read and admired his books. It seemed like an excellent opportunity to rejuvenate my energy and take a fresh look at my life.

So now we were spending two and a half days at the Claremont Resort, a historic hotel that resembles a sprawling white castle. It had a full-service spa, two swimming pools, and the terrace where we now were walking. This would have been a good place to revive ourselves even if there had been no seminar.

The seminar, though, was proving to be a transforming experience. In a supportive group of forty people, I began to untangle all the frustrations that were tying me into knots and tap into the sources of my own strength.

I'd been afraid that I would lose my lawsuit and that this would mean I was a total loser in life. When I expressed this fear, someone told me, "That's not true at all, Diana. You've pursued an international case against a large, corrupt company. Just taking on the fight makes you a winner." I nodded, but I was still unsure.

As the weekend progressed, several profound ideas began to take hold of my consciousness. I realized that we fear the future because we can't control it. We're afraid we won't be able to deal with whatever happens. But we can deal with it, and we will, because we have to. If we pay attention, we will notice how synchronicity works in our lives. Things happen to us for a reason. We draw to ourselves the people and the resources we need at any given time.

In one of the sessions, Dr. Chopra told us, "Your soul has the solution to everything you face in life." I raised my hand. "How can you tell when it's your soul speaking?" I heard other people murmur and saw them nod their heads. I was voicing a question that many of us wondered about. Taking a deep breath, I continued. "I know I have a good heart and a good brain, but so often they tell me conflicting things, and I get confused. I understand that what my soul tells me is always right, so I want to listen when it speaks to me. But how do I know which message is coming from my soul?"

Dr. Chopra said calmly and simply: "Your soul does not have fear."

I wasn't sure what that meant but I hung on to the remarkable words. Even after the seminar was over, I kept turning them over in my mind, trying to figure out what they meant to my life. I knew they were a key that could help me unlock a better, more powerful future.

As I'd hoped, the seminar revitalized me. I came home ready to start fresh. I even cleared out some of the old furnishings in my apartment to create a new environment. I rededicated myself to my training routine of singing and dancing. No more delays, no more missing classes.

In the fertile soil within my mind, a seed I'd planted a while ago began to sprout. A couple of years before, as I was finishing the ten-day self-awareness program in Southern California, I'd told my new friend Patty that I wanted to bring a seminar to China that would help people tap into their potentials and passions. "Go for it," Patty had said.

Perhaps now was the time.

* * *

I returned to my music studies with renewed vigor. The seminar reminded me that music speaks to my heart, that it's one of the ways I can best express my true nature. I made a resolution: no matter what else I might choose to do with my life, singing and dancing will always remain near the top of my list of priorities. It makes sense to work hard to develop my talent and find opportunities to perform—when I do, I'm giving a precious gift to my soul.

One day, as I was walking home from my singing lesson, I passed a new Chinese store on Market Street. A window display of exquisite porcelain objects caught my eye, and I went in to browse. I was amazed—there were hundreds of delicate vases, teapots, bowls, and plates in all sorts of shapes and sizes and a multitude of colors—classic blue and white, pale celadon green, and bright hues of spring and summer. They were adorned with pictures of flowers, birds, and landscapes, and scenes of traditional Chinese people living their daily lives.

I introduced myself to the owners of the shop. I was not surprised to learn that they came from Jingdezhen. This city in southeastern China is known as the porcelain capital of the world. For two thousand years it has been a center for the manufacture of ceramics. The porcelain produced by the artisans there is described in a famous saying: "It is as white as jade, as bright as a mirror, as thin as paper, and sounds as clear as a bell."

So what was this shop filled with beauty doing on a seedy stretch of Market Street? It was a terrible location, blocks away from the neighborhoods frequented by the tourists and art-loving locals who would be the likely customers, and there was no place to park. Instead of being attractively displayed, the merchandise was jumbled helter-skelter into the space. And the prices were way too low, far below what the items were worth.

As I got to know them, I realized that the poor proprietors had no clue about how to do business in the United States. They had come to San Francisco to make their fortune, lured by glittering promises that big money could be made easily in America. They had already paid dearly—almost half a million dollars—for their dream. An unscrupulous Chinese-American operator had charged them that outrageous sum to bring them here and help them set up shop. This crook had arranged for their visas and helped with some minor paperwork. Then he stuck them in a shabby store he'd rented in a poor location with no parking spaces for customers, giving the shopkeepers a short-term sublease with bad terms. He had pledged to help them with marketing, advertising, and other basics of operating a business, and he had even bragged that he would get the mayor of San Francisco to come to their grand opening. But most of his promises were lies; very little had been done.

For their huge investment, they'd received almost nothing of value. Their lack of business knowledge had placed them in this trap. Feeling desperate when no customers showed up, they had dropped their prices, hoping in vain to draw buyers into the store. Soon their lease would be up, and they would have to leave the store, their hopes in ruins.

Their situation pained me tremendously. Just as I had done, they were suffering because of a liar. They had placed their trust in the hands of someone who abused it.

I offered to help them. When I reviewed their agreement with the operator who brought them to San Francisco, I was shocked to realize they didn't even have a formal contract. They had paid him that large sum of money without receiving any guarantee that the services would be delivered or agreeing to any means of recourse when his promises turned out to be made of smoke.

After looking over all the documents they had, I recommended that they gather their strength and courage and negotiate with the business operator for better terms. I also suggested that they ask the Chinese consulate for help, and I gave them some advice on marketing. But they resisted most of my ideas. Having lost so much money already, they didn't want to pay the price to resolve their problems.

Finally they arranged to stay in their storefront for an extended time in order to sell as much as they could of their inventory. They knew they wouldn't be able to sell everything, and whatever was left would be a complete loss. There was no practical way to ship the goods back to China.

Seeing their tragic situation convinced me of the need for the seminar that was beginning to take shape in my mind. I knew the porcelain dealers were not unique. So many Chinese businesses, large ones as well as small ones, are dazzled by dollars. They want to come to the United States to make quick bucks without spending the time, effort, or money to learn how to do business properly in that country. Since they don't lay a proper foundation, their plans backfire and they end up with nothing.

My seminar could help them succeed. The more I thought about the idea, the more excited I became. I could offer them the benefits of my business experience and my own journey to success. The key, I thought, would be to look at the way we define *success*. There is a strong entrepreneurial spirit in China; so many Chinese people are eager to run businesses. But too often they have only one motivation, which is to make money. They never bother to ask or even think about some very important questions: What does success really mean? Can having money really be enough to guarantee a successful life? How do we achieve a success that is lasting and satisfying?

Through my years working with Chinese businesspeople and enterprises, and as someone born and raised in China, I understood deeply how, even more than in other places, Chinese society runs on money, rank, and material possessions. To a large extent, these external factors define your social status and become the basis of your identity and your personal power. They show other people how they should appreciate and accept you. If you lose these external things, you become nothing. This attitude has profoundly affected the society's moral values and promotes ego- and greed-based competition between individuals and enterprises.

What does success really mean? Can having money really be enough to guarantee a successful life? How do we achieve a success that is satisfying and lasting?

What Chinese people so often miss is the understanding that money is a side product of real success. Material riches are temporary—they can be stolen or lost. I want to help people recognize and value what really counts—their inner wealth. The real sources of success and happiness reside within us—in our heart, our mind, our hands, and our indomitable spirit. Our personal strength and our belief in ourselves are treasures that no one else can take away.

When our only purpose is to make money, and we forget that money is just a tool for making life a bit more comfortable, then, I can assure you, we will forever be money's slave, caged in the jail of our possessions. We will live stressful and unhappy lives, constantly worried about gaining or losing money and power. We will always be making choices for our lives based on other people's opinions and on their terms. The society that results from this approach to life will be full of greed, jealousy, conflict, and hatred. Our children will suffer more depression; the adults will face unlimited battles; and our businesses will be full of corruption and indecency.

Money is a side product of real success.

This is what China is suffering through, and it pains me to see it. These conditions are endemic to many places, of course, but my Chinese people need me most, need this daughter of the Yellow River to give her experience and knowledge and wisdom to assist them in finding their dream life.

The path to success is simple to understand, though following it can sometimes be a challenge. First, discover what we love, what brings us joy, what sparks our passion. Second, based on that passion, determine our goal in life. Third, dedicate ourselves—our thoughts, our dreams, and most of all our actions—to attaining that goal. I achieved my own success by taking this profound journey, and I believe that we all have the power within us to do the same.

If individuals in China were to claim their own strength and power and creative energy, the culture and economy, the country as a whole would benefit. China right now is a high-growth nation, home to more than 1.3 billion creative people, and it has the fastest-growing economy in the world. China makes wonderful products—not only traditional expressions of Chinese culture like Jingdezhen porcelain, but housewares, fashions, and electronics that rival those produced anyplace else.

But rather than build its own brand names and raise its image in other countries, China has become a low-cost international manufacturing plant for famous foreign brands from the rest of the world. Most Americans have never even heard of Chinese brands, let alone seen top Chinese brands displayed in prestigious retail stores.

> *The real sources of success and happiness reside within us—in our heart, our mind, our hands, and our indomitable spirit. Our personal strength and our belief in ourselves are treasures that no one else can take away.*

Other Asian countries are building their brand names. Look at Japan, home of Toyota and Honda and Sony. Look at South Korean brands like Samsung and Hyundai. In just a few years brands like these have become recognized and respected all over the world. Why can't it be that way for China? Why do Chinese put themselves in such a passive position? Why do they underestimate their true value?

To me, it is clear that the traditional business model and mindset cannot sustain their business for long in today's competitive global economy. Chinese companies have to become more open-minded and allow creativity and innovation to flourish. They need to adopt the best practices and attitudes of Western business culture while retaining what is best about the Chinese approach to doing business. They must develop farsighted vision, long-range strategies, and international integrity to be really accepted in the global market. With my cross-cultural business experience, I could be a resource to assist them in making this powerful transformation.

The misfortune of the porcelain shop owners had fired me up. I was beginning to see the direction in which my life would go next.

* * *

When I floated my idea about a seminar by my contacts in China, their response was very frustrating. They told me that it would be really difficult, almost impossible, to launch such a business on our own.

I understood that it would be difficult, but I absolutely disagreed that it would be impossible. Anything is possible.

"Sponsoring seminars is a good idea," one of my advisors acknowledged, "but it would be so much easier to partner with another business. Rather than create a seminar from scratch, why not bring someone like Anthony Robbins to China? His message would play well there."

That just charged me up more. What could an American seminar offer China that one by a Chinese person could not? This was another typical example of how the Chinese devalue themselves with their blind allegiance to foreign

> *Chinese companies need to adopt the best practices and attitudes of Western business culture while retaining what is best about the Chinese approach.*

brands. Why should something be seen as important and valuable just because it's foreign? I couldn't stand it anymore.

My secret was to think hopeful thoughts, look forward, and move quickly—the same way I approach most things in life.

Since Anthony Robbins had been recommended as a model, I was curious to take a look at what he was doing. In a bit of lucky timing, his famous seminar, *Unleash the Power Within*, was scheduled in San Jose in just a couple of weeks. I quickly signed up. It was a very different kind of experience from the Renewal Weekend in Berkeley. Instead of an intimate group of forty, this crowd was closer to four thousand eager people, all jammed into the San Jose Convention Center over a hot August weekend.

One highlight of the program was a Robbins trademark—the firewalk. In this exercise the participants discover that they can walk barefoot across a bed of burning coals without being burned. The purpose is to demonstrate that it is possible to confront one's fear, plunge into a frightening experience, and emerge without harm. The fire-walking pit was set up on a street outside the convention center, and one by one we took our turns. Everyone's style was different. Some bounded with big strides, barely touching the coals; some trotted as fast as they could; others skittered on tiptoes across the embers. At the other end, their feet were cooled with a spray of water from a hose. When my turn came I didn't feel frightened; I knew I could do it even without the seminar leader to encourage me. My secret was to think hopeful thoughts, look forward, and move quickly—the same way I approach most things in life.

I have to admit Anthony Robbins has a unique talent for motivating people, and he is also a excellent entertainer. I'm sure that many of his seminar participants have come away feeling energized and empowered. But although he claims to help people break through their fears, it seemed to me that in a fundamental way the seminar was based on fear—people's fear that if they do not have enough material goods, money, and status, they will never gain acceptance and respect. While I learned a lot of useful tools, I was bothered that the seminar seemed to have an atmosphere of greed and that it promoted a superficial definition of success.

The achievements that are worthwhile come when we love what we are doing; that is when we gain real rewards: financial, emotional, mental, and spiritual.

On the last day of the seminar Anthony did not even appear; he had left without saying a word. Instead, he used a videotape and some minor celebrities to take his place and do his job for him. The attendees were very upset, and I was disappointed too, because everyone had paid a great deal of money to hear him speak. I felt he betrayed my trust.

I walked out. I didn't want to waste any more time there. I'd gotten what I wanted, and by now I was convinced that I could create better programs than this one.

Why? Because my motivation was to help people find their love, their joy, and their passion—not to gain a kind of false success based on fear. The achievements that are worthwhile come when we love what we are doing; that is when we gain real rewards: financial, emotional, mental, and spiritual. I was going to help people move step by step out of their fears and into their dreams.

* * *

I grabbed the phone and called Patty to tell her about my ideas. She is wise and understanding, and she can read me so well. I knew she'd give me excellent feedback.

"It's time to get serious about launching this new project," I told her.

"What exactly do you plan to do?" she asked, pragmatic and focused as always.

"I'm going to design books and seminars to help the Chinese reach their potential. With the experiences I've had and what I've accomplished, I know I can give them something valuable."

"Why not aim at the U.S. market? This is where you're living now."

"I want to give something back to the country that raised me. Americans have a better life than most Chinese, and my Chinese people need me more than Americans do. Sharing my success with them will help me have a more meaningful life." I told her about the needs I saw in China for the kind of program I envisioned.

She asked, "Will your target be individuals or businesses?"

I was talking fast now, the way I do when I get excited.

"Both. My goal is to open people's eyes to their own worth and show them the steps to formulating and achieving their dreams. And I'll consult with companies, too, especially ones that want to do business with the West."

"Surely China is full of consultants already," Patty said.

"Of course, but they can't offer what I can. Most Westerners don't know the Chinese culture and mindset in depth like I do. They don't appreciate the sophistication of the Chinese people and their business spirit. They don't really understand the infrastructure of Chinese companies, or the traditions and expectations that govern how business is done. So often a Western consultant says, 'Here's how we do business in the West,' and then leaves. That doesn't work. You have to fit your advice into their structure."

"That gives you an edge," Patty agreed. "You're Chinese, and you've achieved success across cultures. So you understand both systems."

"That's right. The Western business mentality has a lot of advantages—high standards of professionalism, reliable regulatory systems, efficient operations, and a real appreciation for creative ideas and innovation. But it's built on an entirely different culture, social structure, and spirit. To work in China, it has to be customized to fit into Chinese society; it has to have practical value."

"And it has to retain what's best about the Chinese business system," Patty said, getting into the swing of my plans.

I laughed. "How did you know I was going to say that? Yes, China has a lot of wisdom that it should never lose and that could also benefit the West."

Patty's enthusiasm was evident in her voice. "You'll give your clients the best of both worlds."

"Exactly." I was waving my hand eagerly, as if Patty could see my gestures through the phone. "In my business operations, I've blended the wisdom, the pragmatism, and the flexibility of China with the professionalism of the West. The combination is unbeatable."

In my business operations, I've blended the wisdom, the pragmatism, and the flexibility of China with the professionalism of the West. The combination is unbeatable.

"It has certainly been beneficial for your business, Diana. And for your life."

"Yes, and I know I can make it work for others. I'll customize my advice to fit my clients' needs. I won't just hand them information and theories and then walk out, like other consultants. I'll give them new skills, more confidence, a grander vision. I'll follow through and help them implement constructive, practical changes that will be of real value to them, in their businesses and in their personal lives."

I could picture Patty nodding in approval as she said, "Sounds great. You're just the one to do it."

As we wrapped up our conversation, she told me something that will be imprinted in my heart forever: "I could never imagine anyone doing a better job of helping the Chinese people than you. Go ahead. I will applaud for you. I will support you. Your passion, your determination, your successful experience will inspire so many people—not only Chinese, but anyone who needs your help in this world. I believe in you."

* * *

The more I thought about this project, the more powerful and fearless I felt. A new strength flowed into me. So many creative ideas were flashing in my mind. I was excited yet calm, a burning desire tempered with a soothing confidence. It was as if my soul was in love—with this great life, with this noble project I was about to launch, with the future and all its possibilities. I understood now what Dr. Chopra told me: "Your soul does not have fear."

Once the skills and tools are acquired, anything is possible. In planning a business or planning your life, the steps are much the same.

I knew I was on the right course, and I couldn't wait to embark on this meaningful but challenging journey.

The first thing I needed was a map, a plan, so I set about to create one. This could be one of my seminar topics, I decided —teaching people how to chart the step-by-step route into the fulfillment of their dream. So often the gap between where they are now and what they dream for their lives seems unbridgeable, but that's not the problem. The problem is that they don't yet have the skills and tools to build the bridge. Once the skills and tools are acquired and used systematically, anything is possible. Whether you're planning a business or planning your life, the steps are much the same.

Step One. Define your goal.

You can't achieve a dream unless you understand what it is. What does your soul tell you about your life's purpose? What strengths and talents do you have to help you express that purpose? The business you launch or the project you undertake will be most rewarding when you make the effort to address these questions squarely.

Step Two. Develop your vision.

Begin to express on paper what you want to do and how you see the project unfolding, whether it's starting a computer software firm, writing a novel, or building a dream home. Just write whatever comes into your head; don't worry about the format. Draw or doodle if you find that helpful. Ask yourself questions:

> What do I want?
> Why do I want it?
> What will it look like when it's accomplished?
> What steps will I take to accomplish it?
> How long will it take?
> In what ways am I prepared to do it?
> What help and resources do I need?
> Where will the help and resources come from?
> What are the potential gains?
> What are the risks?
> What are my fears?

Write the answers without thinking or hesitating. If you just let the words flow, you'll bring up what's in your heart. When you hesitate, you give fear an opportunity to creep in. If there's something you can't answer, skip it and go back later.

If you try this two or three or four times, you'll benefit

more. New ideas will come up each time, and what's worthwhile in your earlier ideas will become more solid and substantial.

Step Three. Assemble a strong team.

Enlist the help of your friends, colleagues, mentors, and business associates. Brainstorm with them to collect more ideas. Think about who has the most to offer in terms of experience, skills, and enthusiasm, and put together a board of advisors. The board will function as your sounding board, your cheerleaders, your reality check.

Ask your team for their help and honest feedback about the feasibility of your ideas. As long as they respond, that's a good sign. Even a negative response indicates that what you're doing is interesting. The worst thing is to get no response at all.

Step Four. Collect information.

Do extensive research. Find out everything you can about your type of business or project. Gather written information from the Internet, from books, and from magazines devoted to your area of interest, but talk to people too—potential customers or users, and people who are doing similar things and can offer expertise. Join a relevant organization or take a class.

The more you learn, the more research you engage in, the better able you will be to craft a feasible plan and make it succeed. You'll become more confident and less likely to give in when fear comes knocking.

Step Five. Gather basic financial figures.

How much will it cost to put your idea in motion? How much revenue will you need to sustain it, or to make a profit if it's that kind of enterprise? You don't need definitive figures yet, but you'll want to look at what your cost categories will be and develop rough estimations in ranges—minimum, average, maximum—of the money involved.

Step Six. Refine your plan, and add three-year and five-year timetables.

Revisit the vision you developed and build it into a real plan. Depending on your project, you may or may not need to develop a formal business plan with detailed financial projections, but even if you don't, using a similar format can give you a valuable perspective on what you need to consider in order to make your plan work.

The heart of your plan is the timetables. Identify the benchmarks that will indicate your progress. Figure out, as realistically as you can, what you need to do to reach that point, and how long it will take. And remember that timing is everything. If you delay, you can miss the opportunity altogether.

This is a good stage at which to reassess the risks and benefits, because you now have more information and a clearer vision of what you want to accomplish. Think about what you could lose or gain by moving forward—not only financially, but emotionally as well.

Step Seven. Bring in the manpower you need.

Few of us can achieve a dream entirely on our own. We need staff, supporters, and guides. The team you assembled in step 2 may be sufficient, but now that you have a more complete plan, you may find you now need additional people or different people, in new or redefined roles. What work needs to be done, and who is the best person to do it? What are their roles? How will you work with them?

Step Eight. Plan your work and work your plan.

Like many familiar sayings, this one contains good advice. You know what needs to be done (step 6) and who needs to do it (step 7). Now it's time to break your long-range plan into yearly, monthly, weekly, and daily accomplishments.

Circumstances can shift, so be sure to obtain feedback constantly and update your information. Be flexible and open to change, so that you can adjust the plan when necessary. When you make your daily and weekly plans, be sure to factor in other aspects of your life so that you can make realistic time commitments and keep your life in balance. Build in deadlines that are reasonable but also make you stretch yourself to give maximum effort. Minimum effort won't bring you to your goal.

Step Nine. Be a leader.

As a good leader, your role is to encourage your team, mobilize their effort, and help them focus on the task at hand. Even if you are a team of one—yourself—it is your job to keep the project on track.

Step Ten. Keep your eye on your dream.

It's important to remind yourself, as you trudge from one day to the next, why you've chosen to be on this path. As you make your daily, weekly, or monthly schedule, include regular visits back to steps 1 and 2—your goal and your vision. Keep track of your progress, and celebrate every benchmark you reach along the way.

Step Eleven. Pursue your dream with your
passion and 100 percent effort.

Stay focused; be determined. Often we are distracted when difficulties arise or other people try to discourage us with judgments and objections. Any new project will face doubts and opposition, simply because it is different. That's normal, and we have to accept it. Using the problems to challenge and clarify your ideas can be good, but never allow them to derail you. Draw on the strengths of your team, and stick with your beliefs and your vision.

Step Twelve. Be flexible and update
your action plan when necessary.

Nothing is as certain as uncertainty. As you work your plan, you can anticipate that you will encounter surprises and sudden changes along the way. When you do, make sure you come up with an alternative action plan so you can continue your progress toward your goal.

* * *

I couldn't wait to get started. Right away, I initiated discussions with my business partners, friends, and colleagues as I began to put together my team. I talked to associates who had helped me do business in the past and sought out the guidance of experts who had experience in international marketing and impeccable reputations.

In September I went to China to research the potential market and lay groundwork for the new enterprise. Going back to the competitive business world was really exciting after three years away. I wanted to find out if my plan would truly be valuable for China. I knew what I wanted to give to the Chinese people, but was that what they needed?

Everywhere I went I talked to people—friends; business acquaintances; strangers I encountered in airports, hotels, restaurants, and shops—and asked them questions: What is your dream life? What stumbling blocks keep you from achieving the life you wish you had? What inspires you? Do you want to find better ways to improve your life, your career, and your happiness? What kind of help do you get from family, friends, school, and work? How do corporations manage to grow their business? What do corporations need to help them sustain their growth and profits? What obstacles are they facing? Based on the encouraging answers I heard, I put together a preliminary seminar and tested it on a group in Beijing.

Back home again I assembled a board of directors and a group of advisors to guide my new company. The team included highly experienced entrepreneurs and senior executives—experts in economics, finance, technology, law, international business, marketing, branding, and seminar design, as well as specialists in the motivational and self-improvement field. Their international business experience spans China and the West. I was thrilled that my plan sparked genuine interest from individuals with such outstanding records of accomplishment.

With their advice and help, I shaped my ideas into a solid, three-pronged business plan:

1. *Personal growth*: Books, seminars, and practical tools to help individuals discover their dreams, fulfill their potential, build their careers, and achieve their goals.

2. *Corporate consulting*: Books, seminars, and customized consulting services to help companies in China and the West do business with one another more effectively.

3. *Networking and connections*: A series of centers or clubs in China where individuals can come together to exchange ideas and experiences, learn about other cultures, and explore ways to improve their businesses and their lives.

We named the new company Image Global Impact—IGI for short.

My team and I believe we have something unique and valuable to offer the business world, especially business enterprises in China, as well as to people in China and elsewhere who want to lead freer, happier, more prosperous and fulfilling lives. We know in our hearts that many people are waiting for us, and we are committed to working together to pursue the challenge of this new venture.

* * *

My voice and my heart were singing in harmony as I greeted the first guests to arrive at my birthday party. The decorators created a magical environment in the banquet hall, and the caterers were laying out a feast of fusion cuisine, with the best flavors from Italy, France, and of course China. The band was warming up with classical music, but soon it would play a livelier number and people would begin to dance.

It was October 31, 2004, and truly an evening for celebration. Three days earlier I'd turned thirty-seven. The long, drawn-out lawsuit was nearly over, and while we hadn't heard the judge's ruling, I was certain that justice would prevail. Most important, earlier that day I'd held the first meeting of my board of directors and presented the formal business plan for my brand-new company—Image Global Impact.

I wanted to make the party a grand occasion. It was my chance to honor my past, give thanks to the friends and supporters who had helped me on my journey, and announce the new adventure that was about to begin. So I decided to make it a black-tie event. I invited everyone to dress up—tuxedos for the men, elegant gowns for the women. My own dress made me feel beautiful with its low-cut, black lace bodice and long, pleated gold skirt.

More than seventy guests from three continents came to celebrate with me. Childhood friends, business associates, my lawyers, my voice teachers—people who loved me, supported me, challenged me, and inspired me. People who had helped me learn and grow and become the person I am now. Some of them had flown in especially for the occasion from destinations like Australia, Canada, China, Boston, and Los Angeles. I was deeply touched that they would journey so far to be with me on this night, and I was filled with gratitude and love for each and every one of them. Good friends, I know, are the greatest wealth you can have.

The evening flew by in a swirl of color and laughter. We

ate, drank, danced, and sang. I joined my music coach and another vocal artist in a mini cabaret act—what an honor it was for me to perform before this very special audience. New connections were made and new friendships formed among the guests.

We made toasts to the new business and to all the people it would reach with its message that the sources of great accomplishments are love, passion, determination, and integrity. Because of my allergy to alcohol, I could drink only the tiniest sip of champagne, but I raised my glass high anyway. I offered a salute to my friends, to my wonderful life, to the new chapter that was beginning right at that very moment, to the infinite possibilities of the future.

* * *

As I look back on my life so far, I am amazed at what an incredible journey it has been. I've undergone so many transformations. My mind flips through the memories as if they were pictures in a photo album: a skinny, pigtailed little girl chases chickens in a coal-mining village at the edge of the Gobi Desert. A schoolgirl in a smoky city by the Yellow River spikes a volleyball over the net to lead her team to victory. A shy child walks up to a Western stranger in a university housing complex and shyly introduces herself in English. A reluctant medical student struggles to save a dying boy in the midnight quiet of a hospital. A dancer dressed like a goddess in filmy fabric bows to an audience's enthusiastic applause. A nervous, inexperienced university instructor begins her lecture in front of her first group of students.

More images, these of a young woman determined to pursue her dreams: in one picture she wanders through a graduate student dormitory, looking for a spare bed or a space on the floor where she can curl up in her blanket. In another she throws away her heavy winter boots as she travels by train to the subtropical city where she intends to work and live. In yet another she is standing in an elegantly appointed office with an ocean view, shaking the hand of a British man who has just offered her a great job with a firm that sells optical fibers.

The images flash faster and faster: a young woman cuddles in the warm arms of the man she loves. A hopeful but lonely bride sits by herself in a dreary motel room. A young entrepreneur opens the door to the Chinese representative office of her very own company.

From there my mind becomes crowded with more and more pictures of places I've been, things that I've done: board rooms of international companies, luxurious hotel suites in glamorous cities around the world, a French-style house in Santa Cruz, a condo overlooking San Francisco Bay, the box seat of an opera house, the stage of a theater where I am the one singing the splendid music, the JAMS arbitration room where I prevail over a bully just as I did as a child, only this time the bully is a huge corporation.

And now this banquet hall, filled with family and friends, all of them extraordinary people, celebrating my success as an international entrepreneur and the beginning of my new dream, my new life, as a motivational speaker and writer, bringing my message of hope and possibility.

This journey so far has been splendid; it has been full of tears as well as laughter, sadness as well as happiness. The physical, financial, and emotional hardships I've suffered make me value my life today more highly. I think of them as assets, because in struggling to overcome them I've gained so much in the way of strength, courage, confidence, and knowledge. Without those challenges, I would never have my accomplishments.

> *In struggling to overcome hardships I've gained so much in the way of strength, courage, confidence, and knowledge. Without those challenges, I would never have my accomplishments.*

I especially want to dedicate this, my first book, to my motherland China, the country that gave birth to me, raised me, and formed me. I am a real Chinese, completely "made" in China and developed by the world. I want to give back what I have learned to help more Chinese people have a better life.

I also want to express appreciation to the Western teachers and businesspeople who expanded my horizons, teaching me so much and helping me grow to be a better person. And I want to thank my ultimate home, the United States of America, where I've been able to build such a dream life.

My life has been a miracle. Though my story almost sounds too good to be true, it is very true. I intend to keep the miracle going through the positive changes my story will inspire in others.

The story of my life is really just beginning. Yours is too.

I hope that when you have finished reading this book, you will not hesitate to follow my lead. Explore fresh, exciting opportunities. Learn new things. Absorb new ideas. Make your own action plan for success and happiness.

Remember, your soul is not afraid. Listen to what it tells you. If you do what you love, follow your passion, and express your authentic self, nothing can stop you from achieving what you dream.

My best wishes to you as you proceed on your life's journey. I will be walking with you hand in hand as we celebrate our lives and embrace a splendid future with confidence and hope. Wherever you are and whenever you are, I will always be there, saluting you with my whole heart.

Recommended Reading

The books in this list are among the many that I have found to be helpful and inspiring. Many of these authors have written other works that also are worth exploring.

BOOKS OF PERSONAL AND SPIRITUAL GUIDANCE

James Bramlett
The Power

Dale Carnegie
How to Win Friends & Influence People

Patricia Carrington
The Power of Letting Go: A Practical Approach to Releasing the Pressures in Your Life

Joe Caruso
The Power of Losing Control: Finding Strength, Meaning, and Happiness in an Out-of-Control World

Deepak Chopra

*Ageless Body, Timeless Mind: The Quantum Alternative
    to Growing Old*

*The Book of Secrets: Unlocking the Hidden Dimensions
    of Your Life*

Creating Affluence: The A-to-Z Steps to a Richer Life

The Deeper Wound

The Path to Love: Spiritual Strategies for Healing

*The Seven Spiritual Laws of Success: A Practical Guide
    to the Fulfillment of Your Dreams*

The Soul in Love: Classic Poems of Ecstasy and Exaltation

*The Spontaneous Fulfillment of Desire: Harnessing the
    Infinite Power of Coincidence*

Vital Energy: The 7 Keys to Invigorate Body, Mind, and Soul

Wayne Dyer

The Power of Intention

10 Secrets for Success and Inner Peace

Mike George

*Learn to Relax: A Practical Guide to Easing Tension
    and Conquering Stress*

1001 Ways to Relax: An Illustrated Guide to Reducing Stress

David R. Hawkins

The Eye of the I

Susan Jeffers

Feel the Fear and Do It Anyway

Dr. Phil McGraw
>*Life Strategies: Doing What Works, Doing What Matters*
>*Self Matters: Creating Your Life from the Inside Out*

Eloise Ristad
>*A Soprano on Her Head: Right-Side-Up Reflections*
>*on Life and Other Performances*

Anthony Robbins
>*Awaken the Giant Within: How to Take Immediate Control of*
>*Your Mental, Emotional, Physical, and Financial Destiny!*

Don Miguel Ruiz
>*The Four Agreements: A Practical Guide to Personal Freedom*
>*The Mastery of Love: A Practical Guide to the Art*
>*of Relationship*

Susan Polis Schutz
>*Always Follow Your Dreams: A Collection of Poems*
>*to Inspire and Encourage Your Dreams*
>*Life Can Be Hard Sometimes . . . but It's Going to Be Okay:*
>*A Collection of Poems*

Eckhart Tolle
>*The Power of Now: A Guide to Spiritual Enlightenment*
>*Stillness Speaks*

Gary Zukav and Linda Francis
>*The Heart of the Soul: Emotional Awareness*

Books on Business and Leadership

Douglas Barry
> *Wisdom for a Young CEO*

Harry Beckwith
> *The Invisible Touch: The Four Keys to Modern Marketing*
> *Selling the Invisible: A Field Guide to Modern Marketing*

Ram Charan, Stephen Drotter, and James Noel
> *The Leadership Pipeline: How to Build the Leadership-Powered Company*

Clayton M. Christensen
> *The Innovator's Dilemma*

Bill George
> *Authentic Leadership: Rediscovering the Secrets to Creating Lasting Value*

Joanne Gordon
> *Be Happy at Work: 100 Women Who Love Their Jobs, and Why*

Micki Holliday
> *Coaching, Mentoring, and Managing: Breakthrough Strategies to Solve Performance Problems and Build Winning Teams*

Larry Johnson and Bob Phillips
> *Absolute Honesty: Building a Corporate Culture That Values Straight Talk and Rewards Integrity*

Milton Katselas
>   *Dreams into Action: Getting What You Want!*

Guy Kawasaki
>   *The Art of the Start: The Time-Tested, Battle-Hardened*
>   *Guide for Anyone Starting Anything*

Jeffrey A. Krames
>   *What the Best CEOs Know: 7 Exceptional Leaders and*
>   *Their Lessons for Transforming Any Business*

John C. Maxwell
>   *Attitude 101: What Every Leader Needs to Know*
>   *Ethics 101: What Every Leader Needs to Know*
>   *Leadership 101: What Every Leader Needs to Know*
>   *Relationships 101: What Every Leader Needs to Know*
>   *The 17 Essential Qualities of a Team Player: Becoming the*
>   *Kind of Person Every Team Wants*
>   *The 17 Indisputable Laws of Teamwork: Embrace Them*
>   *and Empower Your Team*
>   *Thinking for a Change: 11 Ways Highly Successful*
>   *People Approach Life and Work*
>   *The 21 Indispensable Qualities of a Leader: Becoming the*
>   *Person Others Will Want to Follow*
>   *The 21 Irrefutable Laws of Leadership*
>   *The 21 Most Powerful Minutes in a Leader's Day: Revitalize*
>   *Your Spirit and Empower Your Leadership*
>   *Winning with People: Discover the People Principles That*
>   *Work for You Every Time*

Karen Post
> *Brain Tattoos: Creating Unique Brands That Stick in Your Customers' Minds*

Celia Sandys and Jonathan Littman
> *We Shall Not Fail: The Inspiring Leadership of Winston Churchill*

Gerry Spence
> *How to Argue and Win Every Time: At Home, At Work, In Court, Everywhere, Every Day*

James M. Utterback
> *Mastering the Dynamics of Innovation*

Zig Ziglar
> *Over the Top*
> *See You at the Top*

About the Author

Diana Lu was born in China and currently lives in San Francisco. Following a deprived childhood during China's Cultural Revolution, she has achieved a life of financial and personal success. Trained as a doctor, she decided the world of Western business was her goal. After a successful career with the Chinese branch of a British fiber optics trader, she moved to the United States and drew on her cross-cultural experience and business expertise to establish her own consulting company. As the youngest and only female Chinese entrepreneur in this growing high-tech sector, she helped Western manufacturers expand their markets in China. She also successfully helped establish brands and markets for a Chinese optical fiber manufacturer that had no market share, enabling it to become a major player in the optical fiber industry in China. She retired from the industry at the age of 34 and has founded a new company, Image Global Impact, to pass on the philosophy and practices that have made her successful.

PRODUCED BY WILSTED & TAYLOR PUBLISHING SERVICES

Production management by Christine Taylor

Production assistance by Drew Patty

Copy editing by Rachel Bernstein

Design by Janet Wood and Yvonne Tsang

Printing and binding in Hong Kong by

Regal Printing Ltd. through Stacy Quinn of

QuinnEssentials Books and Printing, Inc.